NATIONAL GEOGRAPHIC

TRAVELER

Hong Kong

NATIONAL GEOGRAPHIC

TRAVELER
Hong Kong

Phil Macdonald

National Geographic
Washington, D.C.

Contents

How to use this guide 6–7 About the author 8
The regions 49–234 Travelwise 235–264
Index 265–269 Credits 271–272

Page 1: Dragon lights at the Star Ferry Terminal
Pages 2–3: Hiker ascending Victoria Peak, Central District
Left: Tai chi at sunrise on Stanley Beach

How to use this guide

See back flap for keys to text and map symbols

The *National Geographic Traveler* brings you the best of Hong Kong in text, pictures, and maps. Divided into three main sections, the guide begins with an overview of the area's history, geology, and culture. Following this are six regional chapters with a range of featured sites selected by the author for their particular interest. Each of the chapters opens with its own contents list.

The regions and sites within the regions are arranged geographically. A map introduces each region, highlighting the featured sites. Walks and drives, plotted on their own maps, suggest routes for discovering an area. Features and sidebars give intriguing detail on history, culture, or contemporary life.

The final section, Travelwise, lists essential information for the traveler—pretrip planning, special events, getting around, emergencies, and a glossary—plus a selection of hotels, restaurants, stores, and entertainment.

To the best of our knowledge, all information is accurate as of the press date. However, it's always advisable to call ahead when possible.

TRAVELWISE

Color coding

Each region is color coded for easy reference. Find the region you want on the map on the front flap, and look for the color flash at the top of the pages of the relevant chapter. Information in **Travelwise** is also color coded to each region.

Color-coded region name

Town name

Hotel name & price range

Address, telephone & fax numbers

Brief description of hotel

Hotel facilities & credit card details

Restaurant name & price range

Address & telephone number

Brief description of restaurant

Restaurant closures & credit card details

Visitor information

Hong Kong Museum of History

Practical information for most sites is given in the side column (see key to symbols on back flap). The map reference gives the page number of the map and grid reference. Other details are address, telephone number, days closed, entrance charge in a range from $ (under $4) to $$$$$ (over $25), and the nearest MTR station for sites in Hong Kong. Other sites have information in italics and parentheses in the text.

Map p. 132

100 Chatham Rd. South, Tsim Sha Tsui East

2724-9042

Closed Mon.

$

MTR: Tsim Sha Tsui

Hotel & restaurant prices

An explanation of the price bands used in entries is given in the Hotels & Restaurants section (beginning on p. 243).

REGIONAL MAPS

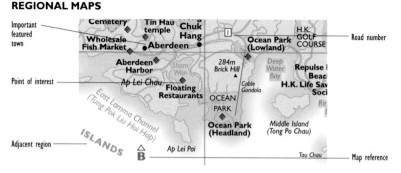

- A locator map accompanies each regional map and shows the location of that region in the country.
- Adjacent regions are shown, each with a page reference.

WALKING TOURS

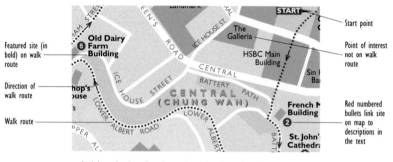

- An information box gives the starting and ending points, time and length of walk, and places not to be missed along the route.

DRIVING TOURS

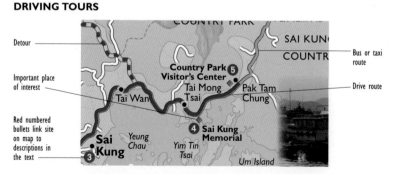

- An information box provides details including starting and finishing points, time and length of drive, places not to be missed en route, or tips on terrain.

NATIONAL GEOGRAPHIC

TRAVELER

Hong Kong

About the author

Phil Macdonald moved to Hong Kong from Sydney, Australia, in 1989 to continue a career in journalism that had begun eight years earlier in the west coast city of Perth. He worked for the *Hong Kong Standard* and the *South China Morning Post* for a number of years before settling—by way of Laos and Singapore—in Phuket, Thailand, in 1996. He now lives in Bangkok, working as a freelance journalist and writer, and contributing to a number of regional and international publications. His interests include Southeast Asian politics and recent history, and the beaches of Southern Thailand. He is author of *The National Geographic Traveler: Taiwan* and co-author of *The National Geographic Traveler: Thailand* guidebooks.

Ian Lyons helped with research for the Hong Kong Island South and New Territories chapters.

History & culture

Chinese New Year decorations

Hong Kong today

IT IS A QUESTION CONSTANTLY REPEATED BY OUTSIDERS EVEN HALF A decade after the event: "Has Hong Kong changed much since its return to China?" Some locals will say "Yes," pointing to political and business deference, even kowtowing, to its new overlord and subtle changes in laws that they see as eroding the territory's taken-for-granted freedoms. Others, however, will give an emphatic "No." Hong Kong, they say, is still the freewheeling, materialistic, hard-edged, cosmopolitan, exhilarating place it was before the handover.

There were doubts in the decade and a half leading up to what Hong Kong people refer to as the "handover," which turned to near panic after June 4, 1989, when troops of the People's Liberation Army violently crushed democracy demonstrations in Beijing's Tiananmen Square. But the dust has long settled. During the ensuing, often painstaking, negotiations that took place between the British and Chinese over the future of Hong Kong, confidence slowly returned.

The transfer to Chinese sovereignty, although not without more than a few rocky moments, was, in the end, remarkably smooth. Hong Kong now exists under the Chinese flag as a Special Administrative Region or SAR. Under the concept of "one country–two systems" coined by China's late leader Deng Xaioping (1904–1997), it is guaranteed near-full autonomy for 50 years beyond the handover.

Hong Kong moves with such unbridled dynamism that even these dramatic recent events are brushed aside, if not actually forgotten. It's a new time with a new landlord, but things remain essentially the same. People still go about their business, and pleasure, with a frantic energy rarely found anywhere else. And when you squeeze more than seven million busy people into just 116 square miles (300 sq km), you get a crowded, bustling, loud, and pushy city in a terrible hurry.

Even by the standards of other Asian cities, where frenetic street life is part of the culture, the sheer number of people on Hong Kong's streets is staggering. They are everywhere, both day and night; shopping, working, eating, walking, chatting loudly. But noise and crowds don't faze the gregarious Cantonese—they revel in it, although many visitors have a hard time coping.

MONEY

So what's the fuel that drives this vitality? Simple. Money. Hong Kong's economic system embodies the purest form of capitalism found anywhere, a laissez-faire policy of almost total non-government interference in business. This suits the hardworking and business-savvy Cantonese, whose obsession with wealth is often regarded as downright obscene by outsiders. But it would be glib to describe this obsession as pure greed. Hong Kong's population was built on successive waves of immigration from neighboring Guangdong Province; poor people escaping famines, wars, and communism arrived in the territory with nothing. Financial security, created through shrewdness and hard work, became the number-one priority.

Wealth is also tied up in the concept of "face" or showing respect. It proffers enormous respect from others who believe those that attain it must carry the admirable qualities of hard work and perseverance. Once this wealth is obtained, it must be displayed in order to earn all-important "face" from others. Hence the ostentatious displays of luxury cars, expensive jewelry and watches, designer-label clothing, and beautiful, immaculately furnished apartments. To the Chinese, show-boating is a way of life, and money does indeed buy happiness.

EAST MEETS WEST

Hong Kong greets East and West with a sleight of hand. Outwardly, it could not appear more Westernized, with its ultramodern airport, the

The shopping experience at the Temple Street Night Market in Kowloon includes lots of haggling, crowds, street theater, and fortune-tellers.

3 1833 04878 845 6

gleaming skyscrapers of Central District, efficient, modern public transportation, clean streets, shady well-kept parks, businesspeople in sharp suits, fashion-conscious women sporting the latest designer brands, and crowded department stores full of everything that is new and desired. But at the core of Hong Kong's vitality lies a culture and traditions that could not be more Chinese.

Ironically, under British rule, Hong Kong became the most Chinese of Chinese cities.

While Mao Zedong's Red Guards laid waste to traditions, festivals, customs, and beliefs on the mainland during the Cultural Revolution of the 1960s and 1970s, Hong Kong, in the main, remained unaffected.

Today, in the shabby, winding streets close to Central, row upon row of Chinese herbalist shops dispense ingredients such as snake musk, pearl powder, lizard skins, and deer antlers. In small shop-house factories Chinese artisans turn out mahjong tiles, company

Atop the Peak at dusk, one of the world's great city vistas sparkles into view.

chops (seals), decorated chopsticks, and coffins. In other places, shopkeepers use abacuses to tally bills on an astonishing variety of rice and teas. Butchers carve up pigs, and old ladies haggle at fish markets. Inside numerous small, nondescript temples, crushed between high-rise residential towers, devotees burn joss sticks and offer fruit to Taoist gods before seeking counsel with fortune-tellers who read faces and palms. In Victoria Park— Hong Kong Island's largest green space—

hundreds of people gather together at dawn and again at dusk to practice the Chinese martial art of *tai chi*.

Hong Kong's numerous festivals (see pp. 46–48), steeped in centuries-old Chinese traditions, do a lot to define the spirit of the place. Almost always elaborate and colorful, and invariably accompanied by a snaking

Tsim Sha Tsui's stereo, camera, fashion, and souvenir shops are a hit with bargain-hunters.

dragon dance and ear-splitting fireworks, they are approached with an enthusiasm not seen on mainland China.

East does not clash with West in Hong Kong, as happens in other Asian cities, which see Western culture as undermining traditional beliefs. Rather it blends like nowhere else. Here, it is not uncommon for a successful businessman, wise in the ways of Western wheeling and dealing, to hire a *feng shui* master (geomancer) to design his office in such a way that his business will prosper, or for an old lady to make offerings at a temple in the hope her shares on the stock exchange will continue to rise in value.

This successful East–West synergy, and its legacy of a colonial past, which is still apparent, are what give Hong Kong much of its appeal. Here, thanks to a tenacious determination to maintain tradition and a ready acceptance of Western culture, discovering the East could not be easier.

VISITORS' HONG KONG

One of your first stops should be Victoria Peak, not only for its magnificent views but also to get some perspective of Hong Kong. From these lofty heights, the territory spreads out at your feet. Remarkable views sweep down steep wooded slopes to the skyscrapers of Central and Wan Chai, across busy Victoria Harbor to the Kowloon Peninsula, and beyond to the hills of the New Territories. Take a walk around the shoulder of the Peak to view the verdant hills, deep valleys, and the convoluted coastline indented with coves and beaches of Hong Kong Island South. Having seen Hong Kong laid out before you, it's time to explore.

Its compactness, along with its excellent public transportation, glut of inexpensive taxis, and streets safe from crime make the territory very visitor friendly. Many areas of Hong Kong can be discovered on foot, especially on Hong Kong Island North and parts of Kowloon.

One of the great delights of the city is to lose yourself in the warren of side streets and alleys that run through Western District and Wan Chai on Hong Kong Island North, and Yau Ma Tai and Mong Kok in Kowloon. This is street life at its best: A barely controlled confusion of thronging crowds spilling off the sidewalks; food vendors selling chicken feet, fish balls, and pieces of cuttlefish on sticks; huge, gaudy overhanging neon signs; and street after street of small shops selling all manner of exotic and mysterious goods, from herbal remedies to religious paraphernalia.

The third largest of Hong Kong's 230 islands, Lamma is an easy escape from the urban hum.

This appears be a world away from sophisticated and glitzy Central—where modern skyscrapers housing Hong Kong's corporate movers and shakers, opulent hotels, and shopping malls full of designer-label goods cluster on reclaimed land between Victoria Harbor and brooding Victoria Peak— but in some cases, it's only a few blocks. This is where Hong Kong's material wealth is unashamedly on show.

A wall of high-rise buildings runs almost the full length of Hong Kong Island's northern corridor, but over the peaks that run along the spine of the island and down on its south side, things are decidedly different. Villages nestle in bays lined with tidy beaches and backed by forested hills. Roads climbing over these peaks offer spectacular views of the country-side and the South China Sea beyond. Not surprisingly, Hong Kong Island South is where Hong Kong's wealthy have chosen to build their mansions.

The subway or Mass Transit Railway (MTR) burrows under Victoria Harbor in three different places, making access to Kowloon easy. But if you aren't in too much of a hurry, hop on the wonderful Star Ferry (see p. 120) for the short trip across the harbor and take in the magnificent panoramas offered by Central's skyline and the backdrop of Victoria Peak. The Star Ferry takes visitors to the tourist district of Tsim Sha Tsui, an exuberant place of hotels, bars, restaurants, and an unbelievable number of retail stores lining the streets, inside arcades, and multi-level shopping centers.

What surprises many first-time visitors is the amount of space given over to national parks, or country parks—as they are known in Hong Kong—about 40 percent, mostly in the New Territories. Characterized by rugged peaks dropping off to wooded valleys and the sparkling waters of the coastal areas, these country parks are crisscrossed with miles of well-marked and well-maintained hiking trails. Allow a day for a trip to the New Territories—if not for the hiking, at least to enjoy the cleaner air, quietude, and less frantic atmosphere. Sai Kung Peninsula in the eastern New Territories is recommended.

Spend a day or two exploring the outlying islands, too; Hong Kong has 234 islands, the vast majority uninhabited. The main ones are easily reached by ferry from Central and the ferry trip itself is a delight. The two most easily accessible islands are Lantau—Hong Kong's biggest—and the smaller and more rural Lamma.

THE PEOPLE

Ninety-eight percent of Hong Kong's population of more than seven million are Chinese, and the vast majority are able to trace their roots back to the neighboring province of Guangdong. Cantonese dialect, food, and culture make up the fabric of society here. Since the British arrived in the 1840s, Hong Kong has been a magnet for immigrants from mainland China seeking a better life. Many faced extreme hardships in China, and Hong Kong was the place where they could better their lives and those of their children. Rags-to-riches stories are commonplace.

A strong will to succeed can be traced back to these hard times, and parents have instilled these values in their children. People in Hong Kong have an incredible work ethic. It's not unusual for them to work 10 to 12 hours a day, six days a week. People who run their own business, big and small, often work even longer hours.

These long hours, teeming streets where you often have to battle just to stay on the sidewalks, and crowded living conditions—with families of five or six sometimes sharing a tiny apartment—have given many Hong Kong people a competitive and strident nature, often manifest, outwardly at least, in a brusqueness that can offend visitors. Don't always expect a smile and an exchange of pleasantries when making a purchase, or an apology when accidentally jostled or bumped.

Crowds mill about Hennessy Road in Causeway Bay, one of Hong Kong's most popular shopping districts.

There is no outward display of hospitality shown to visitors as there is in most other parts of Asia, but neither is there hostility, for that matter. Although Hong Kong people will show a generosity of spirit toward their family and friends, if you are outside that circle, don't expect much.

The very rich social elite at a party in Hong Kong

But Hong Kong still remains a cosmopolitan city, made so by the diverse groups of foreigners who have made their home there, contributing to business, commerce, cuisine, culture, and religion, and giving Hong Kong its sophistication and uniqueness. Filipinos, numbering about 140,000, make up the largest group of foreign nationals. They are mainly women who work as domestic helpers for middle- and upper-class Chinese. Many Thais and Indonesians fill the same role. Large numbers of Americans, Australians, Canadians, British, and Europeans, collectively known as *gweilos* in Cantonese, make up the majority of the foreign business community. *Gweilos* is a derogatory term meaning "ghost people" or "foreign devils," although its meaning has softened somewhat with use.

Hong Kong also has a sizable population from subcontinental Asia. This mixture of mainly Indians and Pakistanis, many of whom have been in Hong Kong for generations, speak fluent Cantonese, hold Hong Kong passports, and are generally involved in retailing and trade.

BEHAVIOR
Constant contact with foreigners for the last 160 years has made the people of Hong Kong pretty much shock-proof when it comes to the strange ways of Westerners. But Asian concepts of "face" or showing respect, and a non-confrontational approach to life are still strong. Although you are unlikely to encounter tense situations or bumbling bureaucracy, if you do, try to solve the situation calmly. Losing your temper will get you nowhere, and you will probably be regarded as a "stupid gweilo," not worth dealing with.

Hong Kong people dress well and you are expected to do the same. Clean T-shirts, shorts, and sandals are acceptable streetwear, but flip-flops and sleeveless vests are not. Neat casual wear will get you into all but the most exclusive restaurants.

LEISURE
People work hard for their money, but they also know how to spend it, so much of their leisure time revolves around eating, drinking, and shopping with friends and family. Brunch at a noisy dim sum restaurant, followed by a shopping expedition, then possibly a movie and a big dinner at another restaurant is a popular way to spend Sunday—the only full day off for many.

Movies are extremely popular, especially the homegrown ones (see p. 146). Movie

From exotic to plain, it's on sale in Kowloon.

theaters showing such films are full most nights of the week.

The young and middle-class have taken to the growing number of upscale Western-style bars, where they often spend a few hours in the evening, unwinding after a busy day at work. Trendy and expensive nightclubs, where possession of wealth can be displayed with abandon, are also popular. There are hundreds of noisy karaoke bars and dimly lit pubs where the young spend their evenings drinking and playing hand games such as "rock, paper, scissors."

In summer, legions of people head to Hong Kong Island's beaches on weekends, while the hiking trails and picnic areas in the country parks in the New Territories are popular for those wanting to escape the frantic urban areas.

Hong Kong's citizens love to gamble, and horse racing and the lottery—known as the Mark Six—are two of the legal outlets. Horse racing (see p. 90) is especially popular. During the race season, between mid-September and June, tens of thousands of betting enthusiasts pack the stands at Happy Valley and Sha Tin racetracks, while those who don't make it to the track bet at one of the hundreds of off-track betting outlets. At each of the twice-weekly race meetings, a staggering six million bets are laid—quite incredible for a place that has a total population amounting to only a little more than seven million.

RELIGION & SUPERSTITION

Cynics may say that the major religion in Hong Kong is money, and there is surely more than the usual amount of adoration for it here. But there are about 600 temples, shrines, and monasteries throughout the territory, many combining the detached view of life offered by Buddhism, the humility and non-assertiveness of Taoism, and the high principles of Confucianism.

The high-mindedness of these philosophies is often eschewed for more temporal needs. Great attention is paid to appeasing the dead—through ancestral worship—and the spirits, with the aim of improving your own lot. The Chinese don't like to leave things to chance. *Joss,* or luck, has to be kept on your side by mollifying a plethora of gods and spirits with gifts and prayers. By keeping the gods and spirits happy, or at bay in the case of the bad ones, joss, and its natural partner, wealth, come your way.

Similarly, the counsel of fortune-tellers, who are found mostly in or around temples,

is often sought as a way to plan one's life and attain wealth. Dates and numbers that are believed to be auspicious in Chinese culture are central to many actions. Weddings are planned, offices and restaurants opened, foundation stones of buildings laid, and newly built boats launched on dates that are seen to guarantee success.

Numbers are hugely symbolic, based on their sounds in multitonal Cantonese. The number eight *(baat)*, for example, sounds

similar to the word for prosperity *(fat dat)*, and to have it in your telephone number or your license plate is indeed fortunate. The number three *(saam)* sounds like the word for lively or flourishing *(saan)*, so is another lucky number. However, four *(say)* is similar in sound to death *(say*—different tone), so it's a number to be avoided.

The sound principle also works with food—for example, *fat choy,* a dark, fibrous vegetable, is often cooked at Chinese New Year

to bring wealth *(fat)*. *Kung hei fat choi* (good wishes, good fortune) is the standard New Year greeting.

Hong Kong's British colonial past has left it with a sizable and active Christian community of about 527,000, with Protestant and Catholic faiths spread evenly. There are numerous denominational churches scattered throughout the territory. The majority of Hong Kong's 80,000 Muslims are Chinese, although there are significant numbers of devotees originally

Many of Hong Kong's 600-odd temples combine Buddhism, Taoism, and Confucianism into a spiritual whole; the atmosphere is much more relaxed than in a Christian church.

from the Indian subcontinent, many of whom came as soldiers attached to the British army and police. Also from the subcontinent are Hong Kong's 12,000 Hindus and Sikhs, and there are some 1,000 of the Jewish faith. ■

Food & drink

ALONG WITH SHOPPING, EATING IS ONE OF HONG KONG'S GREAT PASTIMES.
It's usually treated as a social occasion, with lots of friends and family gathered around a
large table, eating amid much toasting, chattering, and laughter. The territory is Asia's
culinary capital. It has one restaurant for every 700 people, the highest ratio of any city
in the world, with a cosmopolitan selection befitting an international city.

REGIONAL SPECIALTIES

Hong Kong is a great place to sample China's
huge variety of regional specialties, whose
ingredients tend to reflect their geographical
location. In cooler northern China, where
wheat is the predominant crop, noodles,
dumplings, and steamed breads often replace
rice as the staple.

In the south, with its warm and wet climate, rice is plentiful; so, too, are tropical
fruits. Coastal areas, naturally enough, use
a lot of seafood in their dishes, while farther
inland pork and chicken replace seafood. In
some regions, such as Sichuan, spices grow
in abundance and these are used liberally in
the cooking.

Street food

Hong Kong has no end of open-air food
stands, from which vendors dispense all
manner of food including fish balls, cuttlefish-
on-a-stick, brightly colored sausages, noodles,
roast chestnuts (in winter), chicken feet,
fermented fried tofu, and various grilled,
steamed, and deep-fried tidbits. *Dai pai dongs,*
tiny restaurants with a few rickety tables and
chairs inside and out on the sidewalk, can be
found all over Hong Kong. Some serve excellent noodle soup, although the entrails and
stomach linings hanging from hooks in the
exposed kitchens of some of these places can
be a turnoff.

Cantonese

This distinctive style from Hong Kong's
neighboring province of Guangdong is the
most popular and the most varied of all
Chinese cuisines. It places a strong emphasis
on fresh food, using vegetables, chicken, and

seafood as its main ingredients. Meals are
prepared either by steaming or quickly stir-
frying in a wok on a high flame to enhance the
taste. Spices are rarely, if ever, used, but there
is an emphasis on sauces.

Favorite Cantonese dishes include shrimp
with chili sauce, crab in black bean sauce,
whole steamed fish, roast pigeon, fried noodles with beef and green bell peppers, stir-
fried broccoli with scallops, drunken shrimp
—that is to say, shrimp steamed in rice wine—
and barbecue pork.

**A typical Hong Kong meal incorporates
many flavorful dishes shared among family
and friends.**

Beijing

In Beijing's cooler northern climate, wheat is more commonly grown than rice—meaning noodles and dumpling are more prevalent in its regional cuisine. Restaurant chefs often put on an entertaining show of noodlemaking for diners, twisting and twirling the stuff as thinner and thinner strands are peeled off.

The most famous Beijing dish is Peking duck, served on pancakes with plum sauce. Also delicious is beggar's chicken—so called because it is said to have originated when a beggar stole a chicken, smothered it in clay because he had no pot, and baked it. The bird is stuffed with a mixture of black mushrooms, pickled cabbage, herbs, and onions, then wrapped in lotus leaves, coated in wine-soaked clay, and baked. Mongolian hotpot, usually eaten in the winter, is another Beijing favorite. Meat and a variety of vegetables are cooked in a pot on a burner at the diner's table.

Chiu Chow

Chiu Chow cuisine originated in the coastal region of Shantou in Guangdong Province. Its preparation is similar to Cantonese, but there is a strong emphasis on seafood, and sauces tend to be sweeter—tangerine and orange are typical. There are some dishes Westerners may find unpalatable, such as coagulated pig blood stir-fried with green onions, and chicken blood sliced and served with an array of sauces. Duck and goose are popular, and the baked lobster in pepper sauce is a delight. The best known Chiu Chow foods are shark's fin soup and bird's nest soup, the latter often served with coconut milk as a dessert.

Sichuan

Lots of herbs and spices—among them chili, peppercorns, fennel, anise, coriander, and garlic—go into making one of the most fiery

cuisines in China. Time is taken to soak and simmer the dishes so the chilies can leave their mark on the diner.

Most dishes come accompanied either by a chili sauce or a spicy sauce. Because Sichuan Province is located so far from the coast, seafood is rare; chicken and pork are usually featured instead.

Dishing up steamed dumplings, a popular dim sum dish, at an outdoor restaurant on Lamma Island

Hunan

Hunan cuisine is similar to the fiery dishes of Sichuan with liberal use of chilies and garlic, and an emphasis on freshness and fragrance. Rice is used as a staple, but northern-style side dishes such as bean curd rolls, dumplings, and savory buns are often served. Fish, shrimp, lotus root, and turtle are some of the main ingredients. Dishes include Dong'an chicken, shark's fin in red sauce, hot and spicy chicken, and lotus seeds in sugar candy.

Dim sum

A trip to a dim sum restaurant on a Sunday morning is a must if only to see the gregarious Cantonese at their clamorous best. The noise is incredible as people shout their way through a meal of delicious steamed dumplings, buns, spring rolls, and delicate rice-flour wrappings encasing a glorious array of fillings. Waiters wheel trolleys loaded with bamboo baskets of dim sum around the restaurant. You simply stop the waiter and choose what you want. The waiters tally up your bill as you order.

Other specialties

There is more to the food scene in Hong Kong than Chinese restaurants. People also enjoy Western, Middle Eastern, African, and other Asian fare. Many restaurants serve Indian, Japanese, Vietnamese, Thai, Korean, Malaysian, Indonesian, Singaporean, and Filipino food. Western restaurants cover a gamut of styles. Hong Kong is also an excellent place for fusion cuisine, combining Eastern and Western ingredients cooked using the Asian stir-fry method.

WHERE TO EAT

Hotels: Here you'll find some of Hong Kong's and Asia's best and most exclusive restaurants; Chinese, Asian, and Western. You will enjoy excellent and consistent quality cuisine, and impeccable service.

Causeway Bay: Along Tang Lung, Matheson, and Percival Streets, and Sunning Road are plenty of quality regional Chinese restaurants, plus a number of sushi bars and restaurants specializing in shark's fin soup.

Kowloon City: Clustered around Nga Tsin and Nam Kok Roads are dozens of Cantonese, Chiu Chow, Vietnamese, Korean, and Thai eateries offering tasty food and good value.

Lan Kwai Fong & SoHo: These two areas above Central District are full of trendy bars and restaurants offering a wide selection of international cuisine, including French, Italian, Middle Eastern, Spanish, Australian, American, and Mexican.

Sai Kung, Lamma Island & Lei Yue Mun: These seaside locations specialize in fresh seafood with a waterside ambience. You can buy your seafood from fish tanks and take it to a nearby restaurant to be cooked.

Stanley Village: Here you'll find a laid-back atmosphere at the bistros lining the waterfront.

Tsim Sha Tsui: Hillwood and Austin Roads are great places for Chinese fare.

DRINK

Tea

There is a huge variety of Chinese tea (see pp. 66–67) as befits a country that invented the art of tea drinking. The three basic types are green, black, and oolong. Lighter green tea is often scented with chrysanthemum, rose, or jasmine. It is usually served free with meals, and sugar, lemon, or milk are never added.

Coffee

Hong Kong has fallen in love with coffee. There are numerous coffee shops in the more cosmopolitan parts of the territory selling a staggering array of brews. These shops feature stools, benches, tables, and comfy sofas in an airy atmosphere, and plenty of reading material is at hand to encourage lingering.

Alcohol

Hong Kong's native beer is San Miguel, although visitors and expatriates are not impressed by its "chemical" taste. Imports of Blue Girl and Tsingtao from mainland China are very acceptable. Carlsberg is produced locally and Heineken is widely available. British, Irish, Dutch, U.S., Australian, and German beers can be found on tap in many pubs and bars. Some bars have a staggering variety of international beers, so it's unlikely you'll be left high and dry without your favorite brew. A local microbrewery produces hearty ales, including the wonderfully named and tasty Dragon's Back.

Many people in Hong Kong are partial to cognac and expensive brandies, often mixed with cola, lemonade, or soda and drunk in large quantities. An expensive bottle of cognac on one's table is a status symbol.

Wine is expensive in restaurants, but supermarkets often sell bottles from Europe, California, Australia, New Zealand, South Africa, and Chile at marked-down prices. Most restaurants let you bring a bottle, although a hefty corkage charge is often levied, especially if the restaurant has its own wine list.

DINING ETIQUETTE

Dishes are brought to the table as soon as they're cooked, and served communally, although diners get their own bowl for rice. It's polite to wait for someone else to start eating or be invited to do so. In some cases, the host will place a small portion of food in your bowl to initiate proceedings.

You serve yourself using chopsticks to take the food from the plate and dip into the small dishes of sauce, which vary depending on what's being served. Don't pour the sauce onto your plate or empty it into your rice bowl. It's

Cantonese cuisine puts snake to a variety of imaginative—and delicious—uses.

acceptable to hold the rice bowl to your lips and shovel the rice into your mouth with the chopsticks. Chewed bones are often placed in a pile next to the diner on the tablecloth. The Chinese are not big on desserts, and don't expect any fortune cookies—an American invention—after your meal.

Tea accompanies most meals and is drunk throughout (people use it to clean their chopsticks, too). Spontaneous toasts are common during a repast involving alcohol. A diner will raise his or her glass, say a cheery *"Yum seng!"* ("Down the hatch!"), and others will follow suit. Beer, brandy, and cognac are preferred libations. Expect your glass to be topped up continually. ■

History of Hong Kong

WHEN HONG KONG BECAME PART OF QUEEN VICTORIA'S DOMINIONS IN 1841, the monarch was amused by the notion that her daughter Princess Victoria Adelaide Mary Louise may become the "Princess of Hong Kong." The foreign secretary Lord Palmerston, on the other hand, was "greatly mortified and disappointed." He sacked the man responsible for Hong Kong's acquisition, Capt. Charles Elliot, representative of the British Crown in China.

Palmerston was interested in greater spoils along China's prosperous coast, not "some barren island with hardly a house on it." The Chinese, for their part, were bemused by the whole affair. Qing dynasty emperor Emperor Daoguang (R.1821–1850), acceding to the loss of this speck of inconsequential land by the compelling argument of Royal Navy guns leveled at the walls of Nanjing (Nanking), treated the affair casually. But his dismissive tone masked a great feeling of shame and anger by China (it was the first part of China to be taken by force by a Western power), which was not fully appeased for another 156 years when Hong Kong was handed back. The Union Jack was unfurled on January 26, 1841, at Possession Point in the now teeming Western District of Hong Kong Island. Two years later, the cession of Hong Kong to the British was ratified in the Treaty of Nanking.

When the British arrived, Hong Kong Island had a population of about 3,650 scattered around 20 or so villages and hamlets, while another 2,000 lived on their boats in the harbor. The place was hardly conducive to a large population, given its barren, mountainous terrain and lack of fresh water.

But evidence has been unearthed of habitation dating back some 6,000 years. Artifacts discovered along the coast indicate Hong Kong's neolithic citizens fished and panned for salt and carved geometrical images on rocks. Weapons, knives, arrowheads, fishhooks, and socketed axes dating back to 2000 B.C. have been excavated. On the islands of Lantau and Lamma, stone molds indicate metal was worked locally. In 1999, archaeologists unearthed a neolithic workshop in Sai Kung in the New Territories, revealing hundreds of stone cores, flakes, and stone tools such as oyster picks and carving tools, as well as polished implements such as adzes and rings.

Increasing numbers of people settled in Hong Kong during the Qin (221–206 B.C.) and Han (206 B.C.– A.D. 220) dynasties. Coins from the Han period have been found, and Han relics were also unearthed in a brick tomb discovered in 1955 in the Lei Cheng Uk District of Kowloon.

China was visited by trading ships from India, Arabia, and Persia by the time of the Tang dynasty (618–907). They used Hong Kong's sheltered harbors as anchorage while acquiring silks and porcelain from ports along China's east coast and the Pearl River Delta.

EARLY SETTLERS

During the Song dynasty (960–1279), the Cantonese Punti people (Punti means "locals") began moving into the territory of present-day Hong Kong from the southern part of the Chinese mainland. They were followed by the seafaring Hoklo from Fujian, farther north along the coast, and the Hakka who originated from northern China. People tilled the fertile soil of the New Territories and built sturdy walled villages for protection against pirates, robbers, and their neighbors. The area, which fell under the administration of Canton (Guangzhou), was visited by a local administrator, Tang Fu-hip, in 1069. Tang was so taken by the beauty of the countryside and the village of Kam Tin that he later moved his family and ancestral graves there, and his sons became powerful landowners. Over the next two centuries, four other clans—the Hau, the Pang, the Lin, and the Man—arrived, eventually carving out most of Hong Kong between them, although the Tangs remained the most powerful.

A vintage poster depicts the Chinese and British celebrations that occurred on Queen Victoria's Golden Jubilee in January 1888.

EUROPEANS

European ships began arriving along China's southern coast in the early 16th century. The Portuguese, driven by the prospect of lucrative trade, were among the first. In 1517, a flotilla sailed up the Pearl River to Canton. Chinese officials were eventually persuaded to hand over Macau, a small piece of land on the Pearl River Delta, where the Portuguese established a trading post and settlement in 1557.

China, under extreme pressure from Western maritime powers, gradually and reluctantly allowed foreign shipping into four ports. Canton was opened in 1699 and Britain's East India Company was allowed to build a warehouse or "factory" there. The Europeans followed their example. However, only 13 *hongs* (trading companies) could trade at one time. They built their factories on the outskirts of the city.

A multitude of restrictions were placed on foreigners living in Canton: They were only allowed to remain there during the trading season, dictated by favorable winds between October and January, and could not bring their wives ashore, venture from their factory compounds, or learn Chinese.

Despite this, commerce flourished and huge profits were made. But the trade flowed mainly one way. While European traders could not get enough tea, silk, and porcelain, the Chinese were indifferent to woolens, furs, and spices being brought in by the foreign traders.

The only thing that interested them was the vast amounts of silver paid in exchange for their exotic goods.

OPIUM TRADE

All this changed. In 1773, the East India Company secured a monopoly on opium, which it sold to British merchants at auction in Calcutta. That year the first shipment arrived in Canton—200 chests, each containing 160 pounds of Bengal opium—where it found a ready market. Opium had been banned in China since 1729, except for medicinal use, and was forbidden outright in 1800. The ban was easily circumvented with the connivance of a never-ending stream of corrupt Chinese officials. Clippers arriving in Canton simply unloaded the contraband onto floating stores before heading into port for customs inspection. The drug was later smuggled ashore.

The use of opium became widespread in China; between 1810 and 1830, yearly shipments increased from 5,000 to 23,000 chests. At its height, there were an estimated one million opium addicts in China, from coolies, ordinary Chinese, traders, and rich merchants to government officials.

William Jardine (1784–1843) of the preeminent hong, Jardine, Matheson & Company, glibly commented that since "opium is the only real money article sold in China," it had to be smuggled in.

China's dynasties

Xia ca 2205–1766 B.C.	Northern Qi 550–577	Later Han 947–950
Shang ca 1766–1122 B.C.	Northern Zhou 557–581	Later Zhou 951–960
Zhou Western ca 1122–771 B.C.		
Eastern ca 771–256 B.C.	**Southern**	**Song** Northern 960–1127
Qin 221–206 B.C.	Song 420–479	Southern 1127–1279
Han Western 206 B.C.–A.D. 9	Qi 479–502	
Xin (Wang Mang) A.D. 9–23	Liang 502–557	**Yuan** 1279–1368
Eastern A.D. 25–220	Chen 557–589	
Three Kingdoms period		**Ming** 1368–1644
220–265	**Sui** 581–618	
Jin Western 265–316		**Qing** 1644–1911
Eastern 317–420	**Tang** 618–907	
		Republic of China 1911–
		1949 (maintained in Taiwan)
Northern	**Five Dynasties**	
Northern Wei 386–534	Later Liang 907–923	**People's Republic of China**
Eastern Wei 534–550	Later Tang 923–936	1949–present
Western Wei 535–557	Later Jin 936–947	

British navy boats laid siege to Canton (Guangzhou) during the First Opium War to force trade concessions from the Chinese.

By the 1830s, China was suffering a huge outflow of silver that was being used to pay for the drug, and a major economic crisis loomed. In March 1839, Lin Zexu (1785–1850), a high-ranking official, was appointed by Emperor Daoguang to deal with the problem. With his soldiers, he lay siege to the hongs' factories, refused entry, and stopped food supplies until the opium was surrendered and traders signed pledges vowing to discontinue the trade. The British, under the command of Capt. Charles Elliot, held out for six weeks before handing over more than 20,000 chests of opium. The drug was dumped into trenches by a river, mixed with lime, and flushed out to sea. The British merchants halted all trade with China and headed for Macau.

FIRST OPIUM WAR

Opium traders began lobbying the sympathetic foreign secretary, Lord Palmerston, for help in solving the trade problem. Palmer-ston ordered the mobilization of an expeditionary force from India to blockade Canton and demanded a commercial treaty that would swing trade in Britain's favor or the cession of Chinese land where the British could live free from threats. Meanwhile, a Chinese was accidentally killed in a brawl with British seamen on Kowloon Peninsula opposite Hong Kong Island, and Captain Elliot refused to hand over those responsible for trial in a Chinese court. Enraged, authorities in Canton ordered the British off Macau. By August 1839, about 200 merchants and their families found themselves crammed into boats on Hong Kong harbor within gunshot of Chinese war junks.

An expeditionary force of 4,000 arrived in June 1840 and set about blockading Canton. The First Opium War (1840–42) had begun. When treaty negotiations failed, the British began a show of military force, killing 600 Chinese soldiers at a garrison island in the mouth of the Pearl River. Under increasing threat by Britain's naval might, China agreed to a draft treaty at the Convention of Chuenpi in January 1841, which ceded Hong Kong to the British. Captain Elliot, who negotiated the treaty, wasted no time in dispatching Captain Belcher to Hong Kong Island to plant the flag on its western shore. A few days later he proclaimed: "Full security and protection for all British subjects and foreigners residing in and resorting to the island, so long as they shall continue to conform to the authority of Her Majesty's government."

Both sides were unhappy with the treaty. Palmerston blasted Captain Elliot for being too soft and not extracting enough concessions from the Chinese. He was recalled in disgrace and replaced by Henry Pottinger (1801–1875), Hong Kong's first governor, who set about forcing more concessions.

After further shows of strength by the British—in which Dinghai, Xiamen, and Ningo fell to British gunboats, Shanghai and Zhenjiang were occupied, and Nanjing was threatened—the Chinese gave in to demands. The Treaty of Nanking was signed on August 29, 1842, and ratified ten months later. It forced China to pay compensation, open the five ports of Canton, Xiamen, Fuzhou, Ningbo, and Shanghai—the first of the Treaty Ports—to foreigners, and cede Hong Kong to Britain in perpetuity so that the British might have "some Port whereat they may careen and refit their Ships, when required, and keep Stores for that purpose."

NEW COLONY

Building in Hong Kong started soon after the flag was planted. Fifty lots of land along the northern frontage of the island, later to become Queen's Road, were snapped up, many by the hongs who had shifted their businesses from Canton and Macau. By the end of 1841, 28 foreign merchants had settled in Hong Kong, including Jardine, Matheson & Company, which bought the first plot for £565 pounds and found a safe haven for its stores of opium. The navy acquired a plot of land on the seafront, and the army moved in behind, on the lower slopes of what became Victoria Peak. The settlement was called Queen's Town, later renamed Victoria. Unexpectedly, many

Chinese moved to Hong Kong. Soon 12,000 workers and tradesmen had settled to the immediate east and west of the European settlement. A few months after, a raging typhoon swept away much of the new construction. Disease was rife: Malaria wiped out hundreds of troops.

The population reached about 25,000 by 1845, and continued to swell as people fled China's Taiping Rebellion (1851–1864). The rebellion was led by Hung Xiu-quan (1814–1864), an aspiring bureaucrat who came under the influence of Christian missionaries in Guangzhou in the 1830s.

Hung believed he was the brother of Jesus and son of God who had been sent to Earth to destroy the "demons" of the Qing dynasty. He gathered a sizable force of fanatical believers and set about leading a revolt, eventually taking control of large areas of south and central China, including the capital Nanking, where he set up a theocratic-military government.

His strict moral laws together with political infighting led to divisions, weakening the Taiping. In 1864 the Qing retook the capital and Hung's army of 100,000 committed suicide rather than surrender.

Hong Kong's early failure to live up to expectations irked the hongs, who incurred great expense moving their operations from Canton and Macau. Ships were bypassing Hong Kong, heading straight for the Treaty Ports, and frustration was compounded by the obstinacy of Chinese officials, who paid little heed to the Treaty of Nanking.

SECOND OPIUM WAR

Goading by the hongs to revise the treaty led to the Second Opium War (1856–1858), which was sparked off with the arrest of the Chinese crew of the *Arrow*, a Hong Kong ship flying the British flag, which was anchored off Canton. In August 1865, the Chinese seized the ship, searching for a notorious pirate they

Hong Kong's busy harbor soon after British settlement. Some ships bypassed the colony in favor of the Treaty Ports.

believed to be on board. The British were suitably outraged, claiming it was an insult to Queen and country.

Britain, this time in league with France, once again flexed its naval muscle along the China coast. Skirmishes ended in 1858 with the signing of the Treaty of Tientsin, which won the British a lease on Kowloon and diplomatic representation in Beijing. But when the first British envoy, Sir Frederick Bruce, was fired at on his way to Beijing to present his credentials, China had effectively reneged and hostilities resumed.

British and French troops occupied Beijing in October 1860. The Chinese once again succumbed and the Convention of Peking was signed, allowing the cession of Kowloon Peninsula up to what is now Boundary Road,

Sedan chairs and rickshaws were a popular mode of transportation for the colonialists.

and Stonecutter's Island, in perpetuity. Critically, the convention treaty allowed the British to import opium—for a modest tax—into China. Hong Kong's future suddenly looked very rosy.

GROWTH

By 1865, the population had risen to 122,000 and Hong Kong had attained a distinctly colonial profile. Government buildings, a police station, jail, post office, and a hospital had been constructed. The spires of handsome churches poked above the large compounds of the hongs, the lawns of rambling Government House swept down toward the harbor, and a grand gentlemen's club was built on the shoreline. Mansions began appearing on the slopes of Victoria Peak, and a cricket ground, polo club, and horse racetrack were laid.

In true British colonial style, snobbery and class distinction took hold. The elite chose the cool confines near the summit of Victoria Peak to live, while the less affluent Europeans and wealthy Chinese settled at the Mid-Levels. The Portuguese, Jews, Armenians, and Parsis built their homes at the foot of the Peak, and the vast majority of Chinese continued to live in squalor in the slums of Western and Wan Chai districts.

The 1890s was a turbulent decade. Turmoil in China depressed trade. In the face of worldwide economic depression, the Colonial Office demanded more money from Hong Kong for its military defense and the price of silver against sterling was falling. In 1894, the colony was struck by bubonic plague and half of the Chinese population of about 200,000 fled to China. Five hundred people died; Hong Kong was declared an infected port and shipping turned away. Over the next 12 years, the plague took 13,000 lives.

The British grew increasingly worried that their precious harbor would become vulnerable as other European nations began demanding concessions from China. They received land north beyond Kowloon Peninsula to the Shum Chum (Shenzhen) River, and the surrounding 234 islands through the Second Opium War. But this time it was to be a lease, not outright ownership, for 99 years. This land and islands, later known as the New Territories, was given over on July 1, 1898.

At the turn of the century, Hong Kong busied itself with public works as it tried to match the needs of a population that had grown to 325,000. A tramline along Hong Kong's foreshore was built, land reclamation was completed, reservoirs were planned, power utilities were set up, and port facilities

After four years of Japanese occupation, the British retook Hong Kong in August 1945.

were improved. By 1910, the colony had become the world's third biggest port, and the railroad line from Kowloon to the border with China was completed.

Meanwhile China was being wrenched apart by political upheaval, economic chaos, rebellion, and civil war, and waves of immigrants continued to make their way to Hong Kong. In 1911, Sun Yat-sen, recognized as modern China's founder, led a nationalist revolt that eventually toppled the Qing government and established the Republic of China in 1912.

Born to a farming family in Guangdong Province, Sun had studied earlier in Hawaii and practiced medicine and fermented revolution in Hong Kong. In 1913, his Nationalist Party (Kuomintang) won the most seats in China's first national elections, but later that year he was forced into exile by the military and his party was expelled from Parliament. Backed by Russia, Sun regained momentum and was on the verge of success when he took ill and died in Beijing in March 1925.

Between World Wars I and II, the Chinese in Hong Kong began to make their mark in business. Chinese companies moved away from insurance, shipbuilding, shipping, and real estate and into other enterprises such as banking, finance, and transportation. A Chinese elite

prospered and accumulated vast sums of money, although their acceptance among the upper echelons of British society in Hong Kong was guarded. All the money in the world, it seemed, still could not buy a mansion on the Peak if you were Chinese. This was to be forever a part of England unsoiled by "foreigners." The Peak Ordinance of 1904, which was not repealed until 1945, banned Chinese, except the servants of Europeans, from living on the Peak.

JAPANESE OCCUPATION

In 1937, the Japanese—who had occupied Manchuria in northeastern China since 1931—took Beijing and Shanghai and by 1938 controlled major cities in China's eastern coastal regions, including Canton. Refugees came pouring over the China–Hong Kong border, and by the outbreak of World War II, Hong Kong's population had surged to 1.6 million, with 500,000 of these sleeping in the streets. On December 8, 1941, the day after Pearl Harbor was bombed, Japanese forces swept into Hong Kong from the Chinese border. (The British earlier realized they had no hope of holding the colony, and refused to send reinforcements to bolster its ill-equipped defenses, while at the same time Prime Minister Winston Churchill demanded the colony hold out as long as it could.) British forces on the China–Hong Kong border, faced with overwhelming odds, were pushed back through the New Territories and Kowloon, with the last of them being evacuated to Hong Kong Island on December 13.

Before attacking Hong Kong Island, a Japanese officer, Lt.-Gen. Takashi Sakai, sent a note to Governor Mark Young demanding surrender. It said in part: "It [the surrender] will be honorable. If not, I, repressing my tears, am obliged to take action to overpower your forces."

After heavy bombing, the Japanese attacked the island on December 19. British, Canadian, and volunteer troops fought bravely and many were killed. On Christmas Day, Governor Young crossed the harbor to the Peninsula Hotel on Kowloon, which the Japanese were using as headquarters, and signed the surrender document.

What followed was over three miserable years of occupation. Most of the Europeans were interned at Stanley and Sham Shui Po, while the occupiers routinely terrorized the local people. Trade virtually disappeared, and the local currency was almost worthless. Power shortages were common and the island lived under the constant threat of starvation. To ease the strain on resources, the Japanese ordered mass deportations. By the end of the war, Hong Kong's population had been reduced to 600,000.

Following the news of the formal Japanese surrender on August 4, 1945, the colonial secretary Frank Grimson, who had been interned at Stanley, set up a provisional government. Echoing the adventures of Capt. CharlesElliot just over a century earlier, Grimson acted without authority from London, which was considering requests from the United States to return Hong Kong to Chiang Kai-shek's nationalist China. British rule was soon restored.

POSTWAR GROWTH

People flooded back into Hong Kong at the rate of 100,000 a month, and by the end of 1947, there were 1.8 million. With the imminent defeat of Chiang's nationalists by Mao Zedong's (1893–1976) communists, hundreds of thousands flooded over the border. When Mao took power in 1949, establishing the People's Republic of China, refugees continued to arrive, many fleeing from the commercial center of Shanghai. The flood was eventually stemmed when the communists sealed off the border between the New Territories and China.

In 1952, Hong Kong's future as an entrepôt (intermediary center of trade) looked shaky because of the trade embargo instituted by the U.N. against Communist China. Fortunately, many of the new arrivals from China were businessmen and entrepreneurs with capital. Aided by a willing workforce, the colony turned to manufacturing. It started with textiles, then moved into plastics, electronics, and watches. Throughout the 1950s and 1960s, economic growth was 10 percent a year and many of Hong Kong's rags-to-riches stories took place during this period. A "Made in Hong Kong" label may have indicated to the world something cheap and tawdry, but booming Hong Kong cared little.

CULTURAL REVOLUTION

By the mid-1960s, China's Cultural Revolution was under way, driven by Mao to instill a revolutionary spirit in the young. From it evolved the Red Guards, who, for the next decade, spread chaos throughout the country. Millions of people were persecuted, imprisoned, or killed, and China's cultural heritage was all but destroyed. The troubles spilled over into Hong Kong. In 1966, people rioted over a small increase in fares on the Star Ferry. Strikes by unionists and demonstrations by communist sympathizers followed. Curfews were imposed in 1967 when over 8,000 suspected bombs were defused. Hundreds more exploded; 50 people died and many more were injured. But the communists had little support from the majority of Hong Kong people, who were by now tired of this disruption to their daily lives. China, too, offered little support to the leftists, and toward year's end, the turmoil had petered out.

By the late 1960s, China began to move away from its isolationist policies. With the backing of the United States, it gained a seat on the U.N. Security Council. In 1971 the United States lifted trade sanctions and resumed diplomatic relations, setting Hong Kong on a path of unprecedented economic growth and prosperity.

THE 1970s & '80s

Increasing amounts of money in Hong Kong's coffers led to a massive improvement of the

Beijing's 1989 Tiananmen Square demonstrations led to protests in Hong Kong.

quality of life. Murray MacLehose, governor between 1971 and 1982, was the architect. He instituted a massive public housing program, moving hundreds of thousands of people from the colony's slums and re-housing them in multistory apartments, and introduced free and compulsory education to junior high school level, paving the way for an educated and skilled future workforce. He also created the Independent Commission Against Corruption (ICAC) in 1974 and gave it almost unfettered powers to investigate and prosecute rampant graft among police and other government officials. The ICAC was incredibly effective and pivotal to Hong Kong's success in attracting international businesses. MacLehose, a keen hiker, was also mainly responsible for creating the glorious network of country parks (see pp. 39–40) that now cover 40 percent of Hong Kong's total area.

By the late 1970s, China was continuing to open its doors. Most of Hong Kong's factories producing cheap manufacturing products were shifted across the border to Guangdong Province. The territory concentrated on building up its finance and service industries, and attracting international companies wanting to take advantage of the burgeoning economies of Asia, and particularly the new, trade-liberal "Open Door" policy introduced by China's paramount leader Deng Xaioping (1904–1997) in 1978. Things had never looked better; the economy was booming and gleaming new skyscrapers were altering the skyline of Hong Kong's Central District. By the early to mid-1980s, a new-look, cosmopolitan Hong Kong had earned its stripes as an international city.

British Prime Minister, Margaret Thatcher, visited China in 1982, setting off two years of often-bitter negotiations leading to a deal that eventually handed Hong Kong back to China. By 1984, the deal had been struck with the Sino-British Joint Declaration. Hong Kong was returning to China on July 1, 1997, the day the 99-year lease on the New Territories expired. It was to become a Special Administrative Region (SAR), with a high degree of autonomy. It could have its own currency, elect its own government, maintain its judiciary, and keep its capitalist economy and its freedoms for 50 years following its return to Chinese sovereignty. All these rights would be enshrined in a mini-constitution called theBasic Law. Deng tagged this arrangement "one country–two systems."

The Joint Declaration aimed to maintain the confidence of the people of Hong Kong, but given that a significant proportion of its population had fled communism in the mainland, more than a little nervousness was to be expected. The Joint Liaison Group, consisting of Chinese and British diplomats, was formed to agree arrangements for the transitional period. Constant assurances by both sides helped dispel doubts, but unease simmered.

TIANANMEN SQUARE

Doubt turned to near panic after June 4, 1989, when troops of the People's Liberation Army violently crushed democracy demonstrations in Beijing's Tiananmen Square. In the weeks leading up to it, millions of Hong Kong people had taken to the streets to demonstrate their support. The events that followed were extraordinary. At first there were public outpourings of grief never before seen in Hong Kong, as hundreds of thousands of citizens again took to the streets, wearing black arm bands and dressed in mourning in honor of those killed in Tiananmen Square. But then fear took hold. Thinking the same could happen in Hong Kong, many looked for a bolthole. Crowds jammed the foreign consulates of the United States, Australia, Canada, and Singapore seeking residency visas. Tiny countries in the Pacific and Caribbean started selling passports for $10,000 a time, and the territory was flooded by "immigration consultants" who became rich by guaranteeing to smooth the way for would-be emigrants. In the few years following the bloodshed in Tiananmen Square, over 100,000 people left Hong Kong. But things gradually calmed down. Hong Kong got back to business, and confidence in the future, even under the Chinese flag, gradually returned.

THE HANDOVER

Chris Patten, Hong Kong's last governor, arrived in 1992 with a political agenda unseen in previous governors. A politician—he was a Conservative member of Parliament in Britain, but lost his seat in the 1992 elections—Patten set about trying to institute political reforms that the British thought would offer safeguards for Hong Kong after the handover. The Hong Kong legislature, the Legislative Council, was at the time made up of appointed members, elected by their professional peers in "functional

constituencies," and about a third who were directly elected by universal franchise. Patten introduced a package that allowed for the election of all members of the legislature, much to the outrage of China, who saw it as a dismantling of the political processes set in the Basic Law. Elections under these reforms were held in 1995, but China refused to accept the authority of the new Legislative Council, and appointed its own Provisional Legislature.

Although initially very popular among the ordinary people of Hong Kong, not least for his social reforms and his down-to-earth nature, Patten polarized much of the powerful business community, which had been more than eager to please its future masters in Beijing. He was regularly pilloried by the Chinese government for his outspoken stance on political reform. As 1997 loomed, public opinion

began to side with the businessmen, believing it best to leave things as they were rather than upset China. Patten was replaced by the SAR's first chief executive, Tung Chee-hwa, following a somewhat muted handover ceremony on the evening of June 30, 1997.

Tung, a millionaire shipping magnate, was seen as China's pick for the job, although he was chosen from a number of candidates by a selection committee appointed by China's National People's Consultative Committee. Tung rode a wave of popularity following the euphoria of the handover, but things gradually turned sour during his first five-year term as the public saw many of his political decisions more likely made at the behest of China's leaders rather than in the interests of Hong Kong people. But his government did receive plaudits for the way it managed to stifle the worst

Beams of light illuminate a Chinese junk as part of the handover celebrations on July 1, 1997.

ravages of the 1997–99 Asian economic crisis, which severely affected neighbors Taiwan, Korea, and countries in Southeast Asia.

However, Tung's popularity continued to wane. At the behest of China, Tung tried to introduce a security law that brought hundreds of thousands of Hong Kong residents onto the streets in protests in 2003. The planned law was shelved but huge street protests against Tung's rule continued on and off, finally forcing him to step down midway through his second five-year term in early 2005. He was replaced by the territory's financial secretary Donald Tsang in June 2005. ∎

The land

GEOGRAPHICALLY, HONG KONG IS AN EXTENSION OF CHINA'S GUANGDONG Province. It sits at the tip of the province just to the east of the major waterway, the Pearl River Estuary, and just south of the Tropic of Cancer on a similar latitude to Hawaii. The territory covers only 424 square miles (1,098 sq km), but manages a remarkable variety of topographical features; from precipitous peaks plunging down to deep valleys laced with streams, to rocky, convoluted coastlines and numerous islands.

These peaks, with summits regularly rising above 1,640 feet (500 m), characterize Hong Kong more than any other natural feature. You can hardly look anywhere without some sheer mountain rising into the view. Hong Kong's most famous sight, the view across Victoria Harbor to the gleaming skyscrapers of Central District on Hong Kong Island, is made even more stunning by 1,811-foot (552 m) Victoria Peak looming in the background. And from the crests and shoulders of these often mist-cloaked peaks, one of the great surprises opens up to the visitor—remarkable vistas of crowded urban areas existing cheek by jowl with lush, green, mountainous countryside.

When the British arrived in the 1840s, the peaks of Hong Kong Island plunged into Victoria Harbor. Subsequent land reclamation projects pushed the island further into the harbor; Central District's high-rises are built on reclaimed land. Most of the island's 1.5 million people are squeezed along the narrow northern corridor.

The flat peninsula of Kowloon has also been increased by landfill. Gleaming Tsim Sha Tsui East was part of Victoria Harbor until the 1980s, and a huge landfill project on the western side of the peninsula has claimed more of the harbor. This area, along with adjoining New Kowloon, is one of the most densely populated places on Earth.

The New Territories is relatively uncrowded, although a series of "new towns," built since the 1970s, has increased the population significantly. This part of the territory is dominated by tall peaks—including Hong Kong's highest, Tai Mo Shan at 3,140 feet (957 m)—which fall to isolated wooded valleys and a heavily indented coastline of bays, coves, attractive beaches, and natural harbors. The northwest New Territories has Hong Kong's only extensive flatlands, an alluvial plain spreading out from Tai Mo Shan to the South China Sea.

Hong Kong's 234 outlying islands, the vast majority unpopulated, total 67 square miles (175 sq km). The largest, Lantau, is twice the size of Hong Kong Island and is the site of Hong Kong's International Airport. These islands, dotted with small towns and villages, are mostly a peaceful escape from Hong Kong's frenetic urban areas.

COUNTRY PARKS

Hong Kong has 23 country parks covering 40 percent of the territory's land area. Much of this land, originally at least, became country parks through accident rather than through any concerted effort to preserve natural heritage. During the 1950s and 1960s, as development spread from the main population centers, steep terrain got in the way. In the 1970s, these areas gradually became incorporated into country parks.

The parks are laced with a network of hiking trails and nature walks passing through beautiful scenery to the top of windswept peaks, down to wooded valleys, and along rocky coasts. There are four extended trails, linking up with local ones, within these parks. The longest, at 60 miles (100 km), is the MacLehose Trail, which crosses the New Territories. The 31-mile (50 km) Hong Kong Trail traverses Hong Kong Island, the 44-mile (70 km) Lantau Trail winds over Lantau Island, and the Wilson Trail, at 48 miles (78 km), heads from Hong Kong Island South, north across the territory. All trails are well maintained and signed with distances between points. Entry to the country parks is marked

Mirror Pool in Plover Cove Country Park is just one of Hong Kong's hidden refuges.

by map boards indicating the trails, while some have visitor centers. There are plenty of easy walks along nature paths.

WILDLIFE

Hong Kong is home to 47 species of native land mammals. Many of these are nocturnal (bats, for example, make up 22 of the total). Among them are barking deer, long-tailed macaque monkeys, mongooses, leopards, armadillo-like pangolins, civet cats, squirrels, Chinese quilled porcupines, and wild boars.

The territory is also surprisingly rich in birdlife, with more than 440 species, accounting for a third of the total species found in China. At Mai Po Nature Reserve, a protected wetland area in the northwestern New Territories, huge numbers of waterbirds shelter, especially during winters, when up to 70,000 birds from 300 species gather.

Much of Hong Kong's waters are either badly polluted or overfished, so they are not

particularly conducive to maintaining a healthy and teeming marine life. Hoi Ha Wan Marine Park, set in a sheltered bay at the northern tip of Sai Kung Peninsula, is a relatively pristine exception to this. The water quality here has allowed stony corals to thrive, with 39 of Hong Kong's recorded corals to be found there.

Populations of Chinese white dolphins are found in waters off the north of Lantau Island, although they are threatened by pollution and

Pokfulam Country Park on Hong Kong Island marries urban and bucolic vistas.

overfishing. The government has created the Sha Chau and Lung Kwu Chau Marine Park there in an attempt to preserve numbers. Another marine reserve, Tung Ping Chau, surrounding the island of Ping Chau in Mirs Bay off the northeastern point of Hong Kong, is home to more than 124 species of reef fish and several varieties of coral. ■

Arts & festivals

THE DEVASTATING CULTURAL REVOLUTION OF THE 1960s AND 1970s SAW the end of the tradition that was once integral to life on mainland China. But Hong Kong has kept alive many of these customs, and continues to celebrate them with all the clamor and color that make for exciting spectacle.

CHINESE OPERA

For the Western ear, the sounds emanating from the stage of a Chinese opera can take some getting used to. Performers sing in shrill falsetto, accompanied by the sometimes erratic and deafening banging of drums and gongs, and the high-pitched twanging and screaming of traditional string and wind instruments. Amid this cacophony, dressed in elaborate, multicolored costumes, heroes battle overwhelming odds, spirits defend the world against evil, and furtive lovers act in defiance of disapproving parents.

Singing, speaking, mime, swordplay, and acrobatics are incorporated into the performances, which are held during most of Hong Kong's major festivals. Makeshift stages are erected in public squares with rows of seats in front. Traditionally, operas can last as long as six hours, but these days most are limited to about three. You don't have to sit through the whole show. People come and go as they please, chat, walk around, and eat.

There are three types of Chinese opera regularly held in Hong Kong. **Beijing opera,** performed in the Mandarin language, is said to be the most refined. **Cantonese opera** is the most popular, owing to the use of the local language and the more down-at-home themes. The most traditional is **Chiu Chow** or **Chaozhou,** which maintains many of the original elements used when it was staged for the courts of the Ming dynasty.

Chinese opera relies as much upon its costumes, makeup, and gestures as it does on its song to relate its story to the audience. When the hands and body tremble, the character is angry; the flicking of a sleeve indicates disgust; while a hand thrown in the air and sleeves flicked back means surprise. Embarrassment is symbolized by the covering of the face with a sleeve. When worried, the character will rub his hands together for several minutes.

Heavy makeup is worn in place of the masks that were once used. In Beijing opera, a red face suggests a loyal and honest character, white is for the cunning, and blue for the courageous and enterprising nature. A yellow face means intelligence, while a black-faced character is honest, and brown is often the symbol of a stubborn and obstinate person. A clown role is indicated by a dab of white on the nose.

Color and headdress also play a symbolic part in costumes. Barbarians are dressed in purple, emperors in yellow. The more elaborate the headdress, the more important the character.

Props are minimal, while actors use exaggerated movement or symbolism to describe actions. Holding a whip indicates the person is riding a horse. A few soldiers can represent an entire army. A character circling the stage means he is on a long journey. Opening a door, walking at night, rowing a boat, eating, drinking, and other activities are indicated by stylized movements. Actors also use facial expressions to help convey specific meanings.

LION & DRAGON DANCES

While the lion is not native to China, it is rich in symbolism as it is considered a divine animal possessing nobility and dignity, able to protect truth and ward off evil. Pairs of lion statues often guard the entrances to large homes or buildings, keeping evil at bay and encouraging good fortune. Lion dances are performed at festivals and on special occasions, such as weddings and the opening of new businesses and enterprises. These are highly athletic affairs involving two people draped in cloth and holding the colorful and

Elaborate, colorful costumes and heavy makeup define Chinese opera performers. The productions—cacophonous and exciting affairs—are popular during festivals.

animated head of a lion. The lion's movements are accompanied by music. The bearded lion's eyes move, its mouth opens and closes, and the head jerks from side to side. Dragon dances, usually held during festivals, involve a larger group of people. The lead performer holds the multicolored head of the smiling dragon aloft with a pole, while others, partially hidden under cloth, flow in a snaking pattern to symbolize the dragon in flight.

MUSIC

Hong Kong's popular music scene is dominated by a style called Canto pop (see sidebar p. 131). These catchy, generally well-produced arrangements are sung in the native dialect of Cantonese and involve all the prerequisite lyrics of teenage angst. Incredibly popular and invariably good-looking performers sing tunes of unrequited love and loneliness and most of Hong Kong's young people sing along. Concerts held at the Hong Kong Coliseum and the Queen Elizabeth Stadium are highly polished affairs and nearly always sold out. Many of the hits are cover versions of popular U.S. and British pop songs, translated into Cantonese (Western pop music does not have a big following in Hong Kong). Canto pop stars make regular appearances on T.V. game and variety shows to maintain their exposure and many cross over into Hong Kong's movie industry to increase the popularity of a certain film. Top of the Canto pops include Leon Lai, Jackie Cheung, Andy Lau, and Aaron Kwok.

FILM

Hong Kong has the third largest film industry in the world after the United States and India, churning out movies at an astonishing rate (see pp. 146–47). While some Hong Kong films have been well received internationally and picked up a number of awards at film festivals around the world, the most popular in Hong Kong itself remain formulaic affairs involving stylized, bloody violence and weak scripts, or weepy romance. Even so, they still manage constantly to outperform Hollywood blockbusters at local movie theaters. The success of action director John Woo, and actors such as Jackie Chan, Michelle Yeo, Chow Yun-fat, and Jet Li in Hollywood over the past few years has brought about increased interest in

Hong Kong films in the West, and the territory has its own version of the Oscars each year at the glitzy Hong Kong Film Awards.

PERFORMANCE ART

While it would be easy to overlook in a place that is more concerned with business and material success than the finer points of the performing arts, Hong Kong does have a number of good-quality performance groups. Dance troupes include the Hong Kong Dance Company, which performs both traditional and modern Chinese dance; the City Contemporary Dance Company, which focuses on modern dance; and the Hong Kong Ballet Company.

The excellent Hong Kong Chinese Orchestra performs Chinese and modern music using traditional instruments, while the Hong

Kong Philharmonic Orchestra is the resident orchestra at the Hong Kong Cultural Center. Theater groups include the Hong Kong Repertory Theater Company, which puts on mainly Chinese works, and the Chung Ying Theater Company, a vehicle for up-and-coming Hong Kong playwrights. Many of these groups perform at the Hong Kong Cultural Center and the Hong Kong Academy for Performing Arts, both world-class venues.

CHINESE ARTS & CRAFTS

Europeans have hankered after Chinese arts and crafts since the country was widely opened up to trade from about the 16th century, and most highly prized were silks and porcelains.

The largest sector of the Chinese arts and crafts market is undoubtedly the embroideries

A large drum, a gong, and cymbals accompany the lion dance, performed on auspicious occasions to bring luck and happiness.

and brocades, recognized for their excellent craftsmanship. The finest silks used in their production come from the southeast and east, as these are the areas most conducive for growing mulberry trees, whose leaves the silk-worms feed on.

Blue-and-white porcelains from Jindezhen county in the central China province of Jiangxi are regarded as the best in the country because of their smooth texture and the intricacy of the designs.

Carvings—jade, ivory, wood, oxhorn, shell, and stone—are much sought after, with jade being the most popular and the most expensive. Jade carvings come in various shapes and

themes, from small figurines to sculptures crafted from huge slabs. Ivory is often used in the deft art of miniature carvings and paintings, and again the range of work is large, from trinkets and figurines to elaborate tableau carvings from a full elephant tusk mounted on timber.

The best places in Hong Kong to find these and other examples are at Chinese arts and crafts stores. There are stores at the China Resources Building, 26 Harbour Road, Wan Chai *(tel 2827-6667)* and Star House, opposite the Tsim Sha Tsui Star Ferry Pier *(tel 2735-4061)*.

FESTIVALS
January
City Fringe Festival: A month-long alternative arts festival at a variety of venues around Hong Kong. You can see off-beat theater, stand-up comedy, performance art, mime, dance, and art exhibits from local

and international artists *(tel 2521-7251, www.hkfringe.com.hk)*.

January/February

Chinese New Year: The first day of the first moon in the Chinese lunar year (dates vary from year to year). Many shops and businesses extend the official three-day public holiday into a week or more as people head abroad or across the border to mainland China for a vacation. It's about the only time of the year

A sleek dragon boat crewed by dozens of frenetic rowers hits the water during the annual June Dragon Boat Race.

when shops are closed. The start of the New Year is the time to wipe the slate clean, so debts are cleared and feuds ended. A spectacular fireworks display takes place on Victoria Harbor and the Hong Kong Island's skyscrapers try to outdo each other with colored-light displays on their towering facades.

Spring Lantern Festival (Yuen Siu): Held on the 15th day of the new moon, the festival celebrates the end of Chinese New Year. Hong Kong glows with lanterns prepared in traditional styles, which are placed in homes, restaurants, and temples.

February/March

Hong Kong Arts Festival: Top international performers gather in Hong Kong for one of Asia's most prestigious arts festivals. There are symphony, theater, ballet, Chinese opera, jazz, and traditional Asian orchestra performances during this month-long festival. Tel 2824-3555, www.hk.artsfestival.org

March/April

Ching Ming: Families head to their ancestors' graves to clean the sites, light incense, burn paper "spirit money," and make offerings of fruit and wine. It is traditionally held at the beginning of the third moon of the Chinese lunar calendar, but the date is usually fixed to early April.

April

Birthday of Tin Hau: Hong Kong's most popular deity—Tin Hau, goddess of the sea and of seafarers (see sidebar p. 93)—is celebrated with decorated boats streaming around the harbor and noisy and colorful street parades. Around 300 temples in Hong Kong are dedicated to the goddess. They were traditionally built beside the sea, but Hong Kong's huge land reclamation project has left many stranded inland, so the focus of the festival is mainly in the New Territories and outlying islands. The image of Tin Hau is often placed on a sedan chair and paraded through the streets, accompanied by ear-splitting fireworks. Chinese opera and traditional lion dances complete this riotous festival. It is held on the 23rd day of the third moon in the Chinese lunar calendar.

Hong Kong International Film Festival: Hundreds of movies from around the world are screened during this two-week-long celebration of cinema, including films from independent filmmakers. The festival is one of the best for those interested in Asian filmmaking (*www.hkiff.org.hk*).

May

Le French May Festival of Arts: Asia's biggest French festival when top talent from France performs theater, song, and dance. Art exhibitions are also held in this big-time promotion of French art and culture (*tel 3196-6209, www.frenchmay.com*).

June

Dragon Boat Race Month: Narrow, 50-foot-long (15 m) ornate boats are rowed by crews of 20 or more who have practiced for weeks beforehand. Crews paddle to a drumbeater who sits at one end of the boat. The event celebrates Qu Yuan, a third-century B.C. Chinese hero.

July

The first of the month is a holiday to mark Britain's return of the former colony to China in 1997. A huge fireworks display lights up the night sky over the harbor, which is best seen from Victoria Peak on Hong Kong Island or along Hong Kong Harbor.

August/September

Hungry Ghost Festival: You'll see people burning wads of paper "money" on little roadside bonfires, usually at sunset, to appease restless spirits—hungry ghosts who are said to wander the world for a whole lunar month. Some communities also stage street parades culminating in food offerings to the ghosts.

September/October

Mid-Autumn Festival: This celebrates the bright full harvest moon that invariably shines over Hong Kong at this time. Children visit open spaces such as parks, hills, and beaches with their families, waving colorful lanterns lit by candles. It's also the time when moon cakes, small but heavy and rich round pies, are made. It's held on the 15th day of the eighth lunar month.

October/November

Chinese Arts Festival: This month-long celebration of Chinese art and culture is the largest festival of its kind in the world. Art and performances from mainland China, Taiwan, Singapore, and numerous Chinese communities in other countries are highlighted. ■

From a "barren island with hardly a house upon it," the northern section of Hong Kong Island has grown into a vibrant metropolis, its stunning skyline recognizable the world over.

Hong Kong Island North

Jade, ivory, and wood seals

Hong Kong Island North

THE FOUNDING OF HONG KONG WAS AN INAUSPICIOUS AFFAIR—A UNION Jack casually planted by a Capt. Edward Belcher of the Royal Navy on what is now Possession Street in Western District on January 26, 1841, followed by a quick toast to Her Majesty Queen Victoria. Back home in England, the foreign secretary, Lord Palmerston (1784–1865), could barely contain his contempt for the acquisition of a "barren island with hardly a house upon it… Now it seems obvious that Hong Kong will not be a Mart of Trade."

Subsequent generations of residents showed little regard for Palmerston's pessimism and have molded the northern stretch of Hong Kong Island into one of the world's most vibrant places. Today 1.5 million people crowd onto this 30-square-mile (78 sq km) island, 7 percent of the total area of Hong Kong. Most are squeezed along its flat narrow northern corridor. From its western tip at Kennedy Town to Causeway Bay at its midpoint is a wall of tall skyscrapers. At Central, landfill has pushed the original shoreline 200 yards (180 m) into the harbor to accommodate modern high-rise architecture. The view of the skyline across Victoria Harbor from Tsim Sha Tsui, with Victoria Peak as a backdrop, is stunning.

Dining with a view at Café Deco, atop the Peak

Hong Kong
Area of map detail

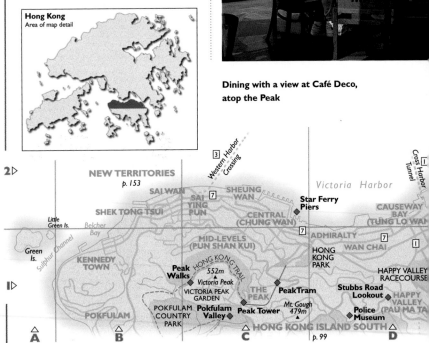

Just beyond the high-rises are the older, bustling, residential and commercial parts of Central, Western, and Wan Chai. Crowds spill from the sidewalks along narrow streets, while at Causeway Bay, shoppers seek the latest fashions in modern department stores. Minutes away, roads and trails wind up steep wooded hills to exclusive residential neighborhoods, the surprising peace of the countryside, and unsurpassed views of urban Hong Kong.

Despite the crowds and the sometimes debilitating heat, this part of Hong Kong is a great place for walking. The area's compactness and the ever changing nature of its streets provide plenty of entertainment. For the foot weary, one of the best ways to take in the sites of the northern corridor is to climb aboard a double-decker tram as it trundles from Kennedy Town in the west to Shau Kei Wan near the northeastern tip of the island. ■

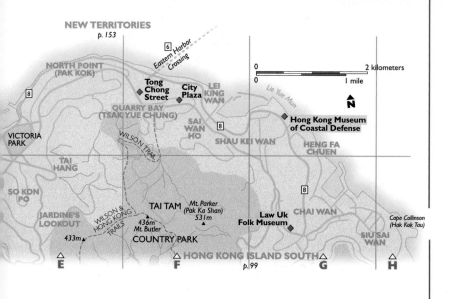

Central to the Peak

Central is the defining image of Hong Kong. It is here where British Hong Kong began in the 1840s and where the dynamism of today's city is at its most evident.

A lion dance celebrates the opening of a Central bank.

When banker Sir Catchick Paul Chater (1842–1923) arrived in Hong Kong in 1864, the overcrowded Central District fell into Victoria Harbor at the foot of Victoria Peak along Queen's Road. The only way to relieve this congestion, he reasoned, was to create more land by filling the lapping waters of the harbor. By 1889, landfill was being poured into Victoria Harbor. Today this reclamation runs for a half dozen blocks through some of the world's most expensive real estate. Around the same time, the government decided to forest barren Victoria Peak. Trees were hauled up the mountain and planted, eventually creating an area of great natural beauty on the doorstep of a frenetic downtown.

Central is an outstanding spectacle. Dozens of office towers are squeezed onto reclaimed land, while residential blocks climb the lower reaches of Victoria Peak at the Mid-Levels, gradually thinning to luxury apartment blocks and mansions among the mists of the Peak.

Hemmed in between these gleaming skyscrapers are pockets of preserved colonial history. Lively markets, noodle stands, restaurants, shop-houses, and worn tenement buildings crowd the back streets. To the east, Victoria Barracks, which once housed the Hong Kong Regiment, has given way to the landscaped beauty of Hong Kong Park.

Just outside the park, the 115-year-old Peak Tram begins its seemingly impossible climb up Victoria Peak. From here, the views are breathtaking. An easy walk around the shoulder of the Peak reveals the green side of Hong Kong Island—lush vegetation, verdant valleys, and vistas of the South China Sea and the outlying islands. ■

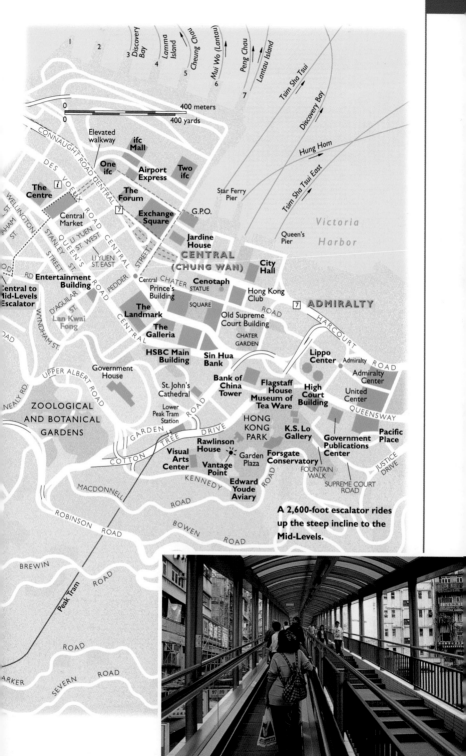

A 2,600-foot escalator rides up the steep incline to the Mid-Levels.

Shopping à la
mode at
Central's chic
Landmark mall

Central District

THIS SMALL, SOMETIMES ABSURDLY CROWDED POCKET OF
reclaimed land is the headquarters of hundreds of financial institu-
tions, home to the seat of government, and prestigious address to a
number of upscale shopping centers.

Central District

Map p. 53

Take the Star Ferry (see p. 120) from
Tsim Sha Tsui in Kowloon across
Victoria Harbor to the ferry's Central
pier for a spectacular introduction to
the area. Just to the west of the ferry
concourse, and at the doorstep of
Connaught Garden and the forceful
Henry Moore bronze sculpture

"Double Oval," is **Jardine House.**
The 600-foot-tall (201 m) building,
with its metallic-colored facade and
trademark porthole windows, was
the highest in Hong Kong when
constructed in 1973. Walk into the
lobby and take the escalator up one
floor to an elevated walkway which

Rickshaws

At the Star Ferry concourse is
an ever dwindling number of
rickshaw pullers, ready to take
tourists on a short ride or let them
pose (for a modest price) in front
of their vehicles.

Invented in Japan, rickshaws
were a popular mode of transportation in Hong Kong during the first
half of the 20th century. By World
War I, some 5,000 carried people

around the streets. Their numbers
plummeted, but were revived in the
difficult days after World War II,
when there was an estimated 8,000
on the streets. Numbers fell again
as motorized vehicles took over,
and by the 1960s they were used
mainly as a tourist attraction. Today,
only a handful of rickshaws are left,
all based at the Star Ferry concourse. ∎

leads to **Exchange Square,** a group of three semicircular office buildings with gold-bronze polished granite and glass exteriors resembling stacked coins. This is home to the Stock Exchange of Hong Kong, Asia's largest bourse, outside of Japan. The entrance is marked by another Henry Moore bronze, the powerful "Oval with Points," sitting in a circular basin surrounded by squirting water jets. Just beyond here, there are more sculptures— "Taichi," a chunky, flowing bronze figure representing *tai chi* exercises from Taiwan's Chu Ming, and Dame Elisabeth Frink's "Water Buffaloes" —sitting at different levels in pools of cascading water at **The Forum** courtyard, a pleasant plaza with outdoor cafés.

In front of Echange Square is the **ifc** (ifc stands for International Finance Centre) complex. It comprises the ifc Mall, One ifc at 39 floors, Two ifc, which, at 88 stories, is one of the highest buildings in the world, and the Four Seasons Hotel Hong Kong.

The **ifc Mall** is a brightly lit chrome and tile collection of cinemas, upmarket retail outlets and restaurants, and encompasses Hong Kong Station MTR station for trains on the Airport Express Line.

The elevated walkway in front of Exchange Square runs all the way to the Macau Ferry Terminal at the Shun Tak Center about 500 yards (1 km) farther west. Take the walkway to the left just beyond Exchange Square, across Connaught Road Central to Pottinger Street and down to the ground-level bustle of Central. Head south up Pottinger Street to Des Voeux Road Central and one block east to the parallel lanes of **Li Yuen Street East** and **Li Yuen Street West,** which cut south to Queen's Road Central. These busy, down-at-heel streets are lined with stands selling clothes, fabrics, handbags, and other goods at knockdown prices, in contrast with the swank shopping centers at the Prince's Building (*corner of Ice House St. & Chater Rd.*), and the **Landmark,** flanked by Pedder Street, Des Voeux Road Central, and Queen's Road Central. Built in 1980, the Landmark contains five floors of designer boutiques framing a giant atrium centered with a lively fountain.

Climb D'Aguilar Street, one block east of Li Yuen Street, to the cobbled laneways of **Lan Kwai Fong,** Hong Kong's lively nightlife center. Dozens of restaurants, bistros, bars, and nightclubs catering to the territory's hip residents cluster in two small lanes.

The pyramid style is echoed at the **Entertainment Building** (*Corner of Queen's Rd. Central & Wyndham St.*). Whimsical touches, like the huge balconies on two sides at the penthouse level and an art deco motif in the frieze around the building, lift the beige granite and gray glass facade above the ordinary. Inside is an elegant colonnaded shopping arcade.

Upscale attire at a Central boutique

STATUE SQUARE & EAST

Follow Queen's Road Central east and cut through the plaza under the Hongkong and Shanghai Bank Building (see p. 62) to the gardens, pools, and fountains of restful **Statue Square.** It gets its name from the number of British colonial statues, including those of Queen Victoria (*R.*1837–1901) and King Edward VII (*R.*1901–1910), which once decorated the small park. The Japanese removed them during World War II (Queen Victoria now rests in Victoria Park in Causeway Bay; see pp. 93–94). The lone holdout is frock-coated Sir Thomas Jackson (1841–1915), a one-time chief manager of the Hongkong and Shanghai Bank. The imposing

Many of Central's most famous skyscrapers tower above the Zoological and Botanical Gardens.

Bank of China Tower
- Map p. 53
- 1 Garden Rd., Central
- 2826-6888

headquarters of the bank lies opposite on Queen's Road Central. Take a look at the two splendid bronze lion figures out front—the one at the eastern end of the bank building is punctured with a number of bullet holes, a legacy of the Japanese occupation during World War II. On the northern side of Chater Road in Statue Square, a **Cenotaph,** built in 1923 and now a monument to troops who died during the two World Wars, sits surrounded by lush lawn in front of the Hong Kong Club, the venerable gentleman's establishment.

Just east of Statue Square, on the opposite side of Hong Kong's seat of government, the neoclassic Legislative Council Building (also known as the Old Supreme Court Building; see p. 60), is **Chater**

Garden. Designed in similar style to Statue Square, with brick and tiled pathways, gardens, shelters, pools, and lawns, it's a good place to escape the stifling daytime heat. Up until 1975, the park was the playing field for the exclusive Hong Kong Cricket Club. Climb the walkway that fringes the eastern end of the garden for excellent views of the towering 1,209-foot (396 m) **Bank of China Tower.** Designed by I.M. Pei in 1982, this 70-story building, notable for its incredibly sharp lines, pristine facade, and bulky intimidating presence, is the dominant building of Central's skyline. Take the express elevator to the 43rd floor for panoramic views of the city and harbor. Next door, the art deco old Bank of China building, now the **Sin Hua Bank,**

is Central's oldest surviving high-rise office tower, completed in 1951.

From Statue Square an underpass leads back under Connaught Road to the Star Ferry concourse. From there, you can stroll east along the waterfront to Queen's Pier—a small, sheltered jetty where chartered junks and cruise yachts pick up passengers for harbor cruises—for unhindered views across the harbor to Tsim Sha Tsui. Behind the pier stands **City Hall,** a nondescript building housing a fine concert hall and theater. Here you can pick up information about upcoming concerts and performances, and buy and reserve theater tickets. A small, pleasant park adjoining the building makes an attractive photographic backdrop for wedding couples who have just tied the knot at City Hall's marriage registry.

ZOOLOGICAL & BOTANICAL GARDENS

The lush tropical vegetation and Victorian-style gardens, gazebos, and enclosures at the Zoological and Botanical Gardens make it an appealing place to visit, although the restricted space of some of the animal compounds can be a bit of a turnoff.

Opened in 1864, the gardens are the oldest in Hong Kong and encompass a total of 13 acres (5 ha). The eastern section is known as the Old Gardens and its attractions include a children's playground, aviaries, a rather sorry-looking jaguar enclosure, a greenhouse, and a fountain terrace garden. The majority of the zoo's animals are kept in the New Gardens to the west.

Despite the forlorn nature of some of the animal enclosures, the zoo has a comprehensive selection of Asian wildlife, and is one of Asia's most important centers for breeding endangered species.

The gardens are bounded by Garden, Robinson, Glenealy, and Upper Albert Roads, and divided into two parts by Albany Road, with a subway linking them. ∎

Zoological & Botanical Gardens

- Map p. 53
- Albany Rd., Central
- 2530-0154
- Bus: 3B, 12M

City Hall

- Map p. 53
- 3 Edinburgh Pl., Central
- 2921-2840

Filipino domestic helpers relax in Central on their day off.

Domestic helpers

Every Sunday, the area around Statue Square and Chater Garden in Central becomes the meeting place of Hong Kong's vibrant community of Filipino workers. Thousands of women crowd the parks and surrounding streets on their only day off, causing Central to drop its serious face for a day and embrace a lively festival atmosphere.

The vast majority of the 140,000 immigrant workers from the Philippines are women, and most of them are employed as domestic helpers by middle- and upper-class Hong Kong families. Here they can earn more than many highly skilled workers back home. ∎

Central to Mid-Levels Escalator
⎙ Map p. 52

Central to Mid-Levels Escalator & around

AT QUEEN'S ROAD CENTRAL, CENTRAL BEGINS ITS STEEP climb toward the residential area of the Mid-Levels. Streets in between are narrow and winding, with some so steep that steps replace roads. Flashy high-rise buildings give way to more modest stores and restaurants topped by tenements.

Central's lively back streets harbor noodle shops, small markets, and other vibrant facets of daily life.

Start your journey at the world's longest covered escalator (2,600 feet/800 m), at Central Market. From here, a first-floor arcade connects you to the Central to Mid-Levels Escalator (*downhill 6 a.m.–10 a.m.; uphill 10 a.m.– 11 p.m.*). The escalator was

completed in 1993 to ease the passage of residents getting home via taxi and minibus through the winding streets linking Central to the Mid-Levels. It rides up Cochrane Street past the second-floor windows of apartment buildings and shops to Hollywood Road (see p. 74). It then doglegs west, continuing south up Shelley Street before reaching its final point at Conduit Road in the heart of the Mid-Levels. Passengers can get off at a number of clearly marked exits en route and explore the narrow streets and alleyways.

Stanley Street is worth investigating for its fragrant outdoor noodle and pastry shops. **Graham Street,** one block to the west, is lined with Chinese herb and medicine shops, and hawkers selling fresh produce. A left turn at **Gage Street** reveals more lively markets. From here, **Peel Street** continues the climb to Hollywood Road past stores selling religious paraphernalia. East along Hollywood Road for one block brings you to **Lyndhurst Terrace.** Continue east on Lyndhurst to rejoin the escalator. At Staunton, Elgin, and Shelley Streets, a trendy restaurant and nightclub precinct called **SoHo**—an abbreviation of South of Hollywood Road—has sprung up in the escalator's shadow to rival Lan Kwai Fong (see p. 55). The journey up the escalator takes about 20 minutes, and steps beside it lead back down the hill. ∎

Admiralty

ADMIRALTY WAS THE SITE OF THE HONG KONG REGIMENT'S Victoria Barracks and, up until the Chinese handover in 1997, the Royal Navy's headquarters at Tamar. After the handover, the Tamar site was acquired by the People's Liberation Army and renamed Central Barracks. A few of the original buildings remain in Hong Kong Park (see pp. 64–65).

The military vacated Victoria Barracks during the 1970s, freeing the valuable land for redevelopment. Shopping centers, hotels, and office towers replaced them. Admiralty can be reached from Central by taking the elevated walkway at the eastern end of Chater Garden. Along this route are the twin towers of the **Lippo Center,** a brash and dominating office building featuring bold "sky windows"—lumpy protrusions hanging from its sides. This building has been nicknamed the "koala tree", as its shape vaguely resembles koalas gripping the trunk of a tree. In the lobby, two dramatic bas-relief murals by one of Hong Kong's best known artists, Gerard D'Henderson, cover the walls.

Next to the Lippo Center, the shopping arcades of the United Center and Admiralty Center join an elevated walkway to **Pacific Place,** a combination of malls, department stores, boutiques, bars, cinemas, offices, luxury hotels, and restaurants. When it was completed in the early 1990s, the boldness and enterprise of glitzy Pacific Place reflected the optimism and growing affluence of Asia at the time, and became the prototype for similar developments around the region. The complex is worth a visit for its sheer size and overstatement.

Adjoining Pacific Place, the **High Court Building** is housed in an unexceptional building, but arouses interest in its courtrooms where barristers and judges still dress in wigs and flowing robes and proceed through cases with the same due formality of British courts. There are public galleries.

On the ground-floor level between Pacific Place and the High Court is the **Government Publications Center,** a good place to pick up maps and publications on Hong Kong. ■

Admiralty
Map p. 53

High Court Building
38 Queensway
2869-0869

Government Publications Center
Room 402, Murray Bldg., Garden Rd., Central
2537-1910

The audacious Lippo Center

The French Mission Building—now housing the Court of Final Appeal—is one of a number of colonial buildings found in Central.

A walk around Central's colonial heritage

Hong Kong has few older buildings of architectural merit, but the scattering of historical remnants around Central provides some insight into the territory's colonial past.

Start in front of the **Old Supreme Court Building ❶** (*8 Jackson Rd.*), which divides Statue Square and Chater Garden. This fine neoclassic building, with its domed roof, was built in 1912 and became home to the Hong Kong government's legislature in 1985.

From here cross Des Voeux Road Central to the Hongkong Bank Building. Walk through its plaza and cross Queen's Road Central to the steps of tree-lined **Battery Path.** The path was built in 1841 to allow British troops to drag their cannon to higher ground. A five-minute climb brings you to the redbrick **French Mission Building ❷**. Rebuilt in 1917, it's also in neoclassic design. It now houses the Court of Final Appeal, set up after Hong Kong was handed back to China in 1997.

Continue up Battery Path to Garden Road and the 1849 **St. John's Cathedral ❸**

(*4–8 Garden Rd., tel 2523-4157*). With its Gothic-style architecture, cruciform shape, and ornate bell tower above the main entrance, it's the oldest ecclesiastical building in Hong Kong.

Climb Garden Road for five minutes toward the Lower Peak Tram Station at St. John's Building, on the opposite side of Garden Road, to the **Helena May Building ❹** (*35 Garden Rd.*). It was constructed in 1916 at the request of the wife of Francis Henry May, who governed between 1912 and 1917, as a hostel for young women arriving in the colony, a function it still serves. It can be difficult to cross Garden Road, so stay on the right and keep climbing to Upper Albert Road and **Government House ❺**, official residence for British Hong Kong governors from 1855 to 1997. The building's colonial look was modified during the Japanese occupation with the addition of a rectangular eave tower. It is used now for official functions but is closed to the public. There are good views of it from its front gates. The new Chief Executive, Donald Tsang, will use it as his official residence, unlike his predecessor. Government House's garden is open to the public six times each year, usually on official holidays. Visitors are also usually allowed to pass by the Drawing Room, Dining Room, and Ballroom on these days.

Backtrack down Upper Albert Road to Lower Albert Road. Follow it to Ice House Street. Opposite is the two-story **Old Dairy Farm Building** ❻ (*Lower Albert Rd.*). Built in 1892 and renovated between 1912 and 1917, it is notable for its horizontal striped walls of red brick and white stucco, first-floor porthole windows, ornate shingles, and bull-nose corner, and is home to one of Hong Kong's best known bars at the Foreign Correspondents Club.

Opposite, near the intersection of Lower Albert and Glenealy Roads and Wyndham Street, is the home of the Anglican Bishop of Hong Kong at **Bishop's House** ❼ (*1 Lower*

Albert Rd.). This 1848 building features a circular tower and lookout at one of its corners. Looking south to Glenealy Road, you will notice the Gothic-inspired spire of St. Paul's Church, from the early 20th century.

From the Old Dairy Farm Building, you can make your way down Wyndham Street to Queen's Road Central. ■

🗺 See area map p. 52
▶ Old Supreme Court Building
↔ 1.5 miles (2.5 km)
⏱ 2 hours
▶ Corner of Wyndham St. & Queen's Rd. Central

NOT TO BE MISSED
- Old Supreme Court Building
- Battery Path
- St. John's Cathedral
- Government House

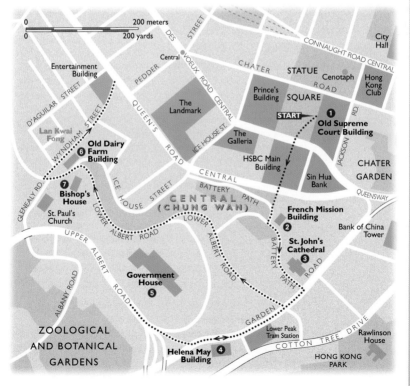

HSBC Main Building

🗺 Map p. 53

✉ 1 Queen's Rd., Central

☎ 2822-1111

🕐 Closed Sat. 1 p.m. & Sun.

🚇 MTR: Central

HSBC Main Building

WHEN THE HEADQUARTERS OF HSBC (FORMERLY THE Hongkong & Shanghai Banking Corporation) was completed in 1985, it had cost one billion U.S. dollars, making it the most expensive building ever constructed at the time. But for the bosses of the bank, it was well worth the cost; its innovation and sophistication make it one of the most recognizable buildings in the world.

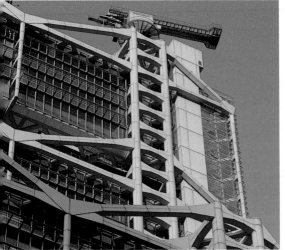

This detail reveals the structure's "coat hanger" framework.

When architect Sir Norman Foster (1935–) took on the challenge to design the building, his major problem was squeezing it into the space made available at 1 Queen's Road Central after the demolition of the previous headquarters (the current structure is the fourth on this site since the bank's founding in 1865. The bank wanted to fit a huge office tower into an area that would normally preclude such design.

Foster got around this problem by eliminating a central core and instead designed a framework that hung from five huge trusses, with eight groups of four-column steel clusters, wrapped in aluminum, supporting them. The "coat hanger" effect resulted in a building whose floors hang from above, rather than ascend from below. This design also allowed for the inclusion of a giant atrium, opening up a huge amount of space and light. Extra natural light is achieved by the use of computer-controlled mirrors that reflect light into the atrium.

The extensive use of non-reflective glass in the design reveals the mechanical workings of the building and has earned it the nickname the "robot building." The gears, chains, motors, and other moveable parts of the escalators and elevators are visible.

Although space may have been a problem, money never was. Bank executives stressed to Foster that they wanted the best possible, implying that cost was a secondary matter. The design had to symbolize the power, stability, and technological proficiency of the bank itself. "The world's most expensive building" tag became their proud boast, rather than an embarrassment of excess and a waste of stockholders' money.

The ground floor is public space you can pass through without entering the building. From there, two escalators rise to the main banking hall. They are carefully positioned to take the maximum flow of *qi* or *chi* (energy) into the building, one of the concessions made to the principles of *feng shui* (see pp. 110–11). Two bronze lions, part of the previous bank building, are placed at each end of the bank, ensuring harmony. ■

The unusual skeletal profile of HSBC's headquarters sets it apart from the other skyscraping marvels that fill Central.

Hong Kong Park

HONG KONG PARK IS A COLLECTION OF GARDENS, MAN-made waterfalls, lakes and ponds, playgrounds, greenhouses, museums, galleries, and aviaries sitting between a wall of high-rise buildings and towering mountains. Exploring this 25-acre (10 ha) jumble of artifice, antiquity, and natural beauty makes a delightful rest from Central's crowded streets.

Hong Kong Park
- 50 DI
- 19 Cotton Tree Dr.
- 2521-5041
- MTR: Admiralty, exit F

Flagstaff House Museum of Tea Ware
- 10 Cotton Tree Dr.
- 2869-0690
- Closed Tues. and some public holidays
- MTR: Admiralty, exit F

Escalators at Pacific Place (see p. 59) bring you to the park's main entrance at Supreme Court Road (there are two other entrances along Cotton Tree Drive). The **Fountain Walk** takes you to the main gates and inside the park.

Walk to the right of the park's restaurant, past a winding artificial lake to a covered walkway that runs up to **Rawlinson House,** one of a few 19th-century Victoria Barracks buildings in the park, and now the Cotton Tree Drive Marriage Registry. Opposite is the **Garden Plaza,** a terraced, open-air theater themed as a Greek amphitheater and built into the hillside. Performances of live music, plays, and puppet theater are held on Sundays and public holidays. Visitors can get free *tai chi* lessons

here *(Hong Kong Tourism Board Visitors Hotline, tel 2508-1234).*

Steps between the marriage registry and Garden Plaza climb to the base of the **Vantage Point,** a circular tower whose spiral staircase leads to an observation deck and stunning views of Central, with glimpses of Victoria Harbor. Head through the walled Tai Chi Court. In the cooler hours of early morning and late afternoon, its courtyards fill with tai chi practitioners.

Beyond is the park's most impressive feature, the walk-though **Edward Youde Aviary.** Named for one of Hong Kong's nature-loving colonial governors, it is one of the largest of its type in the world. This huge meshed enclosure, simulating a tropical rain forest, houses 800 birds from 100 species. Beneath the enclosure is the remarkable mock-up of a 1,000-year-old rain forest. You can get close to birds from the elevated timber walkway, which zigzags through the aviary at tree-canopy level. About 50 feet (15 m) below, a creek bubbles through the forest.

On the southern fringe of the park is the **Visual Arts Center** *(tel 2521-3008, closed Mon.)*, converted from the restored Cassels Block of Victoria Barracks. It is one of Hong Kong's more elegant colonial buildings, with a stepped roof, cool verandas, and a garden setting. A modern gallery annex topped with a steel and glass spine roof has been added. As well as an exhibition gallery, there are studios used by local artists.

Heading back toward the main entrance past the Garden Plaza and the aviary, you will see the impressive **Forsgate Conservatory,** built into a slope. This greenhouse, the largest in East and Southeast Asia, has a number of climate-controlled environments including a tropical rain forest terraced with dense vegetation and flowering plants, a "dry" plant house replicating a desert environment, and an exhibition hall.

FLAGSTAFF HOUSE MUSEUM OF TEA WARE

At the northern perimeter of the park, this museum is housed in one of Hong Kong's oldest surviving colonial buildings. Originally constructed in ungainly Greek Revival style, Flagstaff House has undergone a number of transformations. Today, with its whitewashed, unadorned facade, uncomplicated rectangular shape, columned verandas, huge shuttered windows, and lofty position, it represents one of the finest examples of mid-19th-century colonial architecture in Hong

Kong. The interior layout has changed little from the original, though the military commanders' bedrooms, dressing rooms, library, drawing room, and servants quarters are now replaced by galleries.

A Victoria crown pigeon at the park's rain-forest aviary

The fascinating core of the museum's permanent exhibition consists of 600 pieces of tea ware, from the Western Zhou period (ca 1122–771 B.C.) up until the present. Song dynasty tea ware includes an elegant tea cup on a stand finished in Yingqing glaze, a ewer with a wispy carved peony design, and tea bowls in russet brown glaze and molded designs.

The ground-floor galleries host the "Chinese Tea Drinking" exhibition that shows different methods of tea preparation throughout Chinese history. Exquisite tea ware from the Tang dynasty (618–907) through the Qing dynasty (1644– 1911) is on display here. Temporary exhibitions are held in the upper galleries, and a gift shop just inside its main door sells tea ware, Chinese tea, art books, and exhibition catalogs.

The **K.S. Lo Gallery,** adjacent to the Museum of Tea Ware, contains rare Chinese ceramics from the Song dynasty (960–1279) to the Ming dynasty (1368–1644), as well as seals from the late Ming dynasty to the present. ■

Chinese tea

Ancient Chinese texts attribute the discovery of tea to Emperor Shen Nung, who was believed to have ruled about 2737 B.C. According to legend, he was sipping hot, boiled water in his garden when a leaf from a tea bush nearby fell into his cup. He smelled and tasted the infusion and reckoned it was a big improvement over hot water. Tea drinking was born.

Stores selling innumerable varieties of tea can be found in the Western District.

The practice took a while to catch on, however. Though historians can trace the harvesting, manufacture, and drinking of tea back 2,000 years, its cultural significance did not begin until the Tang and Song dynasties. *The Tea Classics*, the bible of tea, written by Lu Yu during the Tang dynasty, helped to elevate the art of tea drinking throughout China. During the Song dynasty, books, poems, and paintings about tea pushed the act into a cultural experience. Ming-dynasty scholar Li Ri Hua offered instructions on how and when tea should be consumed:

"One should clean out a room in one's home and place only a tea table and a chair in the room with some boiled water and fragrant tea. Afterwards, sit salutarily and allow one's spirit to become tranquil, light, and natural."

The Chinese believe their view on tea drinking is symbolic of their balanced position toward attitudes and behaviors, and that in the interpretation of the art of tea, you can find the source of their open-mindedness.

Unlike the Japanese, who place heavy emphasis on rigid ceremony, the Chinese concentrate more on preparation, taste, and how to drink tea, with a tea master in charge of proceedings. Traditionally, a red clay pot is used to brew the tea. The tea master rinses the pot and tiny cups—which only hold about two swallows—then places the tea leaves in the pot. Hot spring water from a glass kettle is poured into the pot until the water overflows. The water is quickly drained to enhance the flavor of the tea. More water is poured into the pot and left to steep for under a minute and then poured into the cups ready to drink. Much detail is paid to the amount of tea used, the temperature of the water—different leaves require different temperatures—and how long the tea steeps; too long or too short affects the aroma and taste.

Types of tea

Of hundreds of varieties of Chinese tea, many of which are sold in merchants' shops in Hong Kong's traditional Western District, there are six major types:

Green tea has the longest history and is most popular, with a freshness and natural fragrance many find appealing. Famous examples include Longjing, Maofeng, Yinzhen, and Yunwu.

Black tea is another popular type, especially outside of China. The fermentation process turns the tea from green to black, offering a more robust taste.

Wulong tea mixes the freshness of green tea and the robustness of black tea. It is reputed to be helpful in losing weight and therefore has gained in popularity. Because it grows on cliffs and is difficult to pick, it is one of the more expensive Chinese teas.

White tea is a silver color and does not cloud when added to water.

Scented tea is made by mixing green tea with flower petals using an elaborate process.

Sweet osmanthus, jasmine, rose, orchid, and plum flowers are used.

Compacted tea is black or green tea tightly packed into brick, cake, or ball shapes. Because it's easier to store, it's popular with China's ethnic minorities—especially nomadic herdsmen—in the border regions. ■

Above & below: Nearly obliterated by the Cultural Revolution, tea drinking is undergoing a mini-revival in Hong Kong. Traditional teahouses, such as this one in Kowloon, are wonderful places to watch a tea master prepare the leaves—then sample the delicious result yourself.

The Peak's
famous vista
over Hong Kong
Island and beyond

The Peak

FROM THE PEAK'S VARIOUS VANTAGE POINTS SPECTACULAR vistas take in most of Hong Kong Island, Kowloon, much of the New Territories, the outlying islands, mainland China, and Macau. A trip to the Peak should be one of the first things visitors do after arriving in Hong Kong, not only for its world-famous views, but to gain a perspective of the city. Pick a cloudless day and make two journeys, one during daylight and another in the evening to catch a memorable image of Hong Kong illuminated.

Peak Tower
🚇 50 C1
✉ 128 Peak Rd.
☎ 2849-0668
🚌 Bus: 15; Minibus: 1

The Peak has been the preferred residence in Hong Kong since the British arrived in 1841. Top government officials and *taipans* (European merchants) built their mansions there to escape the stifling summer heat—it's cooler than the lower reaches of Hong Kong Island—and were ferried up and down its steep slopes in sedan chairs carried by Chinese coolies. The governor's summer residence was built there and anyone who wished to settle in this rarified atmosphere had to gain permission from the governor of the day. Up until 1945, Chinese were forbidden to live on the Peak. These days, the area remains a

fashionable place, reflected in real estate prices that are among the highest in the world.

Most visitors to Victoria Peak arrive by a funicular railway (see sidebar p. 70), which climbs out of Central at an impossible angle to reach the upper station at the **Peak Tower**—a metallic, bowl-shaped landmark. From the terrace on the fifth floor of the tower, the views are quite outstanding, looking down the mountain to the high-rise apartments of the Mid-Levels and the gleaming office towers crowded into Central, and beyond that across busy Victoria Harbor to Tsim Sha Tsui and Kowloon, backed by the green

jagged mountains of the New Territories.

The Peak Tower has souvenir shops, restaurants, a **Madame Tussaud's** wax museum, and a motion simulator ride called the **Peak Explorer.** Impressive views can be had from the restaurants at the adjacent **Peak Galleria,** a shopping and restaurant complex with some outdoor seating.

PEAK WALKS

The cheek-by-jowl existence of Hong Kong Island's countryside and city is at its most evident and dramatic around Victoria Peak. Views from its northern face look down over green slopes to towering residential and office towers. From its southern aspect, you can see wooded valleys, peaceful islands, and cozy water-side communities.

All walks start at the confluence of roads next to the Peak Tower and the Galleria. The paths that spread from here are signposted and give approximate walking times to different destinations.

The summit of Victoria Peak

is actually another quarter mile (500 m) to the west, up steep Mount Austin Road, opposite the Peak Tower. The Japanese razed the governor's mansion here during World War II, and the area is now a pleasant **garden.** The views, which include the neoclassic mansions of Hong Kong's super-wealthy, are magnificent.

One of the most popular walks is a 70-minute amble around the Peak along **Lugard Road** and **Harlech Road.** The 2.2-mile (3.5 km) route encircles Victoria Peak along a smooth, mostly flat pathway. Start at the Peak Tower and head west along Lugard Road through groves of ferns, stunted Chinese pines, rhododendron, bamboo, and hibiscus. As you head west, views open up to Victoria Harbor, the huge West Kowloon reclamation project, the Yau Ma Tei Typhoon Shelter, and Green and Peng Chau Islands. Lantau, Hong Kong's largest island, comes into view to the west, as does Macau (see pp. 216–17). Farther west you will spot Cheung Chau Island and to the southwest,

Madame Tussaud's
✉ Peak Tower, Level 2
☎ 2849-6966
$ $$

Peak Explorer
✉ Peak Tower, entrance Level 4
☎ 2849-0668
$ $

two huge power-plant smokestacks rise from Lamma Island (see pp. 204–205). The pathway rounds to the south side of the island to scenes of lush Pokfulam Valley and the junks and sampans anchored in Aberdeen Typhoon Shelter. The walk ends back at the Peak Tower.

About 1.4 miles (2.3 km) into the walk, you can take a track descending into the thickly wooded **Pokfulam Valley** to Pokfulam Reservoir—the 1.2-mile (1.9 km) route takes about 40 minutes. From just beyond the reservoir, you can catch a bus back to Central.

For views of the eastern and southeastern sides of Hong Kong Island, head south down Peak Road about 500 yards (1 km) from the Galleria to Plunket Road, which forks to the left and leads to Plantation Road. Follow Plantation Road until it meets **Severn Road,** then turn right and start your first descent as it circles almost halfway around the Peak. From here Aberdeen Typhoon Shelter comes into view. Farther to the left is sprawling Ocean Park (see pp. 112–13), the

Deep Water Bay residential area, and Repulse Bay, home to Hong Kong's favorite beach.

As Severn Road swings abruptly left, you will see expansive vistas of the eastern section of Hong Kong Island and Victoria Harbor. Causeway Bay Typhoon Shelter and North Point appear on the right, while across the harbor is the skyline of Tsim Sha Tsui and, to its right, the runway of Kai Tak airport, which was replaced in 1998 with the international airport at Chek Lap Kok. Follow Severn Road west as it climbs back toward the Peak to Findlay Road and on to the Galleria. The 3-mile (5 km) walk takes about 90 minutes.

You can also head down to the Zoological and Botanical Gardens (see p. 57) and on to Central by following the steep and winding **Old Peak Road** down the summit. The road begins between the Peak Tower and Galleria. Stop 100 yards (90 m) down the hill at the Chinese-style **Lion's Pavilion and Lookout** for unhindered views of Central, the harbor, and Tsim Sha Tsui. ∎

The steep slope puts your adrenal system to the test during the heart-pounding tram ride to the Peak.

Peak Tram

Taking the Peak Tram from its lower station at Murray House on Garden Road in Central is a memorable way to get to the Peak. Completed in 1888, the tram was the first power-driven form of land transportation in the colony. It was built to satisfy the needs of the colonial elite, who sought a more comfortable way home from Central other than a shaky sedan-chair ride up Old Peak Road. Five lateral stations were built en route, enabling passengers to hop off the tram for the trip to their mansions by foot or sedan chair—or, in the case of one resident, by camel.

These days, the modern carriages of the Peak Tram funicular railway carry visitors up from the bustle of Central through the smart apartment blocks of the Mid-Levels at an unbelievable angle. Before the tram glides into its upper station at the Peak Tower, the striking panorama of Central, the harbor, and the Kowloon Peninsula is laid out below as the tram clears tree line at the mid-reaches of Victoria Peak.

After more than a century of operation, the tram has never had an accident. The 12-minute ride operates daily every 15 minutes from 7 a.m. to midnight. ∎

Hong Kong Trail

Views, views, and yet more views along the Hong Kong Trail

OF HONG KONG ISLAND'S 30 SQUARE MILES (78 SQ KM), JUST over a third is given over to country parks. These parks are linked by the 30-mile (50 km) Hong Kong Trail, which traverses the length of Hong Kong Island, taking in four of the island's six country parks (see pp. 38–40), offering a surprising diversity of natural beauty mixed with stunning glimpses of cityscapes from their loftier points.

When the British arrived in 1841, Hong Kong Island was all but barren. A project to reforest the island began in the 1870s, and the results can be appreciated from walks along the Hong Kong Trail.

The trail starts at Victoria Peak (see pp. 68–70) and follows Lugard Road to the west before dropping down to Pokfulam Reservoir. It then heads east over the island's rugged interior to the seaside village of **Shek O** (see p. 103). The trail runs along the ridges of the peaks dividing the island from east to west. From the upper reaches, grassland descends into scrubland. Farther down, ravines and gullies cut through thick woodlands. Views down the slopes reveal a coastline indented with coves and bays.

Each park has its own characteristics. The peaks of **Pokfulam** command stunning ocean, island, and valley views. Streams crisscross the dense growth in the valleys of **Aberdeen.** Scenic **Tai Tam** (see p. 102) combines forests and Hong Kong's largest (man-made) lake, while the shores of Shek O taper off into the South China Sea.

To cover the whole trail in one day would be too strenuous for most, and there are no camping facilities. It's better to break up the walk, or choose one section. The Hong Kong Trail is well maintained and signposted. You can obtain maps from the Government Publications Center (*Room 402, Murray Bldg., Garden Rd., Central, tel 2537-1910*). ■

Hong Kong Trail
- 50 C1
- Starts at Lugard Rd., the Peak
- 2708-8885 (Country Parks Management Ofc.)
- Bus: 15; Minibus: 1

West of Central

Soon after British settlement, the colonial government set aside the area to the west of Central for the thousands of Chinese emigrants flocking to Hong Kong. Artisans, shop-keepers, traders, and coolies made their home and set up businesses in this Western District and it became a raucous and industrious place. In storefront workshops, artisans and tradesmen turned out their goods, while the less productive spent their time in the opium dens, drinking halls, and gambling parlors.

Despite modern development spreading west from Central, the Western District has managed to hang on to much of its character. The opium dens, drinking halls, and gambling parlors may have gone, but much of the enterprise of the area remains.

Along its narrow streets and alleyways you will get a glimpse of a more traditional way of life. This is one of the few places left in Hong Kong where you can see Chinese craftsmen

Some of Hong Kong's oldest houses cling to the steep slopes of stepped Ladder Street.

working in balconied shop-houses, turning out everything from mahjong tiles to company chops (see sidebar p. 75) and coffins. The shelves and timbered cabinets of Chinese medicine shops are full of bewildering and exotic potions and ingredients such as snake musk, pearl powder, lizard skins, ginseng roots, and deer antlers.

Some people take meals and snacks on rickety stools and tables in *dai pai dongs* (side-walk restaurants); others enjoy *yum cha* (tea drinking) in spartan teahouses. Abacuses snap and clack into action as wholesalers strike bargains on a startling variety of rice and teas.

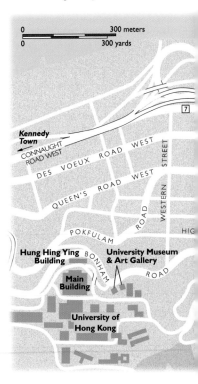

Outside the shops on Western's crowded streets, robust "Flying Pigeon" bicycles weave through traffic delivering wicker baskets full of goods door to door. Wizened old ladies push carts layered with recyclable cardboard and metal, while muscular porters propel their vehicles at a lively pace. Brightly painted trams sound their clanging bells as they trundle along.

In the midst of this lively tone, Western presents good shopping opportunities. Antique shops selling genuine and fake antiquities line Hollywood Road and its side streets, along with carpet and silk retailers, art galleries, and crowded stores full of inexpensive bric-a-brac. This is a good place to pick up a copy of *The Thoughts of Chairman Mao* by Chinese communist leader Mao Zedong (1893–1976), along with other Mao paraphernalia. ∎

Built sometime before the British arrived in 1841, Man Mo Temple in Western is Hong Kong's oldest place of worship.

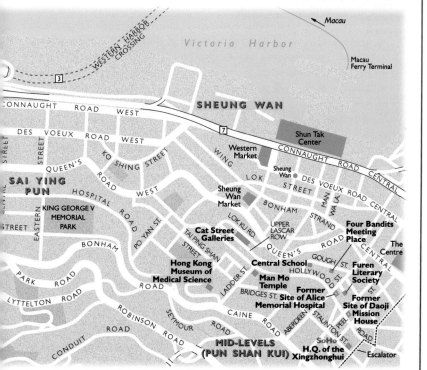

Western District

WESTERN IS OFTEN REFERRED TO AS HONG KONG'S "Chinatown." Although this may sound absurd in a place where 98 percent of the population is Chinese, it does have a ring of truth. The area, with its narrow maze of streets, old buildings, crowds, and constant buzz of shopfront mercantile activity, brims with atmosphere.

**Cat Street
Galleries**

🗺 Map p. 73
✉ 38 Luk Ku Rd.,
Sheung Wan
☎ 2543-1609
🚌 Bus: 26

HOLLYWOOD ROAD

Hollywood Road, carved along the hillside above Western, was built in 1844 for the British regiment attached there and named after the holly wood trees that used to line the street. It winds its way down from the upper section of Central into the heart of Sheung Wan at Queen's Road West, and makes for a fascinating stroll.

The road and its side streets are lined with dozens of antique stores and other shops selling all manner of merchandise. (Beware, not all antiques for sale are genuine.) Here you can buy snuff bottles, carpets, birdcages, name chops (see opposite), paintings, and teapots.

Most of the stores along the eastern part of Hollywood Road are

for the serious collectors, but as you move farther west, the glass-fronted stores with expensive displays give way to more gritty shop-houses selling Chinese knickknacks, or making and selling coffins, funeral wreaths, and antique reproductions.

BEYOND HOLLYWOOD ROAD

Cat Street (Upper Lascar Row)—an area once notorious for seamen's lodgings and brothels—is opposite Man Mo Temple, one block north from Hollywood Road. It is lined with stalls selling bric-a-brac and fake antiques. Behind Cat Street, one block farther north on Lok Ku Road, is **Cat Street Galleries** at the Casey Building. Here you will find a convenient five floors of antiques and souvenirs. At the end of Hollywood Road, keep heading west and lose yourself in the maze of bustling streets and alleys running off Queen's Road West in the **Sai Ying Pun** area, where an enthralling glimpse of old Hong Kong opens up. Here you will find old and worn four-story buildings with ornate balconies shading footpaths lined with restaurants, stores selling exotic produce such as shark fins, dried fish, rice, tea, and Chinese herbs, and tiny craftsmen's factories. Cobblers, key-cutters, and barbers work from street stands.

SUN YAT-SEN HISTORICAL TRAIL

This trail takes you past sites commemorating Sun Yat-sen (1866–1925), who spent a number of years in Hong Kong fermenting revolution before founding the Chinese republic in 1912 (see p. 33). Each site has a red plaque describing what activities took place inside. Unfortunately, most of these places have been demolished over the years, taking some edge off this short walk. But animated street activity, markets, curious shops, and artisan workshops still make it a worthwhile amble.

Take the Central to Mid-Levels Escalator (see p. 58) to the Stanley Street exit. Head east into Stanley Street to No. 15, the **headquarters of the Xingzhonghui** (Revival China Society), a revolutionary organization set up by Sun in 1895. Here he and his colleagues plotted the overthrow of the Chinese Qing government.

Backtrack to Hollywood Road and continue west to No. 59, near the Peel Street intersection, to the **Daoji Mission House** where the Christian Sun attended religious gatherings. Farther west, at the intersection of Aberdeen Street, another plaque indicates the site of

the **Alice Memorial Hospital and Hong Kong College of Medicine** where Sun graduated with a medical degree in 1892. Turn right at Aberdeen Street and take another right down Pak Tze Lane. Stone steps lead to the site of the **Furen Literary Society,** where Sun's comrades hatched revolution.

Back on Aberdeen Street, continue down the hill and turn left at Gough Street. At No. 24 is **Four Bandits Meeting Place,** where one floor of the shop on the site was used by Sun and other leading revolutionaries. A little farther west, opposite 51A Gough Street, is the building that housed the **Central School,** where Sun was educated. ■

Name chops

Chops are signature seals generally made of wood, although stone and jade models are available, with a name carved in Chinese on the base. They are dipped in ink or pushed onto an inkpad, then impressed on a document to add a signature. Originally used by artists to sign their works on paper or silk, today they are still widely used in Hong Kong by companies and shop owners on receipts, invoices, and other documents. They make great souvenirs or gifts, and Man Wa Lane in Sheung Wan is a good place to have one made. ■

Ornate name chops (seals) can be made to order.

Curious dried fish and herbs destined for medicinal use fill Sheung Wan shops.

A walk around Sheung Wan

Hong Kong's Chinatown, Sheung Wan reveals an interesting slice of the territory's history. You will encounter some steep hills along the way, so the walk is best tackled in the cool of the early morning—a perfect time to watch one of Hong Kong's most fascinating areas prepare itself for the day.

Start your walk at the **Central Police Station ❶** (*10 Hollywood Rd.*). This imposing, four-story, blue-and-white extension was built in 1919 in neoclassic style with bold columns at the entrance hall, common in Hong Kong around this time. This police compound is now used as the Central District Headquarters of the Hong Kong Police, but there are plans for the historic buildings in the compound to be developed for tourism use, although it has not yet been decided exactly how.

Heading west, the next stop is one of Hong Kong's oldest religious sites, the **Man Mo Temple ❷** (see p. 78), at the junction of Hollywood Road and Ladder Street. After exploring the temple, climb the stepped Ladder Street to the intersection with Bridges Street. Many of the buildings along **Ladder Street** are graced with shutters, timber balconies, and ornate carvings, and are among the oldest remaining homes in Hong Kong.

Turn right onto Bridges Street and the **Chinese YMCA ❸,** a large, redbrick hybrid of European and Chinese architecture. At the western end of Bridges Street, follow the lane to Tai Ping Shan Street and **Blake Garden ❹;** next to the entrance gate a plaque commemorates the outbreak of the plague in 1894.

West, along ramshackle Tai Ping Shan Street, you will see **Kwong Fook I Tze ❺,** or Tai Ping Shan Temple. Built in the 1850s, its solid red concrete facade is devoid of temple ornateness, but inside in the rear hall are ancestral tablets (see sidebar p. 162) of mainland Chinese who died in Hong Kong. The front hall is dedicated to the Ksitigarbha Buddha, whose blessings allow spirits to rest in peace.

At the western end of Tai Ping Shan Street, turn right into Po Yan Street to Hollywood Road and a shaded patch of green at **Hollywood Road Park ❻,** on the site of Possession Point where the British flag was planted for the first

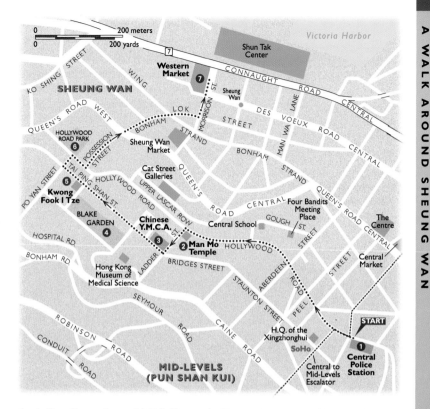

time in Hong Kong on January 26, 1841. The park is bordered on the east by Possession Street, which is closed to traffic and filled with hawkers, market stands, and fortune-tellers. Follow Possession Street north over Queen's Road West to curving Bonham Strand, to Morrison Street and **Western Market** ⑦, an impressive Edwardian building. The market, which was completed in 1906, was refurbished in 1991 and houses shopping arcades selling fabrics, handicrafts, and souvenirs. ■

Many antique stores—this one on Cat Street is an example—offer certificates of authenticity with goods sold.

> 🗺 See area map pp. 72–73
> ► Central Police Station
> ↔ 1 mile (1.6 km)
> ⊕ 1.5 hours
> ► Western Market

NOT TO BE MISSED
- Man Mo Temple
- Ladder Street
- Western Market

Man Mo Temple

MAN MO TEMPLE IS ONE OF HONG KONG'S OLDEST AND, despite its modest size, most important places of worship. Man Mo (literally "civility" and "military") is dedicated to two deities: Man the God of civil servants and literature, and Mo (also known as Kuanti), the god of war and martial arts. The fierce Mo is also the patron saint of both triads and their natural enemies, the police.

Man Mo Temple
- Map p. 73
- Corner of Hollywood Rd. & Ladder St., Sheung Wan
- Donation
- Bus: 26

The exact date of the temple's construction remains a mystery, but it is believed it was well established by the time the British arrived in 1841. The temple underwent major refurbishment in the 1850s.

Outside the entrance to the temple hall are four gilt plaques attached to poles carried during processions. Two of the plaques describe the two gods, while the other two request quiet inside the temple and ask menstruating women to stay away.

Inside, the statue of Man is on the right of the main altar, adorned with red embroidered robes and holding a calligraphy brush. On the left is the red-faced Mo, dressed in green robes and a pearl headdress and wielding a large sword.

The walls are decorated with religious paraphernalia. Huge cone-shaped spirals of smoldering incense hang from the ceiling, and joss sticks burning in polished brass

pots add to the smoky atmosphere. Dull electric bulbs, flickering votive candles, and shafts of sunlight cast an eerie illumination across the hall.

Two brass deer, representing longevity, stand in the temple hall. Near the elaborately decorated main altar are two sedan chairs, which are used to parade the divinities during festivals.

The temple has a smaller shrine dedicated to Pao Kung, the god of justice, with statues of the Eight Immortals (those who achieved immortality and made their homes in the Sacred Mountains of China).

Because of its central location, Man Mo hosts an almost constant stream of tourists and worshipers, but remains tranquil and atmospheric at the same time.

As with most temples in Hong Kong, it is appropriate to leave a small donation after visiting the temple. A shop attached to the temple sells souvenirs. ■

Popular deities

Chinese religion (a mixture of Buddhist, Taoist, and Confucian beliefs) encompasses more than a hundred deities, some more popular than others, and each honored by different sections of the community for their redeeming qualities. Students will honor certain gods who are seen as scholarly; shopkeepers will pray to gods who can bestow riches; fishermen are devotees of deities who

protect them from the dangers of the seas; and the sick pray to gods who restore health.

Hong Kong's most popular deities include Tin Hau, the Queen of Heaven and protector of seafarers; Kwun Yam, the goddess of mercy; Wong Tai Sin, who can bring prosperity; Pak Tai, the guardian of peace and order; and Kuanti (or Mo), the protector of soldiers and police. ■

Opposite: Huge incense coils hang from the ceiling of Man Mo Temple. They can burn for weeks.

Chinese traditional medicine

Visiting a Chinese pharmacy in Hong Kong is like going inside a miniature museum of natural science. Tucked away in row after row of drawers and glass containers lies a mind-boggling array of dead specimens: coiled snakes, tortoises, grasshoppers, dried fish, stag antlers, rhinoceros horns, testicles and penises from various animals, and a selection of herbs, roots, berries, plants, and mushrooms. It seems there is hardly an animal, plant, or mineral that is not used as a curative in Chinese traditional medicine. Over the millennia, the Chinese have documented more than 7,000 kinds of products that possess healing benefits.

Dried sea horses are among the thousands of products used in traditional Chinese medicine.

exists an interdependence and interrestraint that determines their state of constant change. The liver, heart, spleen, lungs, and kidneys correspond with the five elements. The liver, for example, carries the quality of wood, which can be lit up by fire; thus, a person with a liver disorder can easily get angry. In this way illness is explained in terms of the developments and changes in nature.

Doctors emphasize the treatment of the whole body, aimed at restoring its balance sent askew by illness. Attention is also paid to the season of the year, the environment, and living conditions of the patient. Two people with the same complaint may be prescribed different medicines because of their different internal and external conditions.

While people in Hong Kong and the rest of China will probably go to a Western-style doctor when serious ailments strike, they may choose Chinese traditional medicine for minor problems and for preventative and proactive healthcare. After diagnosis, a doctor of traditional Chinese medicine hands his patient a prescription, which is filled by a pharmacist, selecting ingredients from the hundreds in his shop. These are boiled into a soup by the patient, and consumed.

While Western medicine concentrates on treating the area where symptoms occur, traditional Chinese medicine believes in the need for a balance in the entire body to regain and maintain good health. It's based around the theory of the negative force of *yin*, the positive force of *yang*, and the five natural elements—metal, wood, water, fire, and earth.

The human body is made up of the competing and complementing forces of yin and yang, and when the balance between the two is interrupted, illness ensues. Also, the theory holds, among the five elements there

Another theory in traditional Chinese medicine is that of the *jing* and *luo*, which is the basis of treatments such as acupuncture and moxibustion (a heat treatment application of "moxa," derived from the ground-up leaves of the herb mugwort, on acupuncture points of the body). The internal organs and the limbs of the body are related and linked by channels through which blood and *chi* (the vital energy or life force) circulate. The main channels are called *jing* while the branches are called *luo*. If there is a blockage in either of these, the blood and vital energy cannot pass through and in time affect a person's health. To clear the blockage through acupuncture and breathing exercises is the first and fundamental step in curing a disease. ■

Right (above & below): With many people still placing their faith in Chinese traditional medicine, shops such as this one in Central do a brisk trade.

University of Hong Kong

THE UNIVERSITY OF HONG KONG IS THE TERRITORY'S OLD-est and most prestigious university, with a number of grand buildings on its campus. It is also home to one of the least visited, but nonetheless most intriguing, museums whose prize exhibit is a collection of Nestorian bronze crosses collected from northern China.

University of Hong Kong

🅰 Map p. 72

✉ 94 Bonham Rd.

☎ 2241-5500

🚌 Bus: 3B, 23, 40, 40M, 43, 103; Minibus: 8, 10, 11, 22, 28, 31

The 1919 **Hung Hing Ying Building,** which stands opposite the university's main building, is worth a look. A huge white dome and grand columned portico add character to this redbrick, two-story administrative structure. The **Main Building** (1912) is also impressive, with its tiered clock towers crowned with cupolas and its huge Roman

The University of Hong Kong's Main Building evokes the campus's age-old elegance.

columns adding flamboyance to the Edwardian design. The imposing, off-campus University Hall, a blend of Gothic and Tudor influences, was built in 1861 and served as a dormitory, chapel, library, and printing house, until the university acquired it in 1954.

UNIVERSITY MUSEUM & ART GALLERY

The museum is housed in an eye-pleasing, Edwardian-style building, while the smaller art gallery occupies an adjoining building.

Displayed on the museum's first floor are 467 Nestorian bronze crosses, the largest collection of its kind in the world. The crosses belonged to a heretical Christian sect that came to China from Syria during the Tang dynasty (618–907), and date from the time of the Yuan dynasty (1279–1368). They are only about an inch across and vary in shape from crucifixes to swastika.

The first floor also holds bronze pieces from the Shang and Zhou dynasties (10th–8th centuries B.C.), mainly weapons and ritual vessels, along with a series of bronze mirrors from the Early Warring States period (475–221 B.C.).

The second floor is dominated by ceramics spanning 5,000 years. Look for the painted neolithic pottery; Han dynasty (206 B.C.–A.D. 220) clay figures and animals, and lead-glazed burial houses; Song dynasty (960–1279) kiln ware; Sui dynasty (581–618) spittoons; and three-color glazed Tang pottery. Recent work includes early 20th-century Buddhist monk statuettes and pieces from the Chinese pottery centers of Shiwan and Jingdezhen.

The art gallery features works by Ming, Qing, and contemporary painters, and also holds various temporary exhibitions.

Visitors can enjoy a cup of tea in a replicated traditional teahouse. ∎

Hong Kong trams

To avoid getting trampled or trammeled, take the tram.

A TRAM RIDE IS AN IDEAL AND FUN WAY TO CAPTURE THE vibrant and colorful street life along Hong Kong Island's northern corridor. These delightful double-decker trams trundle 9 miles (14.5 km) from Kennedy Town in Western District through residential areas, and shopping and commercial precincts, to the old fishing village of Shau Kei Wan at the eastern end of the island.

Hong Kong's trams began operation in 1904, after earlier concerns about them crowding the colony's narrow streets and putting rickshaw pullers out of work were allayed. The colony's newspapers, the most vehement critics of the plan, later praised the tramway when it opened. The *Hong Kong Daily Press* commented: "The ride was at least three times faster than the best rickshaw, to the blank astonishment of the numbers of Chinese spectators, and the dejected look of rickshaw pullers."

The most interesting section is through the pedestrian-clogged streets of Western to the gleaming high-rises of Central. Hop aboard at the Kennedy Town terminus, climb upstairs, and sit in the front seat for the best view. The trams run close to the harbor along Connaught Road to Western Market before winding south to bustling Des Voeux Road and on to Central. You can ride the reverse section from Des Voeux Road Central (in front of the Hongkong Bank Building) to Kennedy Town or Western Market.

The ride is an incredible bargain—just 25 cents. Enter at the rear of the tram and drop the fare in a box when exiting at the front. Hong Kong Tramways is gradually modernizing its fleet, so take the opportunity to ride one of the older versions while they are still around. Private trams, designed in early vintage style with lots of polished teakwood, are available for private charter. ∎

Hong Kong Tramways

🅜 50 B1

✉ Whitty St. Tram Depot, Connaught St.

☎ 2548-7102

East of Central

Districts just to the east of Central are quintessentially Hong Kong—a mixture of the modern often jarringly juxtaposed against more traditional ways. Steel-and-glass towers lining the harbor give way to the crowded and lively street life of merchants, vendors, and produce markets. Entertainment varies from cultural and performing arts centers to the seediness of hostess bars. People flock here to shop in the modern malls and packed discount stores, and to bet at one of the world's most famous racetracks.

In Wan Chai, new and old are divided by the tram tracks running along Hennessy Road and Johnston Road. To the north and toward the harbor are the skyscrapers built to offset the high rents of Central. South of the tracks, pedestrians spill from the sidewalks on narrow crowded streets that wind their way past innumerable shop-houses and tenements. Be sure to take a tram ride on the top deck to get a bird's-eye view of the action.

Adjacent to Causeway Bay and green and leafy Victoria Park, Hong Kong Island's largest open space, is a thriving shopping, entertainment, and residential precinct notable for its incessant crowds, huge department stores, restaurants, markets, and shopping bargains. It's a better place to shop than often-aggressive Tsim Sha Tsui (see pp. 122–23).

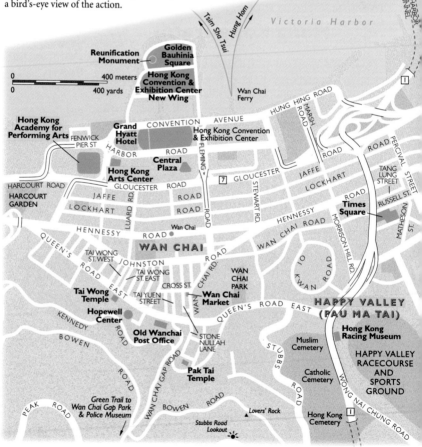

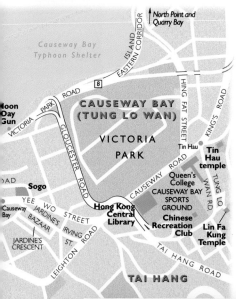

Old-time sampans and luxury yachts crowd Causeway Bay Typhoon Shelter.

Picturesque Happy Valley is home to the Happy Valley Racecourse and, on race days, tens of thousands of passionate betters come here. A night at the floodlit races is a must during your visit.

Farther east, the mainly residential areas of North Point, Quarry Bay, and Chai Wan provide few interesting sites for the visitor, but do give an insight into the living conditions of Hong Kong's people. Here hundreds of residential towers, many with 40 or more floors, rise along the narrow eastern corridor of Hong Kong Island. At the eastern tip of the island is the Hong Kong Museum of Coastal Defense. A bit out of the way, it's definitely worth visiting for a glimpse into the territory's lively maritime past. ∎

Beautifully landscaped Victoria Park is one of Hong Kong's oases.

Wan Chai

WAN CHAI, ONE OF HONG KONG'S MOST FAMOUS districts, earned its less-than-pleasant reputation from its seedy history of bars and bordellos. Although this image has been tempered since its rambunctious days as the haunt of U.S. military personnel on "R and R" during the Vietnam conflict in the 1960s and early '70s, the district still has its share of lively nightlife. But it's also a vibrant residential, business, and commercial community, revealing Hong Kong at its bustling best.

The district can be divided into three sections. Spreading back from the waterfront on Victoria Harbor to parallel Hennessy Road are the sky-scrapers and shopping malls of Wan Chai North, built mainly during the 1980s and 1990s. South, between Hennessy Road and Queen's Road East, are narrow streets and alleyways crowded with tenement buildings, artisan shop-factories, street markets, and small temples. From Queen's Road East, roads and trails wind up the hillside to upscale residential areas and panoramic views.

WAN CHAI NORTH

A good place to begin is at the **Grand Hyatt Hotel** *(1 Harbor Rd., tel 2588-1234),* worth a look for the over-the-top granite and marble art deco opulence of its lobby. From here head to the nearby waterfront and the impressive **Hong Kong Convention and Exhibition Center New Wing** *(Tel 2582-2888)* covering 16 acres (6.5 ha) of reclaimed land in front of the original convention center building. With its elegant winglike roof and five-story-high glass walls that allow extensive views of the Wan Chai and Central waterfront, it has become a landmark building. Completed in 1997, it was the site for Hong Kong's handover ceremony, which is com-memorated at both the harbor-front **Golden Bauhinia Square,** just to the right as you exit the center, and **Reunification Monument,** to the

left. Both these are popular photo-spots with mainland visitors. It has a number of restaurants and cafés with harbor vistas.

Behind the exhibition center and connected by covered walkways stands Hong Kong's tallest building, the 1,227-foot (374 m), 78-story **Central Plaza** *(18 Harbour Rd.).* The silver and gold ceramic-coated sheets on the tower's facade catch the sun's reflection, giving it a glowing aspect. Exaggerated marble colonnades at ground level lead to the vast marble-clad lobby. Head up to the Sky Lobby on the 47th floor for a panoramic sweep across Victoria Harbor to Kowloon.

Follow the walkways south to **Lockhart Road,** an entertainment strip once frequented by U.S. and other military personnel. The area fell into decline by the 1980s, but was revived during the 1990s with the addition of trendy restaurants, cafés, bars, and nightclubs. Plenty of seedy establishments still exist, however, notably the hostess bars. These are overpriced places and rip-offs are common, so it's wise to avoid them.

SOUTH OF HENNESY ROAD

South of Hennessy Road and Johnston Road, Wan Chai shifts into a more traditional Chinese mode with plenty of intriguing narrow roads and alleys to explore. **Tai Wong Street West's** bird market sells crafted bamboo birdcages, some

with pagoda-style roofs and carved dragons, and tiny porcelain water bowls. At the junction of Tai Wong Street East and Queen's Road East, fortune-tellers ply their trade at the unobtrusive **Tai Wong Temple**— also known as Hung Shing Temple. Built about 1847, it honors Hung Lei, a virtuous civil servant during the Tang dynasty who encouraged the study of astronomy, geography, and mathematics.

A block east along winding Queen's Road East, past furniture-makers crafting their products on the sidewalk in front of their shops, is the **Hopewell Center** (183 Queen's Rd. East, tel 2527-7292), at one time Hong Kong's tallest building. You can ride glass-bubble elevators on the outside of the building to the revolving restaurant

and stunning views of the harbor and Victoria Peak at the top.

Another block east is the whitewashed **Old Wanchai Post Office** (221 Queen's Rd. East, tel 2893-2856, closed Wed.), built in 1912. It now houses the government's Environmental Resource Center. Inside you'll find information on the territory's efforts to rescue and preserve its environment.

Cross Queen's Road East and wander down to **Tai Yuen Street,** crowded with shops selling goldfish, aquariums, and Chinese herbs, and watch snake vendors prepare their goods for the pot by cracking them on the pavement like whips. Many of the vendors who used to peddle their wares along this street and intersecting Cross Street now trade from the sprawling **Wan**

Central Plaza, Hong Kong's tallest building, and the glass-curtained Convention Center dominate the Wan Chai skyline.

One of Wan Chai's many herbal medicine shops

Chai Market on the corner of Wan Chai Road and Cross Street.

SOUTH OF QUEEN'S ROAD

One block east from the post office, turn right and head up Stone Nullah Lane to **Pak Tai Temple,** whose grounds are shaded by luxuriant banyan trees. Built in 1863, this three-chambered temple houses a 10-foot (3 m) copper statue of Pak Tai, the Supreme Emperor of the Dark Heaven, cast in Guangzhou in 1604. A second Pak Tai image sports a beard of black horsehair. In the ancestral hall, people burn paper and bamboo offerings expertly folded into airplanes, cars, and homes.

Back at the post office is the start of the **Wan Chai Green Trail,** which climbs through lovely woodlands for about a mile (1.6 km) to **Wan Chai Gap Park.** It gives stunning panoramas at the top but can be tough going. An easier way is to catch bus 7 or minibus 15 from Central to the top of Wan Chai Gap Road, descend by foot to the park at the corner of Bowen Road, and take the trail back to the post office.

Hong Kong Police Museum

🄼 Map p. 84

✉ 27 Coombe Rd. (intersection of Peak, Stubbs, & Wan Chai Gap Rds.)

☎ 2849-7019

🕐 Closed Mon., Tues. a.m.

🚌 Bus: 1; Minibus: 15

Before heading down, check out the **Hong Kong Police Museum.** The four galleries house a wonderful collection of exhibits, including the head of the "Sheung Shui tiger," which was shot in 1915 after killing and chewing on a policeman; weapons, uniforms, and medals; displays of drugs and drug paraphernalia; a mock-up heroin manufacturing plant; and a gallery devoted to Hong Kong's infamous triad societies who run the underworld.

As you head down Wan Chai Gap Road, take a right turn at leafy Bowen Road, originally an aqueduct carrying water from Tai Tam Reservoir (see p. 102) to Central, to the phallic **Lovers' Rock,** in a rocky hillside outcrop. Hundreds of women come on the 6th, 16th, and 26th days of each lunar month to pray for happy marriages for themselves and their children. They burn incense and joss sticks, place paper windmills in sandboxes, hang wine bottles on strings at a nearby tree, and seek the prophecies of fortune-tellers. The spot offers spectacular views of Wan Chai and Happy Valley. ∎

Happy Valley

Happy Valley has been synonymous with horse racing since the first race was run in 1845.

THE RESIDENTIAL AREA OF HAPPY VALLEY DATES BACK TO the founding of Hong Kong as a colony in the 1840s. But settlement there proved a disastrous mistake. Many of the British soldiers billeted in the area contracted malaria and died. Early settlers packed up and headed for higher ground at Central, the mosquito-infested marshlands were drained, and a racetrack built.

Horse races have been held at Happy Valley since December 1845. **Happy Valley Racecourse** *(Tel 2966-8345)* is the best place to witness Hong Kong's obsession with horse racing and gambling. Every Wednesday evening and Saturday from mid-September to June, up to 40,000 people pack the stands in jostling elation or groaning disappointment as millions of dollars are won or lost.

Show your passport at the Badge Office at the main entrance to the Members Enclosure, and get a tourist badge for HK$50. This gives access to restaurants, bars, and boxes. You can also join the Hong Kong Tourism Board's Come Horseracing Tour *(Hong Kong Tourism Board Visitors Hotline, tel 2508-1234)*, which includes transportation, dinner, and seating in the Visitors' Box.

The **Hong Kong Racing Museum** is ideal for delving into the history of horse racing in Hong Kong. Its eight galleries and cinema retell the colorful story of the sport.

Opposite the main grandstands on Wan Nai Chung Road are several cemeteries *(closed at dusk):* **Catholic, Muslim,** and the largest and most interesting, the **Hong Kong Cemetery,** with the remains of early Protestant settlers, missionaries, soldiers, traders, and civil servants. On the gravestones are tragic tales of malaria, cholera, dysentery, and death in childbirth of Russian, German, American, British, and French settlers. ■

Hong Kong Racing Museum

- Map p. 84
- 2/F Happy Valley Stand
- 2966-8065
- Closed Mon.
- Happy Valley Tram

Horse racing

Hong Kong's residents follow horse racing with a passion not seen in other places. Every Wednesday evening and Saturday (and some Sundays) between mid-September and June, tens of thousands make their way to Happy Valley and Sha Tin racetracks. Those who can't be there head to one of the more than 125 off-course betting outlets run by the Hong Kong Jockey Club to lay their bets.

In bars, parks, and restaurants people pour over form guides. Catch a taxi and the cabby's radio will be tuned into the racing. Live race broadcasts on television attract more viewers than any other program. More than 550,000 people hold telephone betting accounts, and a staggering six million bets are made per meeting—nearly one bet for every person in Hong Kong.

The reason for this fervor has more to do with the population's love of gambling than its love of equine sport. Horse racing and the Mark Six lottery are the only forms of legalized gambling in the territory. The Hong Kong Jockey Club—the controlling organization of horse racing and Hong Kong's largest benevolent body—has devised numerous (and often confusing) betting permutations to help people part with their money and, if lucky, win big. Money lost by punters is poured into charity projects. Certain "exotic" bets, such as double quinellas, tierce, triple tierce, and six-up can yield hundreds of thousands of dollars for a wager of a few dollars. Every season, betters spend about 13 billion U.S. dollars, the highest of any horse racing organization in the world.

The sport is nearly as old as Hong Kong itself. The first race meeting was held in 1845 at Happy Valley after a swamp was drained to allow the construction of a track. During the early years of racing in Hong Kong, the horses were Arabs, hunters, and cavalry mounts. Small but hardy Mongolian ponies were soon introduced and became the sport's mainstay for almost a century. (These days most horses come from Australia and New Zealand.)

During the 1850s, a reporter from *The Times* of London visiting Hong Kong wrote: "A Londoner cannot conceive the excitement caused in this island by the race week.... The one mile and a half of road between Happy Valley and the city of Victoria is at the proper time crowded with vehicles and horsemen and pedestrians...."

These words still hold true today. On Wednesday nights, up to 40,000 people crowd the stands at Happy Valley (see p. 89). At the larger Sha Tin track (see p. 176), opened in 1978, numbers reach as high as 75,000. At both tracks, betters are pampered with first-class facilities and state-of-the-art technology, including computerized betting windows, a giant video bet indicator screen, and huge 66-by-19-foot (20 x 5.8 m) screens which show races in progress, replays, and form guides.

The horses, too, enjoy a lifestyle that is nothing short of enviable. Between races, these sleek, expensive Thoroughbreds spend their time in air-conditioned stables that feature soothing music and swimming pools. ∎

Above: Sha Tin Racecourse opened in 1978 to accommodate Happy Valley's overflow.
Right: Creative use of tight training space
Below: Studying the racing form is a pre-race ritual.

Causeway Bay

KNOWN IN CHINESE AS TUNG LO WAN ("COPPER GONG BAY"),
Causeway Bay was one of the first settlements on Hong Kong Island.
Then, it was a deeply indented bay and a haven for fishing boats. It
was here that *hongs* (trading companies) built their *godowns* (ware-
houses). But huge land reclamation projects in the 1950s smoothed
out the coastline.

Causeway Bay

Map p. 85

Victoria Park

Map p. 85

The "Princely Hong," Jardine,
Matheson & Company (see p. 30),
snapped up land, built godowns,
offices, and employee housing, and
set about becoming the colony's
preeminent merchants. Its presence
in Causeway Bay is remembered in
numerous street names. **Jardine's
Bazaar,** formerly a market for the
hong's local employees, is lined with
old-fashioned Chinese provision
stores and traders, noodle shops,
and vegetarian cafés. **Jardine's
Crescent** is crowded with stands
selling cheap clothing.

Jardine's Crescent leads into
Irving Street. Cross the pedestrian
bridge to Tung Lo Wan Road, which
follows the original shoreline of the
bay, past the **Chinese Recreation
Club** (*123 Tung Lo Wan Rd.,*

tel 2577-7376) and, behind it, the
Causeway Bay Sports Ground
(*Tel 2890-5127*). The northeast corner of the ground is taken up with
the Central Library, a block that has
the feel of a shopping mall inside.
Just after the sports grounds, a small
lane on the right, Lin Fa Kung Street,
leads to the 1864 **Lin Fa Kung
Temple** at the top of the hill,
dedicated to the goddess of mercy.
Brightly colored motifs of birds and
fruit decorate the outside walls.

Tung Lo Wan Road curves and
continues east past Shanghainese,
Muslim, and vegetarian cafés,
churches, and Queen's College before
reaching the arterial Causeway Road
and Tin Hau Temple Road. From
here follow Tin Hau Temple Road a
short distance to the junction with

Dragon Road to the 200-year-old **Tin Hau temple,** which honors the Taoist Goddess of Heaven and patron of seafarers (see below), sitting on an elevated stone platform. Before reclamation, this tiny temple was at the edge of the bay.

From here you can backtrack to Causeway Road and sprawling **Victoria Park** *(Tel 2570-6186),* Hong Kong Island's largest public open space, and another place named after Queen Victoria, whose stern-faced statue surveys the park

Burning incense at a temple honors Tin Hau, the protector of seafarers.

Tin Hau

Tin Hau—the Queen of Heaven and protector of seafarers—was the daughter of a government official in Fujian Province in the tenth century. She was said to have keen knowledge and the ability to heal sickness and warn seafarers of impending dangers at sea. When she died, a temple was built in her honor and a cult of worship grew as more were built along the Chinese coast.

She is one of Hong Kong's most popular deities, with dozens of temples devoted to her in areas where fisherfolk work. All the temples were built by the sea, but land reclamation projects have left many stranded inland. ■

from a stone plinth facing Causeway Road. The park has tennis courts, a swimming pool, children's playgrounds, wooded areas, café, bowling greens, soccer fields, roller-skating rinks, and, in the morning, legions of *tai chi* practitioners. During Chinese New Year, it becomes a colorful flower market, while thousands flock here for the Mid-Autumn Festival (see p. 48).

At the northeastern exit of the park, a pedestrian overpass leads to a waterfront promenade where junks and sampans, and luxury yachts from the nearby Hong Kong Yacht Club huddle into **Causeway Bay Typhoon Shelter** (an area protected by seawalls of rocks and boulders, where boats berth when typhoon warnings are given). Head west along the promenade to the Jardine Matheson **Noon Day Gun,** made famous by British satirist Noel Coward's 1924 song "Mad Dogs and Englishmen," a tale about the foolhardiness of colonists venturing out in the heat of the day.

During the 19th century, Jardine's incurred the wrath of a British naval officer by welcoming ships with unauthorized gun salutes. As punishment, the company was ordered to provide a daily time signal for shipping. The tradition is maintained with the sounding of a bell and cannon firing at noon each day.

Beside the gun, a passageway takes you under busy Gloucester Road. Head west to Percival Street and turn left. Follow Percival Street over Hennessy Road to Russell Street and **Times Square,** notable for its gigantic outdoor video screen, chiming clocks, food halls, restaurants, and upscale retailers.

Causeway Bay's department stores, malls, and electronic and clothing retailers offer better deals and less hassle than the shops in bustling Tsim Sha Tsui. The main shopping area is around Lockhart Road and Yee Wo Street and includes the huge Japanese department store **Sogo.** ∎

The famous Noon Day Gun is fired every day of the year.

Hong Kong Museum of Coastal Defense

HONG KONG'S RICH HISTORY OF COASTAL DEFENSE IS illustrated in this delightful museum perched atop a headland at the northeastern tip of the island. The site is the previous location of the British Navy's Lei Yue Mun Fort, built in 1887 to defend the eastern approaches to Victoria Harbor.

What better place to build a museum of coastal defense than somewhere that was once used for that purpose? The museum was completed in 1999, and its main section is housed in the excellently restored Redoubt, the core of Lei Yue Mun's fortifications. A historical trail winds steeply down from the Redoubt, leading through tunnels to ammunition magazines and *caponiers* (bunkers), along defensive ditches and past numerous partly restored gun emplacements and other fortifications.

The Redoubt sits prominently at the highest point of the fort, at the eastern end. Take an elevator from a lobby near the entrance of the museum's grounds and pass over a narrow bridge, with stunning views of the harbor, to the main entrance. The exhibition galleries are housed inside the building's casements, formerly barrack rooms, engine rooms, magazines, and shell and cartridge stores, which surround a large assembly courtyard. From here, stairs lead to an upper gallery.

The museum's standing exhibition is "600 Years of Hong Kong's Coastal Defense," with each of the small galleries devoted to particular periods during that time. You pass neatly through the exhibitions in chronological order.

After the **Orientation Gallery,** just inside the entrance, you enter the **Ming Period Gallery** (1368–1644), with displays

Hong Kong Museum of Coastal Defense

- 🅰 51 G2
- ✉ 175 Tung Hei Rd., Shau Kei Wan
- ☎ 2569-1500
- 🕐 Closed Thurs.
- 🅂 $
- Ⓜ MTR: Sha Kei Wan, exit B

Weapons of war, period military uniforms, and old photographs at the museum help explain Hong Kong's rich maritime history.

erected in Hong Kong (1846). Two adjoining galleries make up the second **British Period Gallery** (1861–1941), which has period military uniforms, swords, guns, and old photographs, and a full-size diorama of a 19th-century British soldier in a typical barrack building of the time.

The **Battle for Hong Kong Gallery** (December 1941) has an excellent audiovisual documentary of the Japanese invasion, with plenty of war footage highlighting the bravery of the vastly undermanned British and Canadian troops, along with war weapons and medals. You can pick up telephones in the **Japanese Occupation Gallery** (1941–1945) and listen to poignant eyewitness accounts of local people who suffered during this time.

The **Volunteers Gallery** (1854–1995) traces the history of the Hong Kong Volunteers—also called the Royal Hong Kong Defense Force—from their formation as an adjunction to the British military until their disbandment in 1995 when they were almost entirely made up of Hong Kong Chinese. There is a full-size diorama of a machine-gun post of the No. 2 Company of the Hong Kong Volunteer Defense Corps.

The final gallery, the **Hong Kong Garrison of the PLA,** is a slightly disappointing exhibit of uniforms, with a Chinese navy flag of no historical importance, a couple of model navy ships, and self-praising history panels.

Upstairs, the **Coastal Defense Weapons Theater** shows a short documentary of the history of Hong Kong's coastal defense. After the film, head outside and check out the gun emplacements and tunnels to the North Caponier before wandering down the hill along the **Historical Trail** to the entrance. ∎

of body armor worn by high-ranking military officers of the time, including blue satin coats, concealed armor vests, and tunics with small metal plates sown into the lining. More of the same is found in the **Qing Period Gallery** (1644–1911), along with crafted bows and decorated spearheads.

The intriguing **First Opium War Gallery** (1840–1842) has a collection of opium pipes and paraphernalia, a model of a Chinese war junk and the British warship *Nemesis* opposing each other, and a diorama of the pivotal Battle of Shajio at Humen in the Pearl River Estuary; in this January 1841 clash, the British 37th Madras Native Infantry overran the Chinese garrison. There is also a copy of the Treaty of Nanjing—the document allowing cession of Hong Kong to the British on August 29, 1842—and a short video documentary of the war.

The **British Period Gallery** (1841–1860) has many weapons from the time and a detailed scale model of Murray House (see p. 106), the first military building

Actors perform a Chinese adaptation of the English drama *The Rivals* at the Academy of Performing Arts. The academy is a major venue for drama and dance.

More places to visit in Hong Kong North

HONG KONG ACADEMY FOR PERFORMING ARTS

Built by the Hong Kong Jockey Club (see p. 90) in 1985, the academy trains Hong Kong's performing artists and is one of the territory's major venues for drama and dance productions. It comprises the 1,200-seat **Lyric Theater,** a smaller drama theater, a concert hall for the academy's instrumental and choral groups, a recital hall, studio theater, and an impressive open-air theater, built in the gardens adjoining the building. The academy has schools of dance, drama, music, technical arts, and television. Public performances are held regularly.

Map p. 84 ✉ 1 Gloucester Rd. ☎ 2584-8500 🚇 MTR: Wan Chai

HONG KONG ARTS CENTER

Opposite the Academy for Performing Arts, the center, built in 1977, was the first multipurpose establishment dedicated to supporting local art groups, and fostering and promoting different art disciplines in Hong Kong. The center incorporates visual arts, performing arts, film, video, and media art.

It hosts numerous performances, exhibitions, concerts, seminars, and film festivals. It has a number of galleries, including the impressive Pao Sui Loong and Pao Yue Kong Galleries. These galleries, on the fourth and fifth floors, display contemporary art by local and international artists including paintings, graphic art, sculpture, photography, crafts, and calligraphy. The center's basement Lim Por Yen Film Theater is Hong Kong's most active art film theater, while the Shouson Theater is used for drama, dance, concerts, and film.

🅰 Map p. 84 ✉ 2 Harbour Rd. ☎ 2582-0200 🚇 MTR: Wan Chai

HONG KONG MUSEUM OF MEDICAL SCIENCE

Housed in the Edwardian-style former Pathological Institute, which was founded in 1906 to combat the outbreak of bubonic plague which broke out earlier in 1894 in the colony, is a fascinating, sometimes morbid museum tucked away in the side streets of the Mid-Levels. It chronicles the development of medical science in Hong Kong, with an autopsy room and a laboratory filled with old equipment, as well as other rooms tracing the development of dentistry and radiology. Most noteworthy, however, is the comparison of traditional Chinese medicine and Western medicine, with displays on acupuncture and Chinese herbs.

Map p. 73 ⊠ 2 Caine Lane, Mid-Levels ☎ 2549-5123 ⊕ Closed Mon. $ $ 🚌 Bus: 26 from Central to Man Mo Temple, then walk up Ladder St. to Caine Lane

JAMIA MOSQUE

Sitting in a tranquil, cool garden and surrounded by tower blocks, the Jamia Mosque is reached by a short flight of stone steps and an elaborate wrought-iron gate. The first mosque on this site was built in 1849, then rebuilt and extended in 1915. For decades most of the worshipers were Punjabi Muslims, many of whom served in Hong Kong's pre-World War II police force.

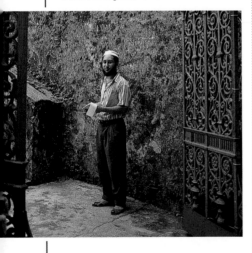

Worshiper at Jamia Mosque. Hong Kong's earliest Muslims were mainly Punjabi who served with the police in the colony.

Map p. 52 ⊠ Corner of Shelley & Mosque Sts. (enter from Shelley St.) 🚇 Central to Mid-Levels Escalator

LAW UK FOLK MUSEUM

The museum is a small and interesting restored Hakka village house. Wax figures in traditional garb, furniture, implements, and farming tools are featured in the museum's living room, bedrooms, cocklofts, kitchen, and storeroom. This particular house, set in peaceful gardens, was the ancestral home of the Law family who settled in the area during the reign of the Emperor Qianlong (1736–1795). The Hakka, still prominent in the New Territories, migrated from northern China from the 18th century. Next to the museum, which nestles in peaceful gardens, is an exhibition gallery with displays and information on traditional Hakka culture and on the restoration of Law Uk.

51 G1 ⊠ 14 Kut Shing St., Chai Wan ☎ 2896-7006 ⊕ Closed Mon. 🚇 MTR: Chai Wan

QUARRY BAY

Hong Kong Island's seemingly insatiable desire for more office space has transformed **Tong Chung Street** from a messy side street of car mechanic's shop-houses and *dai pai dongs* (sidewalk restaurants) into a road lined with gleaming office towers, bars, and restaurants. Most nights, especially toward the end of the week, the bars and restaurants fill with office workers, offering a less pretentious atmosphere than Lan Kwai Fong or SoHo.

Nearby is one of Hong Kong's best shopping malls, **City Plaza.** Shopping at this huge mall is relatively hassle-free compared to Tsim Sha Tsui and Causeway Bay. Visitors rarely shop here, so prices tend to be lower, and bargaining is not necessary. The mall also has an ice-skating rink. The high-rise residential blocks surrounding City Plaza are part of the Tai Koo Shing development and are in a style typical of housing for Hong Kong's middle classes.

51 F2 **Quarry Bay** 🚇 MTR: Quarry Bay **City Plaza** 🚇 MTR: Tai Koo Shing

STUBBS ROAD LOOKOUT

If you want more stunning views, head up to Stubbs Road Lookout. Here you will get uninterrupted panoramas of Victoria Harbor to Kowloon, Happy Valley Racecourse, Causeway Bay, Central, and Wan Chai, equally beguiling at night. The lookout has a handy map board that allows visitors to pinpoint attractions below.

50 D1 🚌 Bus: 7; Minibus: 15 ■

It doesn't take long to swap the bustle and concrete of Hong Kong Island's urban areas for the slower pace, beaches, and green hills of the island's southern half.

Hong Kong Island South

Door god at a Tin Hau temple

Hong Kong Island South

IN LESS THAN 30 MINUTES BY BUS or taxi from Central District on Hong Kong Island's northern shore, a completely new aspect of the island opens up. The contrast could not be more staggering. Relentless concrete and steel towers give way to luxuriant countryside, winding roads, spectacular scenery, pretty beaches, and laid-back villages. With a few exceptions, Hong Kong Island South remains remarkably pristine and uncrowded.

Traveling from the north of the island to the south is an experience in itself, especially when taken from the upper floor of a double-decker bus. The journey climbs over the green hills that separate the two parts of the island and along snaking roads lined with lush foliage. White-sand beaches curving between rocky headlands come into view, then disappear as the single-lane roads wind their way down to the coast.

Most of the shore on the southern side of the island has not suffered from the huge land reclamation projects carried out in other parts of Hong Kong, and its rugged and convoluted coastline, indented with stunning bays, beaches, and coves, remains intact.

Hong Kong's wealthy have chosen to live on the island's south side, where they can enjoy a peaceful respite from the hectic pace of the downtown areas. The tower blocks to be seen here are not offices; they are almost all residential. Those who can afford it have built their mansions along the headlands at Shek O, secluded Deep Water Bay, and the Stanley Peninsula.

Because of the startling contrast between north and south, it is almost inevitable that on weekends and during holidays these communities overflow with day-trippers from the north side of the island. The beaches can get very packed, the walking trails crowded, and the restaurants crammed. Come on a weekday if you want to enjoy the slower pace and atmosphere found here.

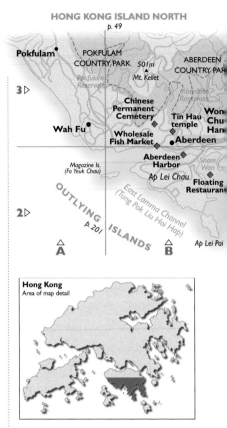

Hong Kong Island South has some of the territory's most popular attractions. Rambling Stanley Market is a hit with both visitors and locals, and there is a great range of restaurants and a number of historical sights.

Hong Kong's most popular beach at Repulse Bay gets so crowded some days, it's hard to see the sand for all the sunbathers, while the huge floating restaurants at Aberdeen are always busy. Ocean Park, sprawling over a headland just to the east of Aberdeen, is billed as one of the largest oceanariums in the world. ■

The old quay at the southern end of Repulse Bay Beach has been renovated into a modern Chinese Temple theme park with mythical figures of dragons and phoenixes, and statues of Buddha and the Tin Hau goddess.

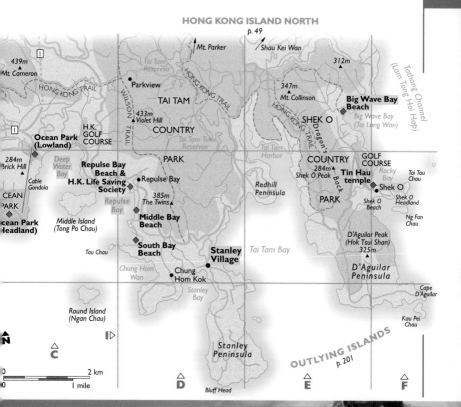

HONG KONG ISLAND NORTH
p. 49

Mt. Parker
Shau Kei Wan

439m
Mt. Cameron

312m

Tai Tam
Reservoir

347m
Mt. Collinson

Big Wave Bay
Beach

Parkview

TAI TAM

Big Wave Bay
(Tai Long Wan)

Ocean Park
(Lowland)

H.K.
GOLF
COURSE

433m
Violet Hill

COUNTRY

SHEK O

Tai Tam Tuk
Reservoir

Tai Tam
Harbor

PARK

COUNTRY

GOLF
COURSE

284m
Brick Hill

Deep
Water
Bay

Repulse Bay
Beach &
H.K. Life Saving
Society

284m
Shek O Peak

Tin Hau
temple

Rocky
Bay

Tai Tau
Chau

Cable
Gondola

Repulse Bay

Shek O

OCEAN
PARK

Repulse
Bay

385m
The Twins

Redhill
Peninsula

Shek O
Beach

Shek O
Headland

Ocean Park
(Headland)

Middle Island
(Tong Po Chau)

Middle Bay
Beach

Ng Fan
Chau

South Bay
Beach

Stanley
Village

Tai Tam Bay

D'Aguilar Peak
(Hok Tsui Shan)
325m

Tau Chau

Chung Hom
Wan

Chung
Hom Kok

D'Aguilar
Peninsula

Stanley
Bay

Cape
D'Aguilar

Round Island
(Ngan Chau)

Kau Pei
Chau

N

C

Stanley
Peninsula

OUTLYING ISLANDS
p. 201

2 km

1 mile

D

Bluff Head

E

F

Tai Tam Reservoir supplies Hong Kong Island with much of its fresh water.

Tai Tam Country Park

TAI TAM COUNTRY PARK, ONE OF FOUR COUNTRY PARKS on Hong Kong Island, is by far the biggest, covering almost a fifth of the island and containing some of its most beautiful countryside. Stretching from Quarry Bay in the north to Repulse Bay and Redhill Peninsula in the south, it straddles the east of the island, offering sweeping scenery and majestic views across Tai Tam Bay.

Tai Tam Country Park

🏞 101 D3

🚍 Bus: 6, 60, 61

Country Parks Management Office

☎ 2708-8885

Tai Tam's valley is cut by numerous streams, waterfalls, and canopied trees over paths, with fantastic views of the jade green waters of the reservoirs that give the park its name—Tai Tam means "big pools" in Cantonese. In 1914, Tai Tam Tuk Reservoir displaced Hakka villagers who had farmed the fertile valley for generations.

The park is traversed by sections of the **Hong Kong Trail** (see p. 71) and the rugged **Wilson Trail,** which runs from Stanley, above Repulse Bay and on to Quarry Bay. It is framed on its northern and eastern sides by a number of towering peaks; the tallest is Mount Parker, at 1,663 feet (507 m) the second highest on Hong Kong Island after 1,811-foot (522m) Victoria Peak.

An easy 2.2-mile (3.5 km) walk through the park, with a short bus journey at the end, is a delightful way to make your way to Stanley Village (see pp. 104–105). You can descend into the valley at the upscale Hong Kong Parkview, a private residential complex, on Tai Tam Reservoir Road. Just follow the road east a short distance from the Parkview until it narrows into a pedestrian path, which drops down to the Tai Tam Reservoir. A small bridge takes you over the reservoir and along the heavily wooded countryside past Tai Tam Intermediate Reservoir, where the road levels out and skirts Tai Tam Tuk Reservoir eventually to join Tai Tam Road. From here, cross the road and take a bus to Stanley Village. ∎

Shek O

Shek O's wide
and sandy beach

ON THE SOUTHEAST COAST OF HONG KONG ISLAND, THE sleepy little seaside village of Shek O is about as remote as it's possible to get on the island. This cluster of houses, separated by narrow alleys, has a population of only about 3,000, although this number swells significantly on weekends when city dwellers seeking a change of scene head for its beach and restaurants.

The town's alleys are worth exploring before heading to the beach or along the headland. You'll find a tiny **Tin Hau temple** (see sidebar p. 93), with colorful deities painted on its doors, soon after entering the village from the traffic circle near the bus stop. Continue along Shek O Road for a short distance and Shek O's sandy beach comes into view on your right. The ramshackle restaurants at the northern end of the beach are a good place to relax.

Keep walking along the road and up a slight incline to where the road moves out onto **Shek O Headland,** which frames the northern end of Shek O beach. Here the large houses and mansions of some of Hong Kong's moneyed line the narrow headland, taking in wonderful panoramas of the South China Sea and the territory's numerous outlying islands.

Walk to the top of the headland for more impressive views of the sea, islands, and the loaf-shaped Cape d'Aguilar, the southeasternmost point on Hong Kong Island. From near the tip of the headland, climb down the steps to a path and onto a small footbridge that crosses over **Tai Tau Chau,** a rocky islet. It takes about 10 minutes to climb to a viewing platform at the top. From here you can see northwest to Tung Lung Chau (see p. 214) and Joss House Bay in Clear Water Bay (see pp. 188–89), southwest to Stanley Peninsula, and south past Cape d'Aguilar to Waglan Island and the Po Toi Islands (see p. 214). ■

Shek O

▲ 101 F2

🚇 MTR: Shau Kei Wan,
then bus 9

Beaches, restaurants, and a famous market are some of Stanley's charms.

Stanley Village

THE PRETTY SEASIDE COMMUNITY OF STANLEY IS ANOTHER enclave of Hong Kong's wealthy; you can't help but be impressed by the opulent mansions and exclusive apartments lining the only road into the village. It is hard now to imagine that Stanley, known as Chek Chu in Chinese, was the largest settlement on Hong Kong Island when the British arrived in 1841.

Stanley Village
101 D2
Bus: 6, 6A, 6X, 260

During those days it was a market town selling produce from the surrounding farms, and a haven for pirates. **Stanley Market** is still here, wedged between a neck of land separating Stanley Bay and Tai Tam Bay, but the goods and the customers have certainly changed. Although not a place to pick up any real bargains, it's still an experience. On weekends, thousands pack the market. Among the mad jumble of stands and elbowing crowds, you'll find clothing, souvenirs, paintings, toys, sports shoes, brassware, rattan, linens, porcelain, crafts, artifacts, swimwear, and much more.

Stanley Main Road, which runs along the edge of a somewhat messy beach fronting Stanley Bay, is more sedate, with a string of bars and excellent restaurants.

Right: Chinese calligraphers in Stanley will turn your name into a framed souvenir.

A few minutes' stroll through the village along Stanley Beach Road on the eastern side of the peninsula is **Stanley Main Beach.** On summer weekends, the beach is packed with people and dotted with the colorful sails of windsurf boards. The quieter and prettier **St. Stephen's Beach,** south of the village along Wong Ma Kok Road, is a better option for swimming and sunbathing.

The trip to Stanley Village is worth it just for the 40-minute bus ride from Central District, regarded as the most scenic trip in Hong Kong. Double-decker buses roll up and down the steep, wonderfully winding, forest-fringed Tai Tam Road, which runs along the border of beautiful Tai Tam Country Park (see p. 102). ■

A WALK AROUND STANLEY VILLAGE

A monk offers prayers at Stanley's ornate Kwun Yam temple.

A walk around Stanley Village

Stanley is one of Hong Kong Island's most pleasing communities for walking. It has a number of attractions, both man-made and natural, all within easy distance, and a laid-back atmosphere not often found in other parts of Hong Kong.

Starting at Stanley Bus Station, cross Stanley Village Road and continue down Stanley New Street, where you will see the start of the famous **Stanley Market ❶** (see p. 104). At the end of the street, turn right onto Stanley Main Road and walk along a line of shops for about 100 yards (90 m) to where the road opens to the water's edge, and a row of brightly painted open-fronted bars and restaurants overlooks Stanley Bay.

Walk a short distance past these along Stanley Main Road to historic **Murray House ❷**, built on reclaimed land at the edge of the bay. This lovely building, now housing the **Hong Kong Maritime Museum** on its first floor and hosting a number of restaurants and shops, is the oldest surviving colonial building in Hong Kong. Built in the early 1840s, it was where the formal surrender of British troops to the Japanese took place in December 1941. It stood on the site of the Bank of China Tower on Queen's Road Central until 1982,

when its 4,000 bricks were dismantled, placed in storage, and put back together again on its current site in 1998.

In an open space between Murray House and Stanley Plaza Shopping Center sits one of Hong Kong Island's oldest **Tin Hau temples ❸**, founded in 1767 and dedicated to the protector of seafarers (see sidebar p. 93). The present bunker-style structure dates from 1938, but the inside is impressive, with some wonderfully crafted model junks.

Take the path to the west of Murray House and continue up the hill to the **Kwun Yam Temple ❹**. Inside a pavilion above the temple is the 20-foot (6 m) statue of Kwun Yam, the goddess of mercy (see sidebar p. 149).

Head back to the bus station via the same route (it takes less than ten minutes). From here, walk east along Stanley Village Road for about 50 yards (45 m); on your right is the 1859 **Old Stanley Police Station ❺**, the oldest surviving police building in Hong

Kong, although it now houses a supermarket.

Just beyond the police station, the road forks onto Wong Ma Kok Road. A short walk along and to your left is the entrance to **Stanley Military Cemetery 6**, whose rows of uniform gravestones set amid neatly manicured lawns serve as a poignant reminder of the lives that were lost during the Japanese occupation here. The cemetery was opened in the early days of the colony—a few colonists' graves still remain—but was closed for 70 years until it reopened in 1942 as the death toll mounted during occupation. Younger people posing for their friends' cameras in front of the gravestones often break the solemnity of the place.

Continue along Wong Ma Kok Road to shaded Wong Ma Kok Path on the right and head down to **St. Stephen's Beach 7**, a pleasant stretch of sand and a better alternative for swimming and sunbathing than crowded Stanley Main Beach, which is a short walk northeast from the bus station along Stanley Beach Road. ■

Looking for bargains at the lively Stanley Market

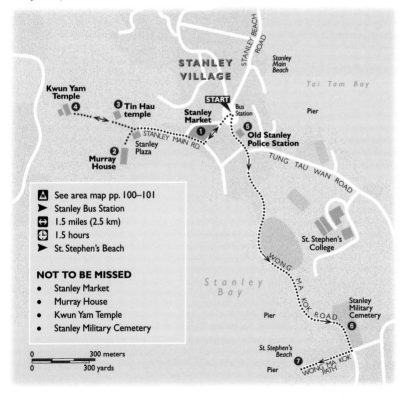

See area map pp. 100–101
Stanley Bus Station
1.5 miles (2.5 km)
1.5 hours
St. Stephen's Beach

NOT TO BE MISSED

- Stanley Market
- Murray House
- Kwun Yam Temple
- Stanley Military Cemetery

0   300 meters
0   300 yards

Repulse Bay

REPULSE BAY GOT ITS NAME FROM THE ACTIONS OF H.M.S. *Repulse,* which took part in a British forces campaign in the 1840s to rid the place of pirates. From the nearby hills, Japanese forces launched an attack in late 1941 on British and Canadian troops based here to keep supply lines opened between Stanley and Aberdeen.

Bizarre and garish statues stand in front of the headquarters of the Hong Kong Life Saving Society.

Repulse Bay Beach

- 101 D2
- Beach Rd., Repulse Bay
- No lifeguard patrols Dec.–Feb.
- Bus: 6, 6A, 6X, 64, 66, 260

Today Repulse Bay is home to Hong Kong Island's longest and most popular beach, **Repulse Bay Beach.** In the summer, this clean, white stretch of sand is packed with thousands of swimmers escaping the territory's sweltering heat—up to 30,000 people come on Sundays. It's also one of the few beaches that get crowded midweek. Oddly, after the official beach season ends in November, it is near deserted even though temperatures can reach the mid-80s (25°C). If you need more room, walk along the shoreline for 10 minutes to the less crowded **Middle Bay Beach,** or another 20 minutes to **South Bay Beach.**

Repulse Bay once served as a playground for Hong Kong's elite. The colonial Repulse Bay Hotel, built in 1920, was regarded as one of the finest beach resort hotels in Asia, the perfect place to take afternoon tea on the veranda and enjoy views across the bay. Despite public outcry, it was demolished in the early 1980s and replaced by one of Hong Kong's oddest buildings, an apartment block called the **Repulse Bay.**

This long and curving, blue-colored high-rise stands out from the other apartment blocks built on the hills behind the beach because of a distinctive pink-framed square hole built in the middle. During its planning, a *feng shui* master was consulted, a common practice in Hong Kong. It was pointed out to the architects that the dragon that inhabited the hills behind the building would be prevented from coming down to drink at the bay if the design went ahead as one long continuous structure. The distinctive hole was created to enable the dragon to pass through, thus quenching its thirst.

In a rather sad concession to the demolition of the graceful old Repulse Bay Hotel, a terrace with lawns, palms, fountains, and a replica of the facade of the hotel has been built at the front of the Repulse Bay apartments. It houses a number of good restaurants including the popular Verandah, where you can still indulge in afternoon tea, or champagne brunch every Sunday, and shop in its upscale shopping arcade.

At the eastern end of Beach Road, which fronts the bay, the training headquarters of the **Hong Kong Life Saving Society** (see

sidebar below) is flanked by huge statues of Kwun Yam, goddess of mercy (see p. 149), and Tin Hau, Queen of Heaven and protector of seafarers (see sidebar p. 93). The bizarre and garish collection of statues on the grounds draws hoards of worshipers burning joss sticks and offering prayers.

The place is filled with imaginative and colorful depictions of elephants, camels, lions, goats, a four-faced Buddha, and Kwun Yam riding a fish.

Each time you cross the **Bridge of Longevity** at the front of the grounds, legend has it that three days are added to your life. ■

South Bay Beach offers a quieter alternative to crowded Repulse Bay Beach.

Lifeguards

Lifeguards perched on lookout towers are a common sight on Hong Kong's beaches. The territory's first lifeguard club was founded in 1956, and today 476 lifeguards, almost exclusively male and young, patrol the 41 official beaches between March and November. To make swimmers feel safer, shark nets have been laid at 31 of the beaches (contact Leisure and Cultural Services Department Customer Hotline, tel 1823). Shark attacks are a real concern in Hong Kong; during the early 1990s, a number of fatal incidents took place off Sai Kung's beaches. ■

Feng shui

The Chinese philosophy of *feng shui* (literally "wind water") has become a worldwide phenomenon in recent years, but it has been a part of the culture of Hong Kong from its earliest days. It aims for harmony, and when this is achieved, good luck, synonymous with health and wealth, will follow.

A feng shui master looks to align the flows of energy called *chi*, considered to be the breath of nature, in a space or building using a special compass called a *lopan*. This determines the

A *feng shui* compass (*lopan*) is used to find the energy of a building.

energy characteristics. Complex mathematical calculations are also involved. Hills, water, and buildings can all affect the flow of chi, as everything in the universe has an energy force.

The first villages built in the New Territories were located in sites that captured the chi, and today feng shui continues to be an accepted part of many aspects of life in the city.

By having buildings or even items in your home in the optimum position to harmonize the energy in and around them, you are able to create areas that protect you from harm and bring you prosperity, good health, or happiness. For example, the head of a bed should not be directly opposite a door, where an enemy could enter in the night and easily see you. A view over water is said to be good for making you prosperous, as water brings with it abundance. If you don't have a sea view, don't worry, the same effect can be achieved by having an aquarium filled with many goldfish.

Doors are important because they are the channels through which bad spirits can enter. For this reason, several clan halls in the New Territories have spirit screens, located behind the main doors to prevent a direct view to the heart of the building.

Also in the New Territories, and sometimes

even in urban areas, you may see a small octagonal mirror above the front door. This, again, is for protection against bad spirits; it is believed that on seeing their reflection the demons will turn tail.

Many of the territory's buildings have been the subject of considerable feng shui debate. Newspapers were full of reports on the allegedly bad feng shui of the Bank of China Building in Central. Its structure of interlocking triangles, ending in sharp points, apparently looked too much like knife blades according to some critical feng shui masters, who warned that if left it could cause economic damage. It was compounded by the fact that the bank was located on part of what is seen as a dragon's back—a line of good fortune that runs past the nearby Cheung Kong Center, the Hongkong Bank building, and into the financial heart of the city. To offset criticism, the Bank of China was opened on the eighth day of the eighth month in 1988 —eight is a lucky number, and that day was divined to be the luckiest of the 20th century.

Another example is the Government House in Central, believed to have one of the territory's best feng shui locations, with uninterrupted views between mountains and sea— that is, until the Bank of China bisected it with an angle. Many suspect this misfortune resulted in a bad fall taken by the visiting British Prime Minister Margaret Thatcher; the building now remains empty most of the year. ■

Top right: Bronze lions flanking the Hongkong Bank in Central, positioned according to *feng shui*, ensure harmony in the building. Bottom right: A square hole cut into the Repulse Bay apartment complex allows the dragon that inhabits the hills behind to drink from the bay.

Ocean Park

Ocean Park

- 101 C2
- Ocean Park Rd., Aberdeen
- 2552-0291
- $$
- Ocean Park bus 629 from Star Ferry, or bus station next to Admiralty MTR

SITUATED ON A HILLY PENINSULA ON THE SOUTH SIDE OF Hong Kong Island, this 200-acre (80 ha) park is a world-class combination oceanarium, zoo, and amusement park and one of Hong Kong's most popular tourist attractions. Each year, four million people visit. The park is sectioned into a number of themed areas linked by paths and a spectacular mile-long cable-car ride.

Entering the park at the Lowland, you come to a cocoon-shaped **Butterfly House,** aflutter with thousands of technicolor butterflies. Nearby is an equally colorful **Goldfish Pagoda,** full of darting, bug-eyed Chinese and Japanese goldfish. At **Dinosaurs—Now and Then** you can check out the living descendents of dinosaurs inside three glass pyramids, including the endangered Chinese alligator and the Chinese giant salamander. Then head to **Amazing Amazon,** an impressive trek through the simulated wilds of South America, with macaws, toucans, and flamingoes. Amazing Amazon also houses the **Caverns of Darkness,** a 3-D mockup of an ancient South American temple, and the **Amazing Birds Show,** where parrots, hawks, owls, and ibises show off their natural behavior with various tricks.

The **Club Giant Panda Habitat** holds two of the rare animals, An An and Jia Jia, gifts from the People's Republic of China in 1999. The couple reside in an indoor, climate-controlled enclosure that replicates their native habitat in the Chinese province of Sichuan. Ocean Park has set up the Hong Kong Society for Panda Conservation and works with reserves in mainland China supporting the conservation of giant pandas and their habitats.

At the **Ocean Park Grand Prix** (requiring a separate admission fee), modern and gast go-karts zoom around a curving course.

Kids love the adjacent **Kids' World,** where they can have a close encounter with dolphins at Dolphin University.

Back at the Lowland, climb on a cable gondola that rises 650 feet (200 m) above the park—the views across the peninsula to Repulse Bay and Stanley are stunning—for an eight-minute ride up to the park's Headland section.

At the end of the ride, head for **Atoll Reef,** one of the park's most popular attractions. It succeeds in making you feel as if you have entered an underwater realm. You get to view more than 4,000 creatures from 400 species swimming, hovering, and bottom-feeding. At the terrific **Shark Aquarium** you come face to face with 250 sharks from 35 species. The park runs a captive breeding program for some of the shark species, including the black tip reef shark and the rare pygmy swellshark.

The 3,500-seat **Ocean Theater** has killer whales, dolphins, and sea lions performing the usual ball-balancing, hoop-jumping, synchronized swimming, and audience-splashing tricks, while at **Pacific Pier,** modeled after the natural habitat of seals and sea lions off the coast of California, there is an underwater viewing tunnel. You can also feed the animals.

At the southeastern corner of the headland are a number of

The Dragon roller coaster

white-knuckle rides, including the **The Dragon** roller coaster. Perched frighteningly on the edge of a cliff, it shoots you through three loops, including one in reverse, at speeds reaching 50 miles an hour (80 kph).

Another roller coaster, the Wild West-themed **Mine Train,** flies alarmingly along a 2,300-foot (700 m) track full of twists, turns, and a gravity-defying 280-foot (85 m) plunge. The pulse-quickening **Raging River** ride swirls through a series of twists and turns down a narrow ravine before lurching into a breathtaking vertical drop at the end of the ride. If that's not enough excitement, thrill-seekers can plummet 20 floors or 200 feet (60 m) freefall at **The Abyss.** ■

An escalator takes visitors past stunning views to the park's Headland section.

Aberdeen

ABERDEEN WAS A SMALL FISHING VILLAGE AND HAVEN for smugglers and pirates when the British arrived. The colonial navy purged the pirates, and the *hongs* (trading companies) built dry docks for their trading fleets. Fishing, along with boat-building, remains the occupation of many families, while visitors flock here to dine at the gigantic floating restaurants anchored in the harbor.

Aberdeen

100 B3

Bus: **70** from Central, 70, 36A, 37B from Admiralty

Aberdeen is known in Chinese as Heung Kong Tsai ("little fragrant" harbor), a name believed to have derived from the village's trade in sweet-smelling sandalwood used in making incense. This term is now used to describe all of the Special Administrative Region—Hong Kong.

The fishing boats start returning to port at 4 a.m. and continue to unload their catches at the frenetic **Wholesale Fish Market** at the western end of the lively Aberdeen Praya Road until noon. From here, live seafood is loaded onto vans with water tanks and transported to restaurants and markets throughout Hong Kong.

Walking a little farther east

along the waterfront brings you to a dock, where inevitably you will be offered a sampan harbor tour. It's easy to negotiate the original price—usually HK$100—down by half, and the 30-minute tour is worth taking.

The sampans motor past boatyards and lanes of anchored boats, giving a brief glimpse into the industrious daily lives of fishing families aboard their vessels (see sidebar opposite). Men repair their nets and hang up fish to dry in the sun, women wash clothes and dishes amid potted plants on deck, chained dogs bark as sampans drift too close, and tethered children play and wander around the deck.

Aberdeen's most famous landmarks are the enormous floating structures, Jumbo and Tai Pak, that make up the **Jumbo Kingdom.** Previously these gaudy Chinese-style buildings housed two cavernous restaurants, but they have been refurbished, and now encompass a variety of fusion and Chinese eateries, along with retail outlets with merchandise aimed at tourists, and a mildly interesting fishing village history exhibition.

The Jumbo Kingdom faces the exclusive Aberdeen Marina Club, with rows of luxury craft to the front and the crowded island of **Ap Lei Chau** to the rear. The island is a major boatbuilding center and huge residential estate. Walk across the bridge connecting it to the mainland for glittering evening views of the harbor and floating restaurants.

Pass through Aberdeen's compact but busy downtown by heading north up Aberdeen Main Road to the junction with Aberdeen Reservoir Road and the **Tin Hau temple** set pleasantly amid trees, shrubs, and potted plants. Originally constructed in 1851, the temple was rebuilt in 2001 after it was found to be sinking into the ground.

Follow Aberdeen Main Road behind the temple to the steep but shady Peel Rise and the enormous **Chinese Permanent Cemetery.** The terraced hillsides are packed with gravestones overlooking the South China Sea, although Aberdeen's high-rise apartment buildings have blocked some of the graves' views. This is an unfortunate aspect of progress in Hong Kong, as being buried on a hillside, overlooking the water, is the most auspicious resting place in Chinese culture. ∎

Boat people

Many of the high-rise apartments in Aberdeen were built in the 1980s as the government encouraged the town's Hoklo boat people to leave their floating harbor homes and settle for a life on dry land. The Hoklo, who came to Hong Kong from Swatow in Guangdong Province in the 19th century, are distinguished by their wide conical hats. Although the Hoklo are a hardy people, those who remain on their boats in Aberdeen Harbor enjoy plenty of creature comforts, which are very much of the 21st century. Many of their boats are equipped with washing machines and dryers, refrigerators, air-conditioners, and satellite television. Life on the sea can still be dangerous, however. Toddlers are often put on a tether to ensure they can't stray to the edge of the boat and fall in. The total number of people living on boats in Hong Kong as of 2001 was 5,895. ∎

Some Hoklo boat people of Aberdeen Harbor still cling to a traditional lifestyle.

The seaside village of **Shek O**, with its sandy beach and ramshackle restaurants, is a favorite spot for a weekend getaway.

More places to visit on Hong Kong Island South

BIG WAVE BAY BEACH

North of the village of Shek O, past the coastal Shek O Country Club and Golf Course, is the excellent and almost entirely deserted Big Wave Bay Beach. Get off the bus from Shau Kei Wan where it curves to meet the golf course at Big Wave Bay Road—the intersection is well-marked. From here, follow the road for about ten minutes to the beach. Alternatively, rent a bicycle in Shek O village and ride the 1.2 miles (2 km) to the beach, backed by a wooded area, rising to the peaks on Mount Collinson and Shek O, both part of the Shek O Country Park. Big Wave Bay can mount a sizable swell given the right weather conditions, usually when typhoons are passing close to Hong Kong. It's one of only two beaches that produce good waves for surfboarding; the other is Tai Long Wan in Sai Kung Country Park (see p. 193).
🅰 101 E3 🚉 MTR: Shau Kei Wan, then bus 9

DEEP WATER BAY

Deep Water Bay bites deeply into Hong Kong Island between the headlands separating Repulse Bay and Aberdeen and is fronted by 500 yards (450 m) of clean white sand and shady trees. It's one of the island's best beaches,

made even more so by the lack of crowds, especially during the week. This super-exclusive area of mansions, outrageously expensive rental apartments, and the terribly upper crust Hong Kong Golf Club has a barbecue area at the eastern end of the beach and a couple of outlets for food and drink. You can reach Repulse Bay by following the waterfront promenade east around the headland for about a mile (1.6 km).
🅰 101 C2 🚉 Bus: 6A, 260, 262

DRAGON'S BACK

The undulating, windswept ridge of Dragon's Back, named for its narrow spine, is a favorite launch site for paragliders. Get off the bus from Shau Kei Wan to Shek O Village at the well-marked entrance to Shek O Country Park. The 90-minute walk (one way) to the ridge is steep in parts but well worth the effort. From the highest point at **Shek O Peak** (932 feet/ 284 m), fantastic views spread along the jagged coastline from the cliffs above Big Wave Bay and carry across to the Shek O Golf Course, Shek O Village, and beyond to Cape d'Aguilar at the island's southeasternmost tip.
🅰 101 E3 🚉 MTR: Shau Kei Wan, then bus 9 ■

The grittier side of Hong Kong lies across Victoria Harbor from Hong Kong Island. Crowded, bustling, and often chaotic, Kowloon is a place of endless fascination.

Kowloon

Freshwater pearls

Kowloon

KOWLOON—CEDED TO THE BRITISH "IN PERPETUITY" IN 1856—IS A corruption of the Cantonese *gau lung* (nine dragons) named for the range of rugged mountain peaks backing the peninsula. Legend holds that when Song dynasty boy-emperor Di Ping arrived here in 1277 fleeing the Mongol hordes, he counted eight peaks and commented there must be eight dragons here. But his consul reminded him that since he was here, and he was also a dragon, there must be nine.

Kowloon's peaks have been mostly ground down to make way for development and fill for Victoria Harbor, and this area of a little over 19 square miles (47 sq km) is now one of the most crowded spots on Earth. From the tourist district of Tsim Sha Tsui to Boundary Street in chaotic Mong Kok, Kowloon is packed with high-rise tenement buildings, people, and traffic. With a few

exceptions, it lacks none of the modern architectural splendor and natural beauty of Hong Kong Island, but does present the grittier face of Hong Kong.

Most visitors will spend time in Tsim Sha Tsui, Hong Kong's best known tourist and shopping district, and glitzy Tsim Sha Tsui East, which rose from reclaimed land in the 1980s and is now a fashionable hotel and nightclub district. Fronting Tsim Sha Tsui and Tsim Sha Tsui East is the Waterfront Promenade, beginning just to the east of the Star Ferry terminal. A walk along the promenade during the cool of the evening reveals glittering vistas of the high-rise office towers on Central.

Wander farther down the peninsula into the more traditional districts of Yau Ma Tei and Mong Kok, where vibrant street life rubs shoulders with the future, the latter embodied in the Langham Place shopping and hotel complex. Among the areas' thronging crowds, you'll find street markets specializing in jade, goldfish, flowers, birds, and clothing, and shops selling a variety of goods, including religious paraphernalia and traditional Chinese wedding attire.

Kowloon also has its share of cultural attractions. The Cultural Center on the Tsim Sha Tsui waterfront plays host to top international performers, while the nearby Museum of Art is one of the best museums in the region. At the excellent Hong Kong Museum of History in Tsim Sha Tsui East, you can learn about the lively history of the territory.

Most places of interest in Kowloon are reached by hopping on and off the efficient MTR (Mass Transit Railway) that runs down the spine of the peninsula. ∎

Festival Walk shopping center in New Kowloon, just one of the area's many shopping possibilities

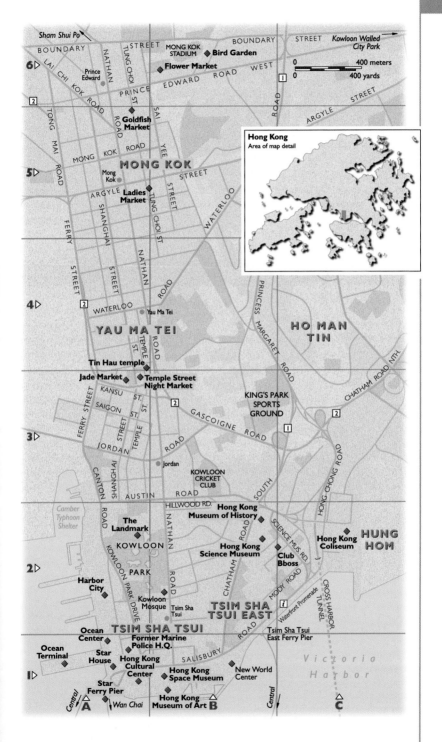

Sham Shui Po

BOUNDARY   STREET   BOUNDARY   STREET   Kowloon Walled
                                                                City Park

BOUNDARY

MONG KOK
STADIUM   Bird Garden

6▷   Prince
              Edward   Flower Market

                    PRINCE   EDWARD   ROAD   WEST

2

                    Goldfish
                    Market

MONG KOK   ROAD

5▷   Mong
              Kok   ARGYLE   STREET
                        Ladies
                        Market

        WATERLOO

ARGYLE   STREET

Hong Kong
Area of map detail

NATHAN   ROAD

4▷   WATERLOO
                        Yau Ma Tei   YAU MA TEI   HO MAN
                                                            TIN

                    Tin Hau temple
        Jade Market   Temple Street
                            Night Market   KING'S PARK
                                                SPORTS
                                                GROUND
        KANSU   ST.
        SAIGON   ST.   GASCOIGNE   ROAD

3▷   JORDAN   ROAD
                        Jordan   KOWLOON
                                    CRICKET
                                    CLUB
                    AUSTIN   ROAD

        Camber   HILLWOOD RD.   Hong Kong
        Typhoon   Museum of History
        Shelter   The
                        Landmark   Hong Kong   Hong Kong
                                KOWLOON   Science Museum   Club   Coliseum   HUNG
2▷   PARK   Bboss   HOM
        Harbor
        City   Kowloon
                    Mosque   Tsim Sha
                                Tsui   TSIM SHA
                                            TSUI EAST
        Ocean   TSIM SHA TSUI   Tsim Sha Tsui
        Center   Former Marine   East Ferry Pier
Ocean   Police H.Q.   SALISBURY   Victoria
Terminal   Star
            House   Hong Kong   Harbor
                        Cultural
                        Center   Hong Kong   New World
        Star   Space Museum   Center
I▷ Ferry Pier
Central   Wan Chai   Hong Kong   Central
        A   Museum of Art   **B**   **C**

0   400 meters
0   400 yards

Star Ferry

A TRIP ACROSS VICTORIA HARBOR ABOARD THE STAR Ferry is one of the world's great travel bargains at just HK$2.20 (25 cents). These hulking, utilitarian green-and-white vessels shuttle across the harbor 450 times a day carrying thousands of commuters between Tsim Sha Tsui, Central, and Wan Chai. Even the most jaded passenger cannot help but look up now and again to catch the remarkable views on this short voyage.

Star Ferry
🅰 119 A1
☎ 2367-7065
🕐 6.30 a.m.–11:30 p.m.
💲 $

The Star Ferry service dates back more than a hundred years and has been plying Victoria Harbor regularly ever since. Riding these ferries, which have whimsical names such as *Celestial Star, Twinkling Star, Morning Star,* and *Electric Star,* evokes a satisfying sense of history and timelessness contrary to the dynamism of today's Hong Kong.

The ferries are double-ended and can be steered by wheelhouses on either end, which allows for surprisingly speedy berthing and departure. There are two decks: the upper, and more expensive first class, and the lower second class. They were originally conceived to allow Europeans to travel apart from the Chinese commuters.

Choose the upper deck for your trip as it offers better views; also, the lower decks have a tendency to smell rather unpleasantly of diesel. One often welcome, if somewhat unexpected, concession to modernity is an air-conditioned room on the top deck.

Old-fashioned the Star Ferry may be, it is still hard to beat for efficiency and sheer fun. You never have to wait more than seven or eight minutes for a ferry. To board, just drop the fare into a slot at the turnstile (first-class passengers can also pay and get change at a cashier's window), and head down the ramp to the gate. Clanging bells and a green light signal boarding time. ∎

Tsim Sha Tsui

The Peninsula Hotel's sumptuous lobby recalls the days of British high society.

AT THE TIP OF KOWLOON PENINSULA LIES THE BRASH AND glittering Tsim Sha Tsui district—the tourists' Hong Kong—a tightly packed and frenetic pocket of shops, hotels, bars, restaurants, camera and electronic outlets, fast food stores, neon signs, street hustlers, tourists, and masses of people. Here you will see the consumerism and relentlessness of Hong Kong at its most rampant.

Tsim Sha Tsui
119 B2

The KCR (Kowloon–Canton Railway) once had its southern terminus adjacent to the Star Ferry Concourse until it was moved to Hung Hom in 1975; its former location is marked by the station's **clock tower.** Looking distinctly out of place, the 144-foot (44 m) square tower, with a clock on each side, was built in 1915 and is topped with a gracefully colonnaded cupola. Opposite the concourse is **Star House,** an unremarkable looking building but home to a huge China arts and crafts store, a great place to buy Chinese handicrafts (see p. 46).

Beside Star House, a short harborside walkway takes you to some escalators and up to **Ocean Terminal,** a combined pier for cruise ships and shopping complex that juts out into Victoria Harbor.

The four-story pier was the first container terminal in Hong Kong, but these days passengers simply disembark their cruise liners and go shopping. It is part of the sprawling complex of hotels and shopping centers—**Ocean Center** and **Harbor City**—that runs for nearly a half mile (1 km) between the harbor and Canton Road. Stores here sell designer clothes, electronics, housewares, books, and perfume.

Back at Star House, walk east along Salisbury Road and cross Canton Road to the **Former Marine Police Headquarters** (*Tsim Sha Tsui Hill*). Built in 1884, it is Hong Kong's fourth oldest surviving building and one of its most impressive colonial relics, with wide, shady colonnaded verandas, huge, arched windows, and bold brickwork. Three buildings make up the headquarters; the main building, stables, and roundhouse, once a time signal station where a copper time ball was dropped daily at noon to enable ships in the harbor to regulate their chronometers.

The **Peninsula Hotel,** another colonial gem, stands a block farther east along Salisbury Road. Opened in 1928, it quickly established itself as one of Asia's premier hotels, and although it has lost its harborside location to land reclamation, it still has a commanding presence. Have a look inside the gorgeous lobby with cornices, graceful pillars, and gilded ceiling moldings. The Peninsula still carries on its very

British tradition of high tea every afternoon from 3 p.m. with the accompaniment of a string quartet (see p. 252).

NATHAN ROAD

When Matthew Nathan, who governed from 1904 to 1907, decided that the Kowloon Peninsula needed a gracious banyan-tree-lined boulevard, the local citizens were incredulous at such a grandiose project in this sparsely populated area. The road was quickly dubbed "Nathan's folly." Now the lower sections of Nathan Road and its maze of side streets and arcades are an extravaganza of consumerism. Thousands of shops are crammed along the strip—camera and electronic stores, tailors, jewelers, shoe and clothing stores, bars and

restaurants, and stereo shops. Street hawkers and hustlers offering "copy watches" line the crowded sidewalks. A walk down this section of Nathan Road (see pp. 124–25), dubbed the Golden Mile, is certainly a worthwhile experience, but as a place to shop, it's overrated. Prices tend to be higher than other shopping precincts, such as Causeway Bay (see p. 92), and rip-offs are common. You are also likely to come across some of the rudest shop attendants on the planet.

Take time to explore the web of side streets off Nathan Road with its maze of shops and arcades. The area to the west, including Lock and Hankow Roads, is full of camera, electronics, and silk stores, while those to the east have a lot of clothing stores. ∎

Neon signs on Peking Road

Nathan Road shops purvey everything from clothing to electronics to jewelry.

A walk down Nathan Road

Join the throngs of shoppers and tourists for a wander down Hong Kong's most
famous strip. You'll be hustled by touts, bustled by crowds, and dazzled by glittering
window displays, but you'll also discover some quiet retreats and get a glimpse into
Hong Kong's past.

Start at the southern end of Nathan Road
where it intersects with Salisbury Road near
the harborfront, and head north alongside the
Peninsula Hotel ❶ (see pp. 122–23). Take
a look at the gracious and opulent lobby, then
continue on past Middle Road. On the opposite side of Nathan Road is the concrete
netherworld of **Chungking Mansions ❷**
(Nos. 36–44), a huge crumbling building with
a labyrinth of guest houses with tiny dormitories, small curry restaurants, sweatshops, and
stores. It has become the bane of the Hong
Kong authorities, who would like to demolish
it. *Chungking Express* (1994) is an excellent
movie exploring the sleaze of this monstrosity.

Back on its western side, past Peking and
Haiphong Roads, Nathan Road becomes less
frenetic. The sidewalk widens at the entrance
to **Kowloon Park ❸** (see p. 130) and the
crowds thin a little. The park is a pleasant
place to escape the noise of Nathan Road.

On its edge, on the corner of Haiphong Road,
is the elaborate **Kowloon Mosque and
Islamic Center ❹,** Hong Kong's largest
mosque. Built in 1984, it replaced a mosque
constructed in 1896 for British Indian troops
garrisoned at the since demolished Whitfield
Barracks—now Kowloon Park.

A little farther north is the upscale shopping strip of mainly clothing stores called

---

▲ See area map p. 119
► Peninsula Hotel
⇄ 0.6 mile (1 km)
⏱ 1 hour
► Hong Kong Observatory

NOT TO BE MISSED
- Peninsula Hotel
- Kowloon Park
- Hong Kong Observatory

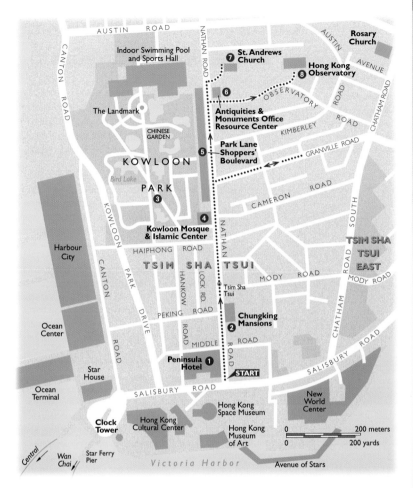

Park Lane Shoppers' Boulevard ❺, shaded with what is left of Nathan Road's banyan trees. Cross Nathan Road at the nearby pedestrian crossing and head north one block to Granville Road, lined with inexpensive clothing outlets and fashion overrun shops, a favorite spot for bargain hunters. Don't expect helpful service, refunds, or the chance to try on the clothes before you buy. Similar stores can be found on Kimberley Road (one block north) and Cameron Road (one block south).

Back on Nathan Road, head north past Kimberley and Observatory Roads to the **Antiquities and Monuments Office Resource Center ❻** *(136 Nathan Rd., tel 2721-2326).* Built in 1902 as the Kowloon British School, the building is reminiscent of the Victorian Gothic design of British schools of that era. Inside are displays of the work of the office in maintaining and restoring historic buildings. Next door is another example of late-Victorian Gothic architecture, **St. Andrews Church ❼.** It was used as a Shinto shrine during the Japanese occupation. After inspecting the church, backtrack to Observatory Road and the 1883 **Hong Kong Observatory ❽** *(Tel 2926-8200),* on the top of a small hill, which still serves as a weather-monitoring station. This graceful, colonial Victorian building has plastered brick and wide, shady colonnaded verandas along its length on both of its two floors. Group tours can be taken by prior arrangement with the Antiquities and Monuments Office. ■

Cultural Center, Museum of Art, & Space Museum

Historic photos, Chinese antiquities, and fine art fill the art museum's modern galleries.

SINCE THE COMPLETION OF THE HONG KONG CULTURAL Center in 1989, the territory has become the preeminent Asian city for performing arts, able to attract top international performers to a world-class venue. The adjoining Museum of Art is one of the best of its kind in the region, while the Space Museum offers a worthwhile diversion for an hour or so.

Hong Kong Cultural Center

🅰 119 A1

✉ 10 Salisbury Rd.

☎ 2734-2009

💲 $ (tour)

🚇 Star Ferry

CULTURAL CENTER

At first glance, the Cultural Center can be viewed uncharitably—all those pink tiles and a magnificent harbor setting but no windows! But it grows on you, especially viewed from different angles. The main feature is its sweeping concave roof, lifting to sharp lines at each end of the building. A plaza set with palm trees, pillars, and ponds enlivens its waterside frontage, and an elevated promenade provides stunning views across the harbor.

Inside, the facilities are world-class. The 2,100-seat, oval-shaped **Concert Hall** has adjustable acoustic curtains and a magnificent 8,000-pipe Rieger Orgelbau organ, one of the largest in the world. Its 1,750-seat **Grand Theater** is equally impressive, with a revolving

stage wagon. There is also a 500-seat **Studio Theater,** exhibition room, rehearsal rooms, and a couple of restaurants. There are regular performances by the excellent Hong Kong Chinese Orchestra, the Hong Kong Symphony Orchestra, and a stream of international performers. Half-hour tours of the center start at 12:30 p.m. daily. You can buy tickets at the information counter in the main lobby.

MUSEUM OF ART

The museum's six galleries do justice to the magnificent collection of artifacts housed here. Five are reserved for Chinese antiquities, fine art, contemporary Hong Kong art, and historical photographs, while the sixth has visiting exhibits.

The fine **Chinese Antiquities Gallery** on the third floor has an extensive collection of ceramics from the neolithic period to the present day. It also displays textiles and costumes, including dragon robes, common clothing, official robes, and Mandarin squares, as well as bronzes, snuff bottles, bamboo carvings, jade, and lacquerware.

Also on the third floor is the fascinating **Historical Pictures Gallery.** More than a thousand oil paintings, watercolors, drawings, and photographs from both Chinese and European artists present a vivid picture of China and the Treaty Ports of Hong Kong and Macau in the 18th and 19th centuries.

On the second floor is the **Contemporary Hong Kong Art Gallery,** Hong Kong's largest collection, mainly from local artists. It presents an interesting fusion of Eastern and Western mediums and styles. Here also you will find the works of the **Xubaizhai Gallery of Chinese Painting and Calligraphy,** a gift to the museum by art collector and patron Low Chuck-tiew (1911–1993). Exhibits date from the fifth century to the present, with the emphasis on the Ming and Qing dynasties.

The **Chinese Fine Art Gallery** on the fourth floor majors on the works of masters from the adjoining Guangdong Province.

The museum offers views across the harbor through a glass wall on the southern face of the building.

SPACE MUSEUM

This museum is housed in an odd-shaped building that looks like one half of a giant golf ball. Inside are two exhibition halls with numerous displays, some interactive.

The **Hall of Space and Science** traces human endeavors in space, including a history of ancient astronomy, science fiction, early rockets, satellites, the space shuttle, and future space programs. There's a lump of moon rock, models of space ships, and videos of space flights and moon walks.

The **Hall of Astronomy** looks at the solar system, solar science, and the stars through a number of displays, and an OMNIMAX screen in the **Space Theater** shows movies on natural history and space. ∎

The Cultural Center has no windows, but the promenade outside capitalizes on its spectacular harborside setting.

Hong Kong Museum of Art
☎ 2721-0116
🕐 Closed Thurs.
💲 $
🚢 Star Ferry

Hong Kong Space Museum
☎ 2721-0226
🕐 Closed Tues.
💲 $
🚢 Star Ferry

Harbor cruises

A VISIT TO VICTORIA HARBOR WHILE IN HONG KONG IS inevitable, even if it's just for a short trip on the Star Ferry. If you want to spend more time on the harbor, there are plenty of options, from private charters to lunch and dinner cruises, or you can just hop on a passenger ferry for a leisurely trip to one of the outlying islands.

Star Ferry
🅰 119 A1
☎ 2367-7065
🕐 Open 6:30
   a.m.–11:30 p.m.
💲 $

The eight-minute cruise across Victoria Harbor on the **Star Ferry** (see pp. 120–21) from Central to Tsim Sha Tsui is one of the world's classic ferry trips. The ferry also plies from Central to Hung Hom in Kowloon and Wan Chai to Tsim Sha Tsui.

New World First Ferry Services (Tel 2131-8181) has a fleet that services the outlying islands. Ferries leave from Outlying Islands Ferry Piers 4, 5, and 6 in front of the ifc building in Central. From here, big, lumbering passenger boats regularly head to Lantau, Cheung Chau, Peng Chau, and Lamma Islands, with most of these trips taking around one hour, although there are some faster vessels. There are two classes, ordinary and deluxe. Buy a deluxe ticket and head to the open-air fantail at the rear of the boat—the air-conditioning in the cabin can be freezing rather than cooling—for a pleasant trip. Snacks and beverages, including beer, are available from a kiosk on board. Trips to the outlying islands are best taken during the week when it's less crowded.

A fast ferry leaves at 20-minute intervals to the satellite community of Discovery Bay on Lantau from Outlying Islands Ferry Pier 3 in Central.

A plethora of private harbor cruise tours are available, and both the day- and nighttime cruise are recommended. Most of the tour companies will pick you up from your hotel and deliver you to a pier on Kowloon or Hong Kong Island for boarding.

C & A Tours *(Tel 2369-1866)* organizes dinner and dancing cruises on the cruise liner *Hong Kong Bauhinia*, while the largest, **Watertours** *(Tel 2926-3868)*, offers a number of evening cruises on its tourist renditions of traditional Chinese junks. One takes you along the northern shoreline of Hong Kong Island, another to Lei Yue Mun Village in east Kowloon for a seafood dinner. It also has a sunset cruise to Aberdeen on the south side of the island. Once there you disembark for a meal at one of Aberdeen's gigantic floating restaurants (see pp. 114–15).

Reliance Tours *(Tel 2731-2068)* offers a cruise highlighting some of Hong Kong's ambitious infrastructure projects, such as the huge West Kowloon Reclamation landfill, the harborside Kowloon Expressway, Stonecutter's Island (no longer an island due to landfill) and its Chinese People's Liberation Army (PLA) navy base, and the impressive Tsing Ma Bridge linking the Hong Kong International Airport at Chek Lap Kok.

Jubilee International Tour Center *(Tel 2530-0535)* has a Chinese junk available for a four-hour private charter to the pleasant beaches and islands of Sai Kung on the eastern side of the New Territories. There are also numerous family-run businesses that charter modern launches for day-trips, known locally as "junk trips," although the boats bear only a faint resemblance to traditional junks. They pick you up from a pre-arranged spot and take you to Sai Kung. Operators are listed in the Hong Kong yellow pages.

Hong Kong Dolphinwatch Ltd. *(Tel 2984-1414)* runs trips every Wednesday, Friday, and Sunday to see the rare Pearl River Delta white dolphins, or pink dolphins (see pp. 206–207). You are picked up from the Mandarin Oriental Hotel in Central or the Kowloon Hotel in Tsim Sha Tsui for a bus ride to Tung Chung, on North Lantau. There you board a boat and head for the dolphins. If you don't spot any on your trip, the company will take you another time for free. ∎

A Victoria Harbor cruise is vital to any trip to Hong Kong.

Pink flamingos are Kowloon Park's most famous residents.

Kowloon Park

KOWLOON PARK OFFERS A WELCOME RELIEF FROM THE clutter and crowds on Tsim Sha Tsui's streets. The park, formerly Whitfield Barracks, an encampment for British troops, combines green spaces, recreational facilities, and a collection of attention-grabbing artifice.

Kowloon Park
- ⬛ 119 A2
- ✉ Austin Rd.
- ☎ 2724-3344
- 💲 $ (swimming pool)
- 🚇 MTR: Tsim Sha Tsui, exit A1

The main entrance is on Austin Road, which runs between Nathan and Canton Roads; you pass a soccer field to an arcade that leads into the park. There are also entrances along Nathan, Canton, and Haiphong Roads. The indoor Olympic swimming pool and adjoining outdoor free-form pools are good places to cool off, but are packed at weekends.

Outside the arcade stands **the Landmark,** a 61-foot (18.6 m), imposing skeletal tower in a shallow pool, created by Canadian sculptor Raymond Arnatt. From the tower, a thoroughfare cuts through the park and well-signposted paths running from it lead to a number of weird and wonderful attractions.

The **Chinese Garden,** with its shrubs and shady trees, snaking covered walkway, and pagoda is worth a visit. On the opposite side of the thoroughfare lies an **aviary** full of colorful parrots and parakeets. Beyond the Chinese Garden is a neatly clipped **maze,** a **sculptured walk** full of works by local and international artists, and a circular **sculpture garden,** featuring a bronze cast of English scientist Isaac Newton, by British sculptor Eduardo Paolozzi (*b.*1924).

At the **Bird Lake,** watch the pink flamingos preening themselves against the backdrop of the high-rise buildings on Canton Road. Beyond Bird Lake, a giant **totem pole** rises incongruously. Opposite, get some perspective from the 121-foot (37 m) **Viewing Cone**. The **Discovery Playground** is the old gun emplacement of Whitfield Barracks. ∎

Tsim Sha Tsui East

The Waterfront Promenade offers front-row seats of Hong Kong's incredible skyline.

TSIM SHA TSUI EAST SITS IN STARK CONTRAST TO ITS MUCH older neighbor, Tsim Sha Tsui. This area of luxury hotels, modern shopping malls, and nightclubs grew from reclaimed land in the 1980s, and it serves mainly as a glitzy entertainment area for those willing to part with large sums of money.

The area is known for its luxurious and expensive Japanese nightclubs, which offer live bands, floor shows, and hostess services. The extravagant **Club Bboss** *(New Mandarin Plaza, 14 Science Museum Rd., tel 2369-2883)* is a fantasyland of indulgence and hedonism. Among its features are a mini Rolls-Royce-styled vehicle that takes patrons to their tables, and a flowing stream full of carp.

Stretching along the waterfront is the **Waterfront Promenade,** a walkway with some of the best views of Hong Kong. It's home to the **Avenue of Stars,** an area along the harbor front, that features plaques and handprints from some of the city's biggest cinematic names, including Hong Kong's most famous Hollywood export, Jackie Chan. Just beyond the promenade's eastern end

is the **Hong Kong Coliseum** *(9 Cheong Wan Rd., Hung Hom, tel 2355-7234),* an odd, inverted pyramid-shaped entertainment center. This 12,500-seat arena is the major venue for Hong Kong's Canto pop performers and fans (see below). ■

Canto pop

The Hong Kong Coliseum is renowned for its Canto pop, which combines the syrupy lyrics of unrequited (and requited) love, with well-groomed, good-looking young performers, slick music videos, and elaborate and expensive stage shows. Only the language—it is sung in Cantonese—distinguishes it from the beat and often corny lyrics of Western pop music. ■

Tsim Sha Tsui East
📖 119 B2

Hong Kong Museum of History

THE HONG KONG MUSEUM OF HISTORY, ONE OF THE newest and most impressive museums in the territory, does an exceptional job of retelling the story of Hong Kong. Visitors are guided through 6,000 years of history with imaginative use of ecological settings, panoramic screens, dioramas, and interactive programs. This purpose-built museum is essential for those with an interest in Hong Kong's fascinating past.

Hong Kong Museum of History

- 119 B2
- 100 Chatham Rd. South, Tsim Sha Tsui East
- 2724-9042
- Closed Tues.
- $
- MTR: Tsim Sha Tsui

Start your tour of the museum just inside the entrance with an overview in the **Landform and Climate Gallery.** Descend into the gallery via the escalator to a globe of the Earth held in a cradle of rock, featuring Hong Kong and the South China area. From there you enter a rock-lined tunnel to begin a "Journey to the Center of the Earth," with multiple theater screens explaining Hong Kong's geological and climatic history and marine environments.

A diorama depicts Hong Kong's earliest inhabitants.

Next, you come to an artificial forest with mounted insects, birds, and small mammals, and all the appropriate sound effects.

Following on from this is the **Prehistory** area, whose exhibits neatly piece together archaeology and prehistory. Dioramas of

archaeological digs and a 140-foot-long (42 m) beach show reconstructions of a stilt-house, a site for making stone tools, a burial site, and a pottery-making site.

Make your way up a ramp, past collections of finds dating from China's predynastic times, to the **Dynasties Gallery,** where artifacts and displays from each of the dynastic periods tell the story of China.

A typical village gateway marks the entrance to the **Folk Culture Gallery.** This lively area highlights Hong Kong and South China's main ethnic groups, with a full-size copy of a boat dweller's fishing junk, a light-and-sound show illustrating the lifestyle of the Hoklo people, and a diorama showing how they harvested salt. The inside of a Punti village house recaptures aspects of this ethnic group's rituals and beliefs, including birth, betrothal, marriage, and religion. There is also a display of the typical farming life of the Hakka, Hong Kong's largest ethnic group.

From here an escalator takes you back to the main lobby. Head up the nearby escalator to the second floor and the **Opium Wars and Early Maritime Trade Gallery.** The first part covers the Opium Wars (1840–42 and 1856–58; see pp. 29–32) and contains a facade from the Bocca Tigris Fort, which

served as a key defensive position for the Chinese forces during the First Opium War. Walk through the facade to the Opium War Theater, where this intriguing story is presented in a multimedia show. Next, a three-story colonial facade dominates the reproduction of the Praya (waterfront) and Hong Kong Harbor in the late 19th century.

The **Growth of the City Gallery** portrays a century of history beginning in 1840. Here you will find copies of banks, trading companies, a colonial clubhouse, post office, tea shop, grocery store, herbal medicine shop, tailor shop, and Cantonese teahouse. A typical apartment set in a re-creation of a Chinese settlement from the 1930s shows living conditions during those days.

An alleyway leads upstairs where period rooms, interactive units, and displays re-create prewar government and administration, law enforcement, early industries, and education. There are also sections on Sun Yat-sen (see p. 33) and the role of Hong Kong in modern Chinese history.

Exiting the teahouse or the alleyway, you come to the street gallery, where a full-scale double-decker tram houses a multimedia show on transportation during the prewar years.

The **Japanese Occupation Gallery** begins with the interior of a bomb shelter. Artifacts and multimedia exhibits recount the dark days of occupation, the Japanese surrender, and immediate postwar events.

The **Postwar Years Gallery** highlights the huge waves of immigration, industrialization, natural disasters, and problems such as water rationing. A 1960s cinema celebrates the growth of Hong Kong's movie industry. Further exhibitions take you through postwar education, the stock market, and other episodes of Hong Kong's explosive growth during this period.

The final gallery focuses on the signing of the Sino-British Joint Declaration in 1984, and the 1997 Handover Ceremony. A multimedia production relives the often turbulent development of China–Hong Kong relations. ∎

The Chinese junk, representing a bygone era of transportation and trade

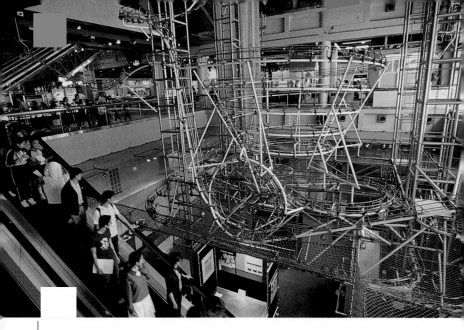

A mad scientist's dream: The curious Energy Machine spirals up through the museum's four levels.

Hong Kong Science Museum

THE HONG KONG SCIENCE MUSEUM IS THE MOST POPULAR museum in the territory, not least for the large number of interactive exhibits on display. It is four floors of fun, and if you bring the children, count on spending a few hours here before you get the chance to drag them away.

Hong Kong Science Museum

- 119 B2
- 2 Science Museum Rd., Tsim Sha Tsui East
- 2732-3232
- Closed Thurs.
- $ (free Wed.)
- MTR: Tsim Sha Tsui

Of the 500 or so exhibits arranged thematically, more than half are hands-on. At the entry level (on the first floor), a giant video screen called a **Vidiwall** plays a short introductory video. At the center of the hall is an **Exhibits and Facilities Directory System** where you can press buttons on a computer screen for layouts of the exhibition halls and location, and a description of each exhibit.

Dominating the museum, beginning on ground floor, a level below the main entrance, is the **Energy Machine,** a 70-foot-high (22 m) contraption of scaffolding, tubing, looping, spiraling tracks, and bronze drums that cuts up through four levels of the museum. When set in motion, a continuous stream of balls roll around the tracks of its two towers like a roller coaster, producing dramatic sound and visual effects along the way. In the **Motion** section, you can lie on a bed of nails or sit in a rotating room and learn how to toss a curve ball. In the **Life Science** section, assess your endurance, hearing, and sight through a number of tests.

The **Electricity and Magnetism** section on the first floor lets you check the amount of static electricity in your body at the Hand Battery, while on the second floor you can take off from Hong Kong International Airport in the **Transportation** section's Flight Simulator. The third floor's **Home Technology** section takes a look at the workings of home appliances from microwave ovens and coffee-makers to flushing toilets. ∎

Yau Ma Tei

YAU MA TEI PRESENTS A ROUGHER SIDE TO HONG KONG than neighboring Tsim Sha Tsui, and most other places in Hong Kong for that matter. It's a district of packed sidewalks, crowded and crumbling tenement buildings, shops, *dai pai dongs* (sidewalk restaurants), street markets, and endless fascination—an ideal place to explore on foot.

Start by exploring the grid of streets between **Jordan Road** and **Kansu Street,** west of Nathan Road. Shops along Canton Road specialize in ivory and mahjong sets, while Ning Po and Reclamation Streets are known for their paper models of houses and cars and notes from "Hell Bank" used for burning at funerals and festivals to aid financial security for relatives in the afterlife. There is a street market at **Saigon Street,** and the shops in other streets do a brisk business selling bronze and plastic deities, brass incense burners, and wooden altars.

At the intersection of Battery and Kansu Streets is the **Jade Market.** More than 450 standholders sell amulets, necklaces, ornaments, beads, and statues made from the green stone, which the Chinese believe has magical healing powers. It's at its busiest in the morning. Unless you know a lot about jade, settle for an inexpensive trinket as a souvenir.

Nearby on Public Square Street, off Shanghai Street, stands a **Tin Hau temple,** which stood on the waterfront until reclamation buried sections of the harbor (see sidebar p. 93). Immense incense coils hang above the entrance to the largest hall, which is dominated by an image of Tin Hau. Also here are 60 identical figures of Tai Sui, a deity entwined in the belief and worship of Chinese astrology, and representing the 60-year lunar calendar. Worshipers slip Hell Bank notes under the deity representing the year of their birth. To the left are

temples to the city god Shing Wong, and To Tei the earth god. Fortunetellers gather nearby to read the *chim* (bamboo fortune sticks).

Along **Shanghai Street,** shops sell traditional red wedding outfits, embroidered pillowcases, and other bridal items, including traditional wedding buns. ■

Yau Ma Tei
▲ 119 A4

Jade for sale in all shapes and sizes at its eponymous market

Martial arts

During the 1970s, legendary Bruce Lee (1940–1973) introduced Western movie-goers to Chinese martial arts. His onscreen exploits projected a confrontational and violent side, but that's just part of the picture.

Kung fu has become the generic term to describe any martial art that comes from China. There are, in fact, hundreds of different styles dating back centuries to relatively recently. Their core is reflected in the name kung fu, which can be used to describe anything that requires a person to invest both time and effort into training to become skillful. Chefs, artists, musicians, and computer programers can all be said to have good "kung fu." The correct name—and literal translation—for martial arts in China is *wushu*.

Wushu is also the name of a particular form of martial art, which experts claim epitomizes the "art" in martial arts. It uses natural movement to exhibit traditional techniques and can be performed by individuals, in pairs, or in groups, either bare-handed or armed with traditional Chinese weaponry, in noncontact competition. Wushu proffers an athletic and aesthetic performance rich in detail, style, speed, power, and level of difficulty. Watching exponents dodge flailing swords and staffs with amazing skill is exciting theater.

At dawn and dusk in Hong Kong's open spaces you will witness the world's most popular martial art as groups of mainly elderly people go through their daily *tai chi* exercises. Flowing movements are performed slowly, as if the practitioner were moving through very thick air. This slow action allows for deep breathing and concentration, which, in turn, promotes a calm, tranquil, and centered disposition as the body's internal energy or life force—*chi*—comes into play.

Regular tai chi exercise keeps joints flexible, muscles toned, and allows for better circulation and balance. The slow-motion movements help neutralize stress and release the tensions that tend to accrue in daily life.

Although it may not seem so, tai chi has its roots in combat. It teaches resistance to force by yielding to it and redirecting it away from the target, hence "the vigorous is subdued by the soft."

Bruce Lee incorporated the martial art *wing chun* into his list of skills before moving on to create his own style. Wing chun was developed by a Buddhist nun, Ng Mui, from the famous Shaolin temple in Henan Province, who passed it on to a young girl named Wing Chun. The art is ferocious and dynamic and relatively easy to learn.

It eschews the more elaborate and flourishing movements of other martial arts and relies on speed, evasion, and economy of action, characterized by short explosive hand attacks, low kicks, and simultaneous attack and defense. It uses the "centerline theory," which draws an imaginary line down the center of the body, including the eyes, nose, lips, mouth, throat, heart, solar plexus, and groin, and directs all attacks and blocks there. Because it places less emphasis on strength, it is popular among women as an effective method of self-defense, the original intention of its inventor. ■

Above: Hong Kong residents traditionally practice tai chi in the city's open spaces, especially parks.
Below: Kung fu's slow, steady, fluid movements are based on ancient combat techniques.

Temple Street Night Market

THE BAZAAR SET UP ON TEMPLE STREET AT NIGHT IS ONE of Hong Kong's favorite and most colorful markets. Locals and tourists flock here for shopping bargains and food, to have their fortunes told, and to listen to amateur performers of Chinese opera. The market officially opens late in the afternoon, but the best time to go is between 8 and 10 p.m., when it's at its liveliest.

Temple Street Night Market
119 A3

During the day, Temple Street is no different from other streets in the area, lined with restaurants and cheap clothing stores. Late in the afternoon, however, it's closed to traffic, and hundreds of vendors move in, erecting makeshift canvas stands and piling them with an incredible array of goods.

The market stretches south from Man Ming Lane, through the grounds of the Tin Hau temple across Kansu Street to Ning Po Street. For sheer variety, it's hard to beat anywhere in Asia. Stands are full of fake designer clothing and watches, cheap jeans and tops, cigarette lighters fashioned into anything from hand grenades to small statues of naked women, silk ties patterned with cartoon characters,

swimsuits, sunglasses, shoes, pirated CDs, audiotapes, alarm clocks that ring constantly, toys, Chinese bric-a-brac, silks, magazines, and untold knickknacks.

Escape the bustle at one of the *dai pai dongs* (sidewalk restaurants) set up at intersections along the street. Here, you can dine on seafood, drink beer, and watch the crowds surge past.

At the Tin Hau temple, people stand around groups of men playing chess, while along Pak Hoi Street fortune-tellers read palms and faces.

The market is also a theater for shrill-voiced Cantonese opera singers and small orchestras of men playing percussion instruments, banjos *(yue chin)*, xylophones, and dragon-headed fiddles. ∎

Mong Kok markets

LIKE ITS NEIGHBOR YAU MA TEI, MONG KOK PRESENTS A coarser side to Hong Kong. The area is an impossibly crowded mix of tenements, people, noise, and traffic-clogged streets. Though it's off the regular tourist route, it's worth heading there for its number of interesting markets.

The most popular of these markets is the **Bird Garden** *(Yuen Po St.),* with its pretty courtyards and moon gates. Birds—especially melodious ones—are favored pets among Chinese. Their owners dote on them, feeding them live crickets imported from China and honey drinks to sweeten their song. The Bird Garden's stands have hundreds of birds including finches, mynahs, sparrows, parrots, and cockatoos. Cages with ornate carvings and delicate porcelain water bowls are for sale, along with special seeds and other bird food.

Next to the Bird Garden, one block back from Prince Edward Road West, off Sai Yee Street, is the **Flower Market,** worth a look for its color, scents, and array of flowers imported from all over the world.

Back on Prince Edward Road West, head west toward Nathan Road and turn left onto Tung Choi Street. The first section of the street is taken up by dozens of shops and a market selling goldfish and aquariums; the area is known as the **Goldfish Market.** There's plenty of color here, with thousands of multihued fish swimming about in tanks. The Chinese believe aquariums filled with goldfish bring good luck and provide calm and beauty.

Farther south along Tung Choi Street, around Nelson and Argyle Streets, the **Ladies Market,** as the name suggests, sells mainly ladies' clothing and cosmetics, but there are also plenty of clothes for men at bargain prices. The market kicks off late in the afternoon. ∎

Sweet birdsong fills Kowloon's Bird Garden, where some 70 stalls vend hundreds of birds as pets.

Mong Kok markets
Ⓜ 119 A5

New Kowloon

Until the British leased the New Territories from the Chinese for 99 years in 1898, the Hong Kong border was at Boundary Street, running east–west along the peninsula and demarcated by a bamboo fence. Land north of here is, strictly speaking, the New Territories, but the area's crowded neighborhoods have more in common with Kowloon.

The highly urbanized, somewhat dour districts of New Kowloon have a number of attractions that will appeal to you, and, like most areas in Hong Kong, are easy to reach by public transportation.

In the middle of high-rise housing estates, people from all over Hong Kong flock to the riotously ornate and active Wong Tai Sin Temple to pray for good fortune and have their

futures predicted. Kneeling in a plaza in front of the temple, these worshipers ask specific gods questions while shaking a container filled with *chim* (numbered bamboo sticks). The number of the one that falls out is matched with a message obtained from a fortune-teller in a nearby arcade.

The amazing Chi Lin Nunnery, built in strict adherence to Tang dynasty form and

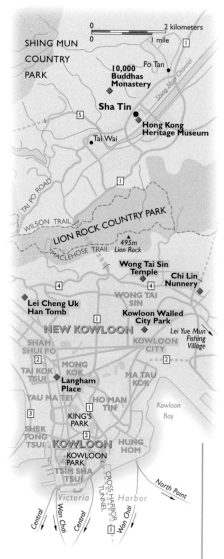

Hong Kong Island forms a spectacular backdrop to a New Kowloon container terminal. The area is a mixture of industry and urban living.

architecture and following the principles of *feng shui,* also has its share of religious followers, but most visitors come simply to wander through the nunnery's beautiful gardens and to admire the magnificently crafted timber buildings. Go early to experience the serenity of the place—and beat the busloads of tourists, who start arriving midmorning.

The streets of Kowloon City—with their abundance of inexpensive restaurants (featuring cuisines from all over Asia, including Cantonese, Korean, Malaysian, Thai, and Vietnamese), cheap clothing outlets, and down-to-earth atmosphere—make an interesting diversion after taking in the gardens of the adjacent Walled City Park, one of Hong Kong's most traditional Chinese-style parks. The park sits on the site of what was once Hong Kong's most infamous area—an impossibly overcrowded, dangerous, and crumbling slum known as the Walled City. ∎

Devotees looking for good fortune pray at the richly ornate Wong Tai Sin temple.

Wong Tai Sin Temple

WONG TAI SIN TEMPLE IS ONE OF HONG KONG'S MOST popular places of worship, because of its resident deity's ability to grant the wishes of its devotees—wishes almost exclusively centered around money. People flock here to earn enough merit for a big win at the horse races, the Mark Six lottery, or any other windfall the powerful Wong, god of good fortune and healing, may bestow.

Wong Tai Sin Temple

- Map p. 141
- 2 Chuk Yuen Village, Wong Tai Sin
- 2327-8141
- $ (donation)
- MTR: Wong Tai Sin, exit B2

The image of Wong, which is housed in the ornate **main temple,** was brought to Hong Kong from Guangdong in 1915 and originally kept in a temple in Wan Chai until it was moved here in 1921. The main temple sits under a roof of bright yellow tiles and pinewood ceilings, supported by bold red pillars. Elaborate painted designs, gilded dragons carved in relief, timber features under the eaves, and altar carvings that depict the life and times of Wong complete the building's impressive features. Buildings in the temple grounds were rebuilt in 1973.

The plaza in front of the main entrance to the temple (you cannot enter the temple, only view the Wong Tai Sin image through the doors) is crowded with devotees offering fruit, burning incense, and shaking out bamboo fortune sticks.

The sound of these rattling *chim* is unceasing. You can get them from a small kiosk at the side of the plaza. Cast them on the ground in front of the temple, write the numbers down on the paper supplied, and take it to the adjacent **oblation and fortune-telling arcade** for a reading. The arcade is lined with dozens of fortune-tellers' booths where you can have your chim, face, or palms read. Some of the fortune-tellers speak English.

Late afternoon on Friday is a good time to visit the temple for the extraordinary sight of hundreds of suited businessmen and well-dressed businesswomen praying, casting chim, and making offerings in the plaza.

To the right of the main hall is the smaller **Three Saints Hall,**

dedicated to Taoist deities, where devotees crowd at an altar in front. Walk past the hall and the large Memorial Hall to the octagonal **Confucian Hall,** with its sweeping eaves and tiled roof features of lions, fish, birds, and mythical creatures. Between the Memorial Hall and the Confucian Hall is the entrance to the elaborately landscaped and peaceful **Good Wish Garden** *(Closed Mon.),* full of colorful pagodas topped with ornate eaves, curved pathways, a bubbling stream, a carp-filled pool, rock gardens, and bridges. A rock archway leads to a bamboo grove and a copy of the Nine Dragon Wall from the Imperial Palace in Beijing set in front of a small pond. The garden also features a 60-foot (18 m) artificial waterfall. ■

Fruit and incense are among the most common temple offerings, while bamboo containers of *chim* (flat numbered sticks) are used to seek advice from fortune-tellers.

Kowloon Walled City Park & Kowloon City

THIS TRADITIONAL CHINESE-STYLE PARK SITS ON THE OLD site of the notorious Walled City, once an enclave of tightly packed, crumbling apartment buildings connected by passageways and dark alleys, and home to a variety of sweatshops and illegal factories. Adjacent to the Walled City Park, the streets of Kowloon City are an inexpensive way to indulge in two of Hong Kong's most popular pastimes—shopping and eating.

The Walled City was originally a garrison town built by the Qing government in 1847. When the British took possession of the New Territories (including New Kowloon) in 1898, the sovereignty of the Walled City remained in the hands of the Chinese, even after the British forced Qing officials out in 1899. The occupying Japanese pulled down the wall surrounding the city to extend nearby Kai Tak Airport. After World War II, thousands of refugees fleeing communist China moved in, and it became a haven for triads, drug users, prostitutes, assorted criminals, and, curiously, hundreds of illegal dentists (Chinese qualifications were not recognized in Hong Kong). After lengthy government compensation negotiations with residents,

and the agreement of China, the city was finally abandoned and bulldozed. In its place the Walled City Park was built.

You enter the South Gate on Carpenter Road to a plaza shaded with banyan trees and the **Yamen Building,** a three-hall structure originally used as the administrative office of the Assistant Magistrate of Kowloon. It now has photographs and a model of the Walled City.

Archaeological digs carried out during demolition revealed two stone plaques bearing the inscriptions "South Gate" and "Kowloon Walled City." These now sit to the east of the entrance to the original South Gate, at one time the main entry to the city. Other relics unearthed, including some of the wall's foundation stones, a cannon, a flagstone path, and drainage ditch, are now features in the park.

The western section features small bridges straddling a carp-filled brook and stream, bordered by a winding covered walkway. Just to the south, a bridge crosses an artificial lake full of turtles to one of eight elegant pavilions spread throughout the park—**Nam Lung Pavilion,** with its sweeping tiled eaves, timber lattice, moon gate entrances, red windows, and patterned walls. Between the water features and the Yamen Building, the enclosed **Garden of Four**

Left: A temple within the dark, dank confines of the old Walled City, which was demolished in 1933

Kowloon Walled City Park

🅰 Map p. 140

✉ Tung Tsing Rd., Kowloon City

☎ 2716-9962

🚇 MTR: Lok Fu, exit B then taxi; Bus: 1 from Star Ferry

Seasons is worth a look for its numerous species of bonsai trees.

The winding paths in the park's eastern section lead to a couple of hillock pavilions—the elaborately designed **Mountain View Pavilion** and **Hill Top Pavilion.** Owing to a recently installed high-rise tower outside the park, views to the imposing **Lion Rock** to the north are obstructed.

Follow the covered walkway from Mountain View Pavilion to the Ming-style **Twin Pavilion** and **Chess Garden,** with four giant stone Chinese chessboards built into the ground.

KOWLOON CITY

The row of parallel streets bounded by Prince Edward Road West, Junction Road, and Carpenter Road is the best place to explore. Start in front of the Regal Kai Tak Hotel on Sa Po Road and zigzag west toward Junction Road. The streets are crowded with people and more than 200 restaurants. You can dine on excellent Chinese, Taiwanese, Korean, Vietnamese, Malaysian, and Japanese food. The area is especially renowned for the quality and number of its Thai restaurants.

There are also a number of cheap clothing stores selling slightly damaged clothing or overruns. With a bit of rummaging, you may come up with designer clothing for a fraction of the price you would pay in a department store or boutique in the more upscale shopping precincts. Most of these stores don't having fitting rooms or offer refunds. ■

Above: Lung Nam Pavilion in Kowloon Walled City Park. The park, which replaced the notorious Walled City slum, was inspired by the Jiangnan garden style of the early Qing dynasty.

Hong Kong movies

Hong Kong churns out more than one hundred films a year, making it the third-largest producer of movies in the world after the United States. Besides entertaining movie-mad audiences in Hong Kong, fans in Taiwan, Singapore, Malaysia, Thailand, the Philippines, and Indonesia lap up the mainly action-packed fare dished out by Hong Kong's producers and directors.

Movies in Hong Kong are turned out at a fraction of the price of Hollywood. A little more than a million U.S. dollars is average, while anything more than five million U.S. dollars is enough for a big production. Film companies can make a movie from first take to post production in a couple of months (compared with anything from six months to a year in Hollywood).

Lead roles are filled by a few dozen actors—often Canto pop stars (see sidebar p. 131)—who are idolized by moviegoers in Hong Kong and other parts of Asia. They are always in huge demand by producers, who know that by assembling a cast of hot actors, success is all but guaranteed, though not necessarily quality. Such easy pickings led to the involvement of the triads (organized crime gangs) in the movie industry, especially during the early to mid-1990s.

To offset movies' low budgets, much emphasis is placed on amazing stunt work and cartoon-like violence, This violence is often incessant and hard to take. Scenes that would be completely unacceptable even by the loose standards of Hollywood are commonplace in many mainstream Hong Kong action movies. The gangster film *The Big Heat* (1988) opens with a power drill piercing a man's hand. In *Run and Kill* (1993), a man incinerates his enemy's 12-year-old daughter then, with a snarling smile, places the charred corpse at the father's feet.

But there are some notable exceptions beyond the splattering violence. Art film director Wong Kar-wai's *Happy Together* won the Palme d'Or at the Cannes Film Festival in 1997, while his excellent *Chungking Express* (1994) replaces mayhem for intense dialogue and insight into modern Hong Kong. While huge on stunts and kung fu action, Jackie Chan's comedic movies replace more graphic violence. His *Drunken Master II* (1994) is a classic of Hong Kong cinema.

Hong Kong movies are growing in popularity in the United States and Europe, and interest has been spurred on by the appearance of a number of Hong Kong actors and filmmakers in Hollywood. Director John Woo, who produced the blood-soaked cult classic *The Killer* (1989), has enjoyed success, replicating the stylized violence of his Hong Kong movies. Kung fu comedian Jackie Chan—by far the most popular actor in Asia—has made a couple of classy comedy action features including *Rush Hour* (1998) and *Shanghai Noon* (2000).

Dramatic actor Chow Yun-fat made his first appearance in Hollywood in 1998 in *The Replacement Killers*. He has since gone on to acclaim in the Academy Awards, winning with *Crouching Tiger, Hidden Dragon* (2000). Other Hong Kong actors, including action superstar Jet Li, have made an impact on Hollywood. High-kicking kung fu expert Michelle Yeoh (also *Crouching Tiger, Hidden Dragon)*, although Malaysian, got her start in Hong Kong movies.

The Hong Kong film industry is gradually recovering from a slump that hit in 1998, precipitated by the Asian economic crisis, rising prices of movie tickets, and unbridled pirating of films, which reduced production by up to one third. In 1999, the government set up the Film Development Board, handing over one hundred million U.S. dollars to help in the recovery of the industry. ■

Above & left: The acrobatic Kung Fu star Jackie Chan is one Hong Kong actor who has succeeded in Hollywood.
Below: The movie industry has been big in Hong Kong for more than half a century.

Chi Lin Nunnery

Chi Lin Nunnery

Map p. 141

5 Chi Lin Dr., Diamond Hill

2354-1882

MTR: Diamond Hill

CHI LIN NUNNERY IS A MONASTIC COMPLEX OF GARDENS, lotus ponds, and magnificently crafted timber structures, modeled after the architectural style of the Tang dynasty (618–907), a period of great cultural achievement in China. A total of 95,000 pieces of timber were used in the construction of this splendid and serene place, which was put together without nails.

The design follows the ancient rules of Chinese architecture and *feng shui* (see pp. 110–11). The main halls, built on a north–south axis, have ancillary halls to the east and west. The main buildings face the sea and back onto a mountain, and are in a style known as "one court, three yards, and three doors." The gilded and flamboyant images of Buddha in the nunnery's monastic halls are typical of the Tang period.

Enter the nunnery complex at the Shanmen ("first door" or "mountain gate") to the first yard, a tranquil place with four large lotus

The magnificent Chi Lin Nunnery copies the graceful Tang dynasty style of architecture.

lead to the **Hall of Celestial Kings**—the "second entrance"—which guards the nunnery and serves as a reception hall. Inside the main door is the Maitreya Buddha, a heavenly being who will descend to Earth to save humanity. The Maitreya is surrounded on its altar by images of the Celestial Kings holding spears, swords, and staffs. From the hall's veranda there's a lovely elevated view of the plaza, lotus ponds, and timber structures.

Passageways on either side of this hall take you through to the "second yard" and the magnificent Main Hall at its northern end. Just beyond the left passageway is the small **Jai Lan Hall** or Drum Tower. The Bodhisattva Jai Lan (the "courageous, vigilant, and diligent guardian" of Buddha's teachings), sits in a grotto on the ground floor.

Opposite the Drum Tower on the right passageway lies the **Ksitigarbha Hall** or Bell Tower, where Bodhisattva Ksitigarbha is housed. The bell on the upper floor has a chime so clear as to "awaken people's minds and soothe suffering spirits." Two halls flank the yard. On the right is the **Hall of the Bhaisajyaguru** (Medicine Master), whose gilded image,

ponds and numerous bonsai plants. Long, colonnaded corridors with mullion windows flank the yard. Beyond the "second door" steps

Kwun Yam

Kwun Yam, the goddess of mercy, is the Chinese incarnation of the Buddhist Bodhisattva Avalokitesvara.

Legend holds that Avalokitesvara was Prince Bu Xun, who lived on the southern coast of India. He renounced the material world and became the disciple of Buddha, vowing to deliver people from all suffering. Bodhisattvas are traditionally asexual, but during the Chinese Yuan dynasty, as they grew in popularity, images of Kwun Yam as a female were erected in temples as it was believed many of the bodhisattva's tasks, such as bestowing and delivering children, were more appropriate for a female deity. ■

holding a medicine bowl in its hands and honored by followers seeking longevity and good health, is attended by the Suryaprabha (sunlight) and Candraprabha (moonlight) bodhisattvas. To the left is the **Hall of Avalokitesvara** (also known as Kwun Yam, goddess of mercy; see sidebar p. 149). Here

transfer gradually to the columns. A team of traditional craftsmen from Anhui Province in China carried out the work.

Inside the Main Hall is a striking image of Buddha Sakyamuni, sitting on an altar flanked by two standing disciples, Mahakasgapa and Anada, and two sitting bodhisattvas, Marjusri and Samantabhadra.

The north door of the Main Hall leads to the "third yard"— unfortunately off-limits to visitors—which holds the Patriarch, Ancestral, Prayer, and Dharma Halls. In the northeastern corner of the nunnery, the **Ten Thousand Buddha Pagoda** houses over 10,000 Buddha images. ∎

Left: A lantern at Chi Lin Nunnery in Tang dynasty style marks the path to Western Lotus Pond.

devotees pray for worldly needs such as health, wisdom, peace, and wealth. The bodhisattva sits on a lotus upon a rock, in the middle of the ocean, pondering the reflection of the moon in the water, a symbol of the impermanent and illusory nature of life.

Chi Lin's grandest structure is the **Main Hall,** an architectural wonder. Twenty-eight columns of thick yellow cedar support a roof made from 28,000 tiles (their weight alone is 160 tons). Instead of nails, a highly elaborate bracketing system, typical of ancient Chinese architecture, was employed, allowing the load of the heavy roof to

CHI LIN NUNNERY

Shanmen

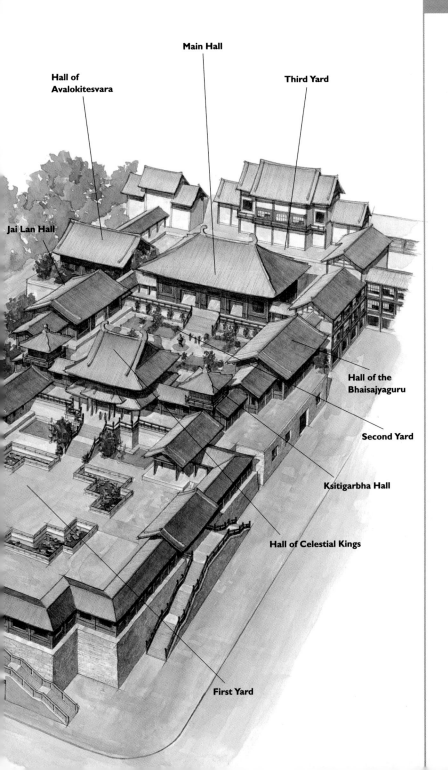

Main Hall

Hall of
Avalokitesvara

Third Yard

Jai Lan Hall

Hall of the
Bhaisajyaguru

Second Yard

Ksitigarbha Hall

Hall of Celestial Kings

First Yard

More places to visit in Kowloon

LEI CHENG UK HAN TOMB

The tomb, a branch of the Hong Kong Museum of History (see pp. 132–33), dates back to the Han dynasty (206 B.C.–A.D. 220). It was discovered in 1955 when workers were leveling the area to make way for a housing project, and consists of four barrel-shaped brick chambers in the form of a cross, centered by another domed chamber. The tomb, about 1,600 years old, lies protected inside a temperature-controlled vault. Funerary pottery and bronze objects unearthed at the site are displayed in an adjacent exhibition gallery. The tomb's inhabitants remain a mystery, but it is thought it was built for a high-ranking Chinese official.

🅰 Map p. 141   ✉ 41 Tonkin St., Sham Shui Po   ☎ 2386-2863   🕐 Closed Thurs. & Sun.   🚇 MTR: Sham Shui Po

Shoppers crowd a fish market in Sham Shui Po.

LANGHAM PLACE

Looking like a spaceship that has landed in one of Hong Kong's most traditional areas, the futuristic shopping center and hotel complex that is Langham Place could not be more incongruous with the frenetic mixture of stores at street level. Inside, floors of shops and a department store attract the city's young into a build-

ing that is crowned by an "outdoor" restaurant area on the 13th level with its own artificial sky.

🅰 Map p. 141

LEI YUE MUN FISHING VILLAGE

The colorful and lively fishing village of Lei Yue Mun, lying at the eastern end of Victoria Harbor, has evolved into one of Hong Kong's premier seafood venues. Although the place has lost some of its character and been dolled up to resemble an ancient Chinese fishing village, it still maintains enough atmosphere to make for a good dining excursion. Buy live seafood from one of the many market stalls—ask the price before buying—and take it to a restaurant to have it prepared.

🅰 Map p. 141 (arrowed from map)   ✉ Lei Yue Mun   🚇 MTR: Kwun Tong, exit A1, then bus 14C

ROSARY CHURCH

The small, whitewashed Rosary Church, built in a well-proportioned Gothic revival style, is one of Hong Kong's oldest Catholic churches. Constructed in the late 1880s, features include pointed arches, tracery windows, buttresses, a bell tower, and two stair towers.

🅰 Map p. 125   ✉ 125 Chatham Rd.   ☎ 2368-0980   🚌 Bus: 2C, 2K, 5, 5C, 8, 8A, 110

SHAM SHUI PO

This impossibly crowded neighborhood on the border with Mong Kok along Boundary Street has an enormous street market along Apliu Street. The dozens of market stands concentrate mainly on computer and electronic goods, including Walkmans, CDs, CD-players, and televisions (both new and secondhand). You will also find cheap clothing, toys, and novelties, among many other things. The market is open from noon to midnight.

Some very good clothing bargains can be found at the **Cheung Sha Wan Road Fashion Center,** between Yen Chow and Wong Chuk Streets. The modern **Dragon Center** at 37 Yen Chow Street is more upscale. The nine-floor shopping mall has a roller coaster on its top floor and an ice-skating rink.

🅰 119 A6 (arrowed from map)   🚇 MTR: Sham Shui Po ∎

Immense new towns rising from what were once paddy fields, walking trails rising to mountain peaks and skirting beaches, ancient buildings, and pockets of rural life can be found in the "Land In Between."

New Territories

Walled village decoration in Kam Tin

New Territories

5▷

THE NEW TERRITORIES TAKES IN A 307-SQUARE-mile (796 sq km) swath of land between Boundary Street in Kowloon and the border with the People's Republic of China—an area twice the size of Kowloon, Hong Kong Island, and the outlying islands combined. This is where many Hong Kongers come to breathe fresh air and escape the clamor of the city.

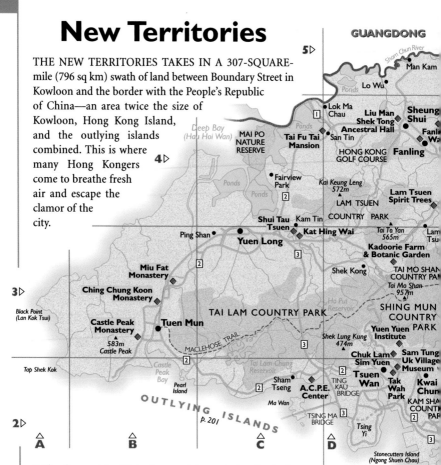

GUANGDONG

Settlers from mainland China began arriving in what is now the New Territories between the 10th and 15th centuries. They gathered in clans, built villages surrounded by sturdy walls for protection, and farmed the fertile soil.

The arrival of the British had little effect on their way of life, even after the New Territories were leased from the Chinese in 1898. The completion of the Kowloon–Canton Railway (KCR) in 1910, and a network of roads built by the 1920s, had only marginal impact, and rural and village life continued more or less unhindered until the start of World War II.

By the 1960s, the population of the New Territories was around 400,000, but Kowloon and Hong Kong Island to the south were bursting at the seams. To ease this, the government embarked on massive infrastructure programs that saw the creation of large-scale housing developments with clusters of residential towers, some as high as 40 floors, rising above what were once paddy fields. These "new towns," including Tsuen Wan, Tuen Mun, Yuen Long, Fanling, Sheung Shui, Tai Po, Sha Tin, and Ma On Shan, now house most of the 3.5 million people living in the New Territories.

Although much of the tradition, architecture, and environment of the area has been lost, a surprising amount still remains. There are gloriously ornate Buddhist and Taoist temples, remnants of 500-year-old walled villages inhabited by descendants of the pioneering clans, imposing clan and ancestral halls, and isolated villages in lush valleys. There are also large tracts of beautiful, protected countryside interlaced with walking trails and set aside as country parks (see pp. 38–40). At Mai Po, on

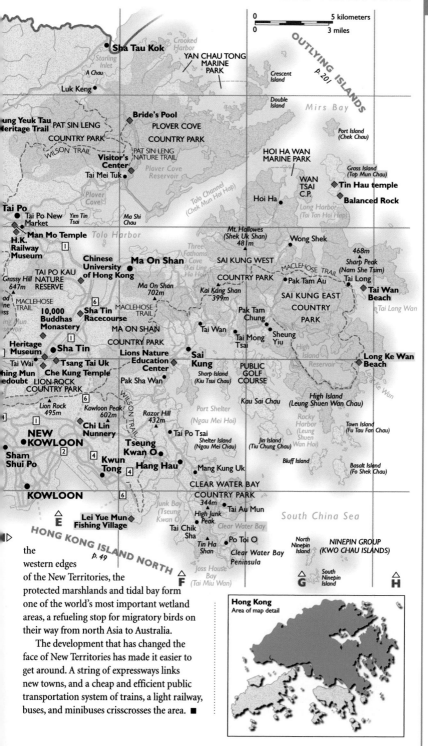

0   5 kilometers
0   3 miles

Sha Tau Kok

YAN CHAU TONG
MARINE
PARK

Crooked Harbor

Starling Inlet

A Chau

Luk Keng

Crescent Island

Double Island

Mirs Bay

OUTLYING ISLANDS
P. 201

ung Yeuk Tau
Heritage Trail

PAT SIN LENG

COUNTRY PARK

WILSON TRAIL

Bride's Pool
PLOVER COVE
COUNTRY PARK

PAT SIN LENG
NATURE TRAIL

Visitor's
Center

Tai Mei Tuk

Plover Cove Reservoir

HOI HA WAN
MARINE PARK

*Port Island
(Chek Chau)*

*Grass Island
(Tap Mun Chau)*

WAN
TSAI
C.P.

Tin Hau temple

Balanced Rock

Hoi Ha

*Long Harbor
(Tai Tan Hoi Hap)*

Tai Po

Tai Po New
Market

*Yim Tin
Tsai*

Plover Cove

H.K.
Railway
Museum

Man Mo Temple

Tolo Harbor

*Ma Shi
Chau*

*Tolo Channel
(Chek Mun Hoi Hap)*

*Three
Fathoms
Cove
(Kei Ling
Ha Hoi)*

Mt. Hallowes
(Shek Uk Shan)
481m

Wong Shek

468m

Chinese
University
of Hong Kong

Ma On Shan

SAI KUNG WEST

MACLEHOSE TRAIL

Sharp Peak
(Nam She Tsim)

Tai Long

TAI PO KAU
NATURE
RESERVE

*Grassy Hill
647m*

MACLEHOSE
TRAIL

*Ma On Shan
702m*

COUNTRY PARK

Pak Tam Au

Tai Wan
Beach

Kai Kung Shan
399m

SAI KUNG EAST

Tai Long Wan

10,000
Buddhas
Monastery

Sha Tin
Racecourse

MACLEHOSE
TRAIL

COUNTRY

PARK

Pak Tam
Chung

MA ON SHAN

Heritage
Museum

Sha Tin

COUNTRY PARK

Tai Wan

Tai Mong
Tsai

Sheung
Yiu

*High
Island
Reservoir*

Tai Wai

Tsang Tai Uk

Lions Nature
Education
Center

Sai
Kung

Long Ke Wan
Beach

hing Mun
edoubt

Che Kung Temple

LION ROCK
COUNTRY PARK

Pak Sha Wan

*Sharp Island
(Kiu Tsui Chau)*

PUBLIC
GOLF
COURSE

*Lion Rock
495m*

*Kowloon Peak
602m*

*Razor Hill
432m*

WILSON TRAIL

Kau Sai Chau

High Island
(Leung Shuen Wan Chau)

*Rocky
Harbor
(Leung
Shuen
Wan Hoi)*

*Town Island
(Fu Tau Fan Chau)*

Chi Lin
Nunnery

NEW
KOWLOON

Tseung
Kwan O

Tai Po Tsai

*Port Shelter
(Ngau Mei Hoi)*

*Shelter Island
(Ngau Mei Chau)*

*Jin Island
(Tiu Chung Chau)*

*Basalt Island
(Fo Shek Chau)*

Sham
Shui Po

Kwun
Tong

Hang Hau

Mang Kung Uk

Bluff Island

KOWLOON

*Junk Bay
(Tseung
Kwan O)*

CLEAR WATER BAY
COUNTRY PARK

344m
High Junk
Peak

Tai Au Mun

South China Sea

E

Lei Yue Mun
Fishing Village

HONG KONG ISLAND NORTH
P. 49

*Tai Chik
Sha*

Clear Water Bay

Tin Ha
Shan

Po Toi O

Clear Water Bay
Peninsula

*North
Ninepin
Island*

NINEPIN GROUP
(KWO CHAU ISLANDS)

F

*Joss House
Bay
(Tai Miu Wan)*

G

South
Ninepin
Island

H

the
western edges
of the New Territories, the
protected marshlands and tidal bay form
one of the world's most important wetland
areas, a refueling stop for migratory birds on
their way from north Asia to Australia.

The development that has changed the
face of New Territories has made it easier to
get around. A string of expressways links
new towns, and a cheap and efficient public
transportation system of trains, a light railway,
buses, and minibuses crisscrosses the area. ■

Hong Kong
Area of map detail

Peaceful gardens and ponds enhance the temple architecture of the Yuen Yuen Institute.

Tsuen Wan & Sam Tung Uk Village Museum

AT THE LAST STOP ON THE MTR LINE, JUST NORTH OF THE enormous Kwai Chung container terminal, lies this bustling new town of factories and towering residential blocks. Tsuen Wan, the gateway to the western New Territories, lies close to several interesting monasteries, country park walking trails, and a vestige of New Territories' history, the Sam Tung Uk Village Museum.

Yuen Yuen Institute

🅰 154 D3

✉ Low Wai Rd., Lo Wai, Tsuen Wan

🚇 MTR: Tsuen Wan, then Minibus 81 from Shiu Wo St.

Sam Tung Uk Village Museum

🅰 154 D2

✉ 2 Kwu Uk Ln., Tsuen Wan

☎ 2411-2001

🕐 Closed Tues.

🚇 MTR: Tsuen Wan, exit 3B

On Tsuen Wan Market Road, a five-minute walk from the MTR station, is **Tak Wah Park** *(take exit B and follow footbridge over Sai Lau Kok and Castle Peak Rds.).* This relaxing area has ponds filled with carp and catfish, Chinese pavilions, grottoes, and an old run-down clan hall.

One of the main attractions in Tsuen Wan is the **Yuen Yuen Institute,** one of a number of monasteries tucked into the hills just north of the town and a ten-minute taxi ride from Tsuen Wan MTR station. The institute is a religious, one-stop shop, catering to worshipers of Buddhism,

Confucianism, and Taoism; its impressive main building is a copy of Beijing's famed Temple of Heaven. You can walk around the pavilions and ponds in the peaceful grounds and enjoy a vegetarian lunch at the canteen.

The monastery of **Cheuk Lam Sim Yuen,** or Bamboo Forest Monastery *(Minibus 85 from Shiu Wo St., just south of Tsuen Wan MTR station, exit B),* was originally built from bamboo matsheds (woven slats of bamboo used as walls for dwellings) in 1927. The monastery is home to three of the largest Buddha statues to be found in Hong Kong.

Shing Mun Country Park, in the hills northeast of Tsuen Wan, has a number of hiking trails. Follow the western bank of the Shing Mun Reservoir through dense forests into Shing Min Valley, on to Lead Mine Pass, and haul yourself up the 2,122-foot (647 m) Grassy Hill to superb views. Alternatively, take an easy amble around the 1.2-mile (2 km) **Pineapple Dam Nature Trail.** The park's visitor center *(closed Tues.)* has displays of the area's primeval vegetation and the building of the reservoir, along with a history of local agriculture and mining.

Adjacent to Shing Mun Country Park is **Kam Shan Country Park,** famed for its bands of macaque monkeys that hang around the road leading into the park. The monkeys have become used to being fed by humans, a practice officials are keen to discourage. They may casually wander up to you and snatch anything you are carrying.

Winding over the hills between the two country parks is the **Smugglers' Ridge Trail** and **Shing Mun Redoubt,** a network of bullet-scarred, crumbling, overgrown pillboxes, bunkers, and trenches, part of a string of defensive positions built across the New Territories in the 1930s and known as the Gin Drinker's Line. The redoubt was overrun within hours of the Japanese launching their attack on Hong Kong on December 8, 1941.

SAM TUNG UK VILLAGE MUSEUM

A part of New Territories' history has been preserved at this restored walled village. A five-minute walk from the Tsuen Wan MTR station *(take exit B3 and walk east along Sai Lau Kok Rd. for a short distance)* are the distinctive tiled roof and whitewashed walls of the Sam Tung Uk Village Museum to the left, providing a somewhat sanitized but interesting look into early life in the New Territories.

Sam Tung Uk was a Hakka village, built in 1786 by the Chan clan. (The Hakka were settlers from the Chinese mainland who arrived in Hong Kong in the late 1600s.) The Chans moved from Guangdong Province in the 1750s and settled in Tsuen Wan. Clan leader Chan Yam-shing built three rows of village houses at Sam Tung Uk, and his descendants added annexes. The family's ancestral altar was placed in a hall at the back of the compound and the Chinese characters for "Chan's Family Ancestral Hall"

Cheuk Lam Sim Yuen showcases the color and craftsmanship of Chinese Buddhism.

were engraved on the granite lintel above the door frame.

The name Sam Tung (literally "three-beam dwelling") comes from the design of the village that incorporates three roofed halls, each with a *tung,* or main supporting beam, along its central axis.

After entering the main doorway, you come to an **Orientation Hall,** which highlights the history of the village and the Chan clan, and charts the work carried out to restore the village. It's interesting to see how plain the village was in the 1970s before restoration began (it was fully restored and opened as a museum in 1987).

On the way from the Orientation Room to the village's Front Lane is one of the structures used as living quarters, with areas for cooking, sleeping, and eating, and a cockloft for storage. The building, one of the four individual houses built beside the main halls, is full of artifacts and reproductions of furniture and cooking utensils collected from

A restored Hakka walled village, Sam Tung Uk gives insight into the New Territory's early settlers.

Hakka villages in Guangdong. The tiny side houses along the village walls also have small exhibits of artifacts such as traditional paper figurines and Chinese New Year prints. You can wander the narrow lanes past these structures.

The **Assembly Hall,** one of the village's three interconnecting main buildings that line up along a central axis behind the entrance to the museum, is hung with brightly decorated lanterns. The other two buildings are the **Entrance Hall,** and the **Ancestral Hall,** at the rear of the village, behind the Assembly Hall. The altar in the Ancestral Hall, where tablets inscribed with the names of ancestors were kept (see sidebar p. 162), still stands, but the tablets have been moved. They are in the new Sam Tung Uk village, built by the government to house residents of the village before it became a museum.

A small park with a pond behind the museum provides a pleasant place to rest under the trees. ■

Airport Core Program
Exhibition Center

The ACPEC's terrace provides stunning views of the 1.4-mile Tsing Ma Bridge, the world's longest road and rail suspension bridge.

DESPITE ITS LESS-THAN-ENTICING NAME, THE AIRPORT Core Program Exhibition Center (ACPEC) is an interesting place. It traces the building of the massive infrastructure projects that went into creating and supporting Hong Kong International Airport on Lantau Island, and has unsurpassed views to the mightily impressive Tsing Ma and Ting Kau Bridges.

When Britain announced in 1989 its plan to build the enormous airport at Chek Lap Kok, it neglected to tell China. Officials on the mainland were outraged, because they were not informed and because they saw the project as too ambitious and expensive, an unnecessary strain on Hong Kong's coffers, which they would soon inherit. At a massive 16 billion dollars, the airport was the most expensive infrastructure program in the world. Originally due to be completed in 1997, symbolically before Britain handed Hong Kong back to China, it did not open until May 1998.

ACPEC has models, diagrams, and photographs charting the progress of many projects, including land reclamation in Central, construction of the Western Harbor tunnel, the Airport Express train line, and bridges, as well as the airport. A 10-minute video in English and Cantonese describes the construction every 30 minutes.

A **viewing terrace** at the back of the center gives spectacular 180-degree views to the Tsing Ma Bridge, at 1.4 miles (2.2 km) the world's longest road and rail suspension bridge, and the smaller Tin Kau Bridge. Beneath and beyond the bridges barges, tankers, tugboats, and numerous other vessels cut a white wake through the busy harbor's deep green waters. ■

Airport Core Program Exhibition Center

- 154 C2
- 410 Castle Peak Rd., Tsuen Wan
- 2491-9202
- Closed Mon.
- Bus: 234B or 53 from Tsuen Wan Ferry Pier; MTR: Tsuen Wan, exit B, then Minibus 96M

Tuen Mun monasteries

AWAY FROM THE ENDLESS ROWS OF HIGH-RISE APARTMENT
towers that characterize Tuen Mun are a number of Buddhist and
Taoist monasteries worth exploring. They vary from the sedate and
rustic to the expansive and busy. All can be reached by the New
Territories' Light Transit Rail (LTR) system.

**Castle Peak
Monastery**
🅐 154 B3
✉ Off Yeung Tsing Rd.,
   Ching Shan Tsuen,
   Tuen Mun
🚈 LTR: Technical
   Institute Station

**Ching Chung Koon
Monastery**
🅐 154 B3
✉ Tsing Chung Koon
   Rd., Tuen Mun
🚈 LTR: Ching Chung
   Station

**Opposite: Ching
Chung Koon
Monastery is one
of Hong Kong's
most famous
Taoist shrines.**

CASTLE PEAK
MONASTERY

Castle Peak Monastery nestles in
the foothills of Tsing Shan (Green
Mountain) overlooking Tuen Mun.
Its elaborate but faded shrines and
worn appearance add character to
the place. The present monastery
was built in 1918, but, according to
legend, it was founded in the fifth
century by the famous and somewhat scurrilous monk Pei Tu, who
is said to have stolen a golden
Buddhist statue from a house where
he was a guest. He was chased to
the banks of a stream, where he
magically turned his rice bowl into
a boat to cross, hence his name,
which translates to "cup ferry." Take
the path behind the temple leading
to a **shrine** and statue of a four-
faced Buddha under an overhanging

rock, and a view over sprawling
Tuen Mun. From Technical Institute
LTR station, save yourself the climb
up the steep hill and take a taxi.

CHING CHUNG KOON
MONASTERY

The atmosphere at this large Taoist
complex, one of Hong Kong's most
important Taoist shrines, is often
hectic; its expansive grounds fill up
on weekends and during festivals
with worshipers and sightseers.
The bold **main temple building**
sports a heavily ornate orange roof,
supported by red pillars, with a riot
of swirling colors under its eaves.
Carved timber fixtures, frescoes,
and antique artifacts complete the
picture. The temple's major image
is one of Taoism's legendary Eight
Immortals, Liu Tung Bun. Liu is

Miu Fat Monastery
154 B3
Castel Peak Rd.,
Lam Tei, Tuen Mun
LTR: Lam Tei Station

Ching Chung
Koon's lavish main
building holds a
collection of
ancient religious
artifacts.

flanked by the sect's founder Wong Chung Yeung, and Liu's student Qiu Chang Chun. On the main altar are the magic sword used by Liu to slay demons, a fly switch to whisk away bad luck, and a gourd of herbs to heal the sick.

At the front of the altar stand two exquisite 300-year-old stone statues of goddesses, and a glass case with a thousand-year-old jade seal. Past the main temple are **two ancestral halls** packed with thousands of wooden ancestral tablets (see below), where paper offerings are burnt during commemorative services. Behind these lie a Chinese garden with a bridge winding over a pond to a small pavilion.

The temple is famous for its bonsai trees, which are said to bring harmony, and a bonsai festival is held each spring.

At the small building to the left of the main temple, you can buy tickets for the monastery's renowned vegetarian lunches.

MIU FAT MONASTERY

Gilded dragons set with mosaics and tiny mirrors wrap around the pillars at the entrance, statues of lions and elephants carved from stone guard the door, and porcelain figurines of mythical beasts line up along the ridges of the sweeping roof and eaves of this elaborate Buddhist temple. Inside, the parade of color continues with painted sculptures of Buddhist scenes in bas-relief on the stairway landings.

Continue up the stairs to the vegetarian restaurant and on to the **main shrine** on the third floor. Here, thousands of gilded Buddha plaques are embedded in the walls, and murals painted on the ceiling depict scenes from Buddhist mythology. The main shrine holds the statues of the **Three Precious Buddhas.** Walk behind it to view the hundreds of ancestral tablets inscribed in gold and the huge statue of Avalokitesvara (see sidebar p. 149), whose thousand hands stretch out to help the suffering. ■

Ancestral tablets

Ancestral tablets—timber slats about 8 inches (20 cm) tall—are found in major clan halls, lined up behind ancestral altars. They are inscribed in gold with the name and brief biography of deceased clan members. The principal tablets, often devoted to the founding members of the clan, are in the most prominent position. ■

Kadoorie Farm & Botanic Garden

SET IN A STEEP, DEEPLY WOODED VALLEY ON THE NORTHwestern edge of Tai Mo Shan Country Park you will find a surprising amount of biodiversity on display. Two brothers, Lawrence and Horace Kadoorie, from one of Hong Kong's most influential families, started this unique place in the 1950s to help immigrants flooding across the border from China learn farming techniques.

Since then, the Kadoorie Farm & Botanic Garden has grown into a place of conservation and education, a sanctuary for the territories' rich variety of plants and animals, and an intriguing place to visit.

A zigzag of roads and paths takes you up the steep slopes of the valley to the summit of **Kwun Yam Shan** at 1,974 feet (602 m). On the lower slopes a road winds past organic vegetable fields to greenhouses and nurseries full of subtropical flowers, enclosures for waterfowl and deer, an aviary, a lotus pond full of carp, and insect and amphibian houses.

Injured birds of prey are nursed back to health in the **raptor sanctuary** at the top of the lower slopes. Here the road narrows to a path and views open onto terraced orchards. A shady path leads to a tumbling cascade of water called the Great Falls. Nearby, colorful butterflies flutter among flowers especially chosen for their specific nectars at the **Butterfly Garden.**

Farther up the slope, a stream runs alongside an enchanting fern walk to gardens growing different varieties of tea and medicinal herbs. Beyond these gardens lies the **Orchid Haven,** the principal site on the farm for flora conservation. From here you can climb to the **Kadoorie Brothers Memorial Pavilion** for marvelous views back down the valley. Cross near to the top of Kwun Yam Shan with its ancient stone altars, believed to have been built about 500 years ago to call upon the blessing of the goddess of mercy, Kwun Yam, and a much more recent statue of the goddess. Call ahead when visiting the farm and botanical garden to see if tours are available. ∎

Kadoorie Farm & Botanic Garden
🗺 154 D3
✉ Lam Kam Rd., Tai Po, New Territories
☎ 2488-1317
🚉 KCR East: Tai Po Market station, then bus 64K

An injured black kite receives attention at Kadoorie Farm's raptor sanctuary.

New Territories drive

The drive begins in Tsuen Wan and follows Castle Peak Road in an arc close to the mainland Chinese border, before heading south through the verdant hills on Route Twisk and back into Tsuen Wan. Along the way you'll take in ocean views and some exceptional natural scenery.

Mangroves give way to mudflats at the protected Mai Po Nature Reserve.

About 1 mile (1.6 km) after picking up the start of Castle Peak Road in Tsuen Wan, you will skirt a scenic coastline on the way to the Ting Kau Bridge, linking Tsing Yi Island. A half mile (800 m) after passing under the bridge is the **Airport Core Program Exhibition Center ❶** (see p. 159). Head out to the terrace at the back for views of the spectacular Tsing Ma Bridge.

Continue on past the bridge to **Sham Tseng ❷**, famous for its roast goose restaurants. A mile (1.6 km) beyond views take in the high peaks rising from the eastern end of Lantau Island. The road then dips under the Tuen Mun Highway to the **Gold Coast ❸**, a modern resort fronted by **Golden Beach ❹**, one of the area's better stretches of sand. From the Gold Coast, you will pass more beaches as the towering residential blocks of Tuen Mun come into view. At the T-junction,

turn right on Castle Peak Road as it starts to head inland and skirts the eastern fringes of Tuen Mun.

After 7 miles (11 km), exit Castle Peak Road to Hung Tin Road on the right and loop onto Yuen Long Highway, bypassing busy Yuen Long town center. Follow the highway for 3 miles (5 km) to Pok Oi Interchange, and take the Pat Heung exit to rejoin Castle Peak Road.

At the next traffic circle, take the Mai Po turnoff. Two miles (3.2 km) farther down Castle Peak Road is the sign for the **Mai Po Nature Reserve ❺** (see pp. 166–69); take a left turn on Tam Kon Chau Road and continue to the entrance. You can only enter the reserve if you have reserved a visit, but the countryside is striking, with patchworks of ponds and marshlands set against a hilly backdrop.

Return to Castle Peak Road and head north for 1 mile (1.6 km) to a narrow road on the left signposted to Fan Tin Tsuen. The village is home to several old clan halls and the **Tai Fu Tai Mansion ❻** (see p. 200).

Back on Castle Peak Road, follow the signs for **Lok Ma Chau ❼,** 1.5 miles (2.2 km) farther north, and enjoy uninterrupted views across the border to Shenzhen. Rejoin Castle Peak Road, this time skirting the Fanling High-

way as it heads east for 3.3 miles (5.3 km). It ends at a T-junction. Turn left and follow the Fan Kam Road, through the Hong Kong Golf Course, for 8 miles (13 km) until it joins Kam Tin Road. Turn left here and after another 1.3 miles (2 km) you join the scenic **Route Twisk ❽,** which winds past Shek Kong, once a British Army base but now occupied by the People's Liberation Army. The route continues through the mist-shrouded hills of Tai Mo Shan and Tai Lam Country Parks for 5.5 miles (8.5 km) before arriving back at the eastern edge of Tsuen Wan. ■

- See area map p. 154
- Castle Peak Rd., Tsuen Wan
- 40 miles (65 km)
- 6.5 hours
- Route Twisk, Tsuen Wan

NOT TO BE MISSED
- Mai Po Nature Reserve
- Tai Fu Tai Mansion
- Lok Ma Chau
- Route Twisk

Tai Fu Tai
Mansion

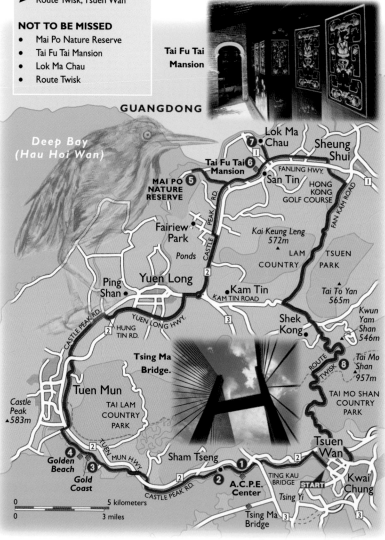

Countless thousands of migratory and resident birds seek haven in Mai Po's wetlands each year.

Mai Po Nature Reserve

IN THE UNLIKELIEST OF SPOTS IN THE NORTHWESTERN New Territories, Mai Po Nature Reserve lies sandwiched between the tower blocks of the new town of Yuen Long to the south and the high-rises of the Shenzhen Special Economic Region across the border to the north. But the marshes of Mai Po and the mudflats of adjacent Inner Deep Bay make up one of the most important wetland areas in the world, designated a Site of Special Scientific Interest in 1983 and a Wetland of International Importance in 1995.

Mai Po Nature Reserve

- 154 C4
- Mai Po Wildlife Education Center, Tam Kon Chau, Yuen Long
- 2526-4473
- $$ (guide fee)
- MTR to Nam Chong, West Rail to Kam Tin, then taxi

The area provides a unique habitat and crucial stopping-off point for vast flocks of migrating birds and huge numbers of resident species. About 60,000 birds gather and feed in the ponds, marshes, mangroves, and mudflats during the winter and more than 340 different species have been recorded here, many of them endangered, including a quarter of the world's remaining 600 black-faced spoonbills.

What brings them to the 3,700 acres (1,500 ha) of Mai Po and Inner Deep Bay is the opportunity to rest and refuel on their long migratory journeys between north Asia and Australia.

A rare sighting of a leopard cat at the reserve

One of the biggest attractions at Mai Po for the birds is the man-made, **earth-walled ponds** known as *gei wai*. Covering about 24 acres (10 ha), they were built by migrants from China during the 1940s to farm shrimp. The ponds attract fish, crabs, and oysters, which flourish in the environment.

The reserve, which is managed by the World Wide Fund for Nature Hong Kong, is active in promoting the importance of the site. The **Education Center** has displays highlighting the area's geology, ecology, and settlement, and the exhibition gallery has interactive exhibits featuring the art of gei wai-building, farming techniques, wetland ecology, the area's abundant land-based wildlife species, and, of course, birdlife and migration.

Mai Po's network of paths, bridges, and boardwalks, with access for the disabled, takes you to within feet of thousands of birds. There are ten **observation hides** near the ponds where you can survey the birds without risk of disturbing them, and a three-story observation tower with panoramic views over the area.

A **floating boardwalk** runs out into the mangroves of Deep Bay. Request a boardwalk permit when you reserve a visit.

Serious bird lovers attend the annual **Big Bird Race**—a competition for four-member teams from around the world who compete to see, hear, and record the greatest number of species in a 24-hour period.

Although it's unlikely you will see any on your visit, Mai Po also attracts a wide variety of mammals, including mongooses, pangolins, and leopard cats.

Despite the determined efforts at conservation and protection, the reserve remains under threat from development in the surrounding areas. Pollution in Deep Bay, flowing

down from the manufacturing centers in southern China, and agricultural waste from Hong Kong, have had an impact, as has air pollution. On some winter days, it's not possible to see across Deep Bay to nearby Shenzhen.

Ironically, the fact that such large numbers of birds use Mai Po and Deep Bay as a break on their migration is not necessarily a good sign. It means that other wetlands on the bird's migratory route between north Asia and Australia are becoming rare.

Access to the reserve is limited, so make a reservation well in advance. You can rent binoculars at the site. Children under five years of age are not admitted. ■

Left: Cormorants cluster among the branches of a casuarina tree.

Mangrove

Pied kingfisher

Japanese yellow bunting

Black-capped kingfisher

Leopard cat

Dalmatian pelicans

Black-faced spoonbill

Pangolin

Spotted greenshank

Spoonbilled sandpiper

Asian dowicher

Shrenk's bittern

Greyheaded lapwing

Mudskippers

Black-faced spoonbills

Oriental stork

A black-crowned night-heron, one of the 340 bird species spotted at the reserve.

Imperial eagle

Chinese egrets

Otter

Mandarin ducks

Silky starling

Blackheaded ibis

Far eastern curlew

Baikal teal

Dragonfly

Bandicoot rat

Reed

Tang clan boys received schooling at the meticulously restored **Kun Ting Study Hall**, one of a number of renovated clan dwellings in Ping Shan.

Ping Shan Heritage Trail walk

The short Ping Shan Heritage Trail offers the chance to see a collection of centuries-old and other related structures without too much effort. The buildings are part of the mini-empire of the Tang clan, the largest of Hong Kong's "Five Great Clans" who settled in the New Territories in the 11th century (see sidebar p. 173).

Hop off the LTR (Light Transit Railway) at Ping Shan and take the crossing over the tracks. Head left along the sidewalk to Ping Ha Road, turn right, and follow it for about a half mile (0.8 km) to a small park on your right. The trail starts behind the park. The first stop is the 1767 **Hung Shing Temple ❶**. Inside the dimly lit building are three carved timber altars, a riot of red and gold embroidery.

Continue along Ping Ha Road for a short distance to the lane on your right. The building standing on the corner, embellished with a brightly decorated lintel and superbly decorated inside, once served as the **Ching Shu Hin Guest House ❷** for important visitors. The gloriously ornate **Kun Ting Study Hall ❸** lies next door. Here boys of the Tang clan were educated. The hall was built in 1870 and has recently been fully restored to show off its carved granite columns, wall and eave

plaster moldings, and wildly colorful murals.

Follow the lane a little farther until a square opens to your right and two large ancestral halls come into view. The one on the left is the **Tang Ancestral Hall ❹**, its sheer size proclaiming the power and wealth the family wielded in the area. Built about 700 years ago and now splendidly restored, its three large halls and two courtyards feature stone pillars rising to support the finely carved painted roof beams 25 feet (8 m) above, while pottery dragon-fish top its sweeping eaves. In the first courtyard you will see a red stone wall leading to the gate, built to keep evil spirits out. Beyond this spirit wall is another courtyard and the main hall where ancestral tablets (see sidebar p. 162) recording the names of this line of the Tang clan stand on a red altar. The hall also features a history of the clan hall and is popular with the many descendants of the Tangs now living in Europe, the United States, Canada, and Australia.

Next door is the smaller 16th-century **Yu Kiu Ancestral Hall ❺**. This hall contains the ancestral tablets of a different branch of the Tang clan, and is designed in similar style to the main hall, although on a less grand scale.

The trail continues from the square for a short distance to the simple **Yeung Hau Temple ❻**. Over a low wall, you can see its three chambers and red altars with an imposing statue of Yeung Hau, flanked by the earth god, and the goddess of expectant mothers suitably adorned with pottery children in her lap.

Retrace your steps to a turn on the right and follow it to the small walled village of **Sheung Cheung Wai ❼** to explore its few narrow lanes. Just beyond the village

is a well-tended and richly ornamented brick shrine to the earth god. The trail now snakes to the three-story **Tsui Shing Lau ❽**, the only ancient pagoda remaining in Hong Kong. The Tangs built this six-sided structure 600 years ago to keep evil at bay; today its impact is all but lost because of nearby development. ■

🏔	See area map p. 154
➤	Hung Shing Temple
↔	0.6 mile (1 km)
⏱	45 minutes
➤	Tsui Shing Lau

NOT TO BE MISSED
- Kun Ting Study Hall
- Tang Ancestral Hall

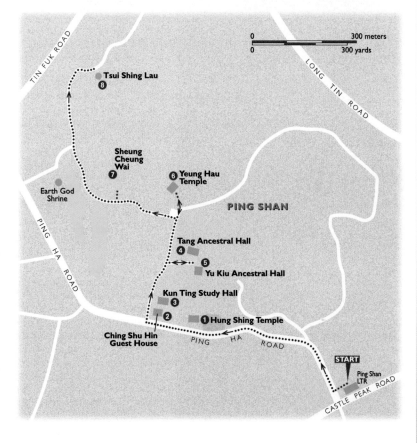

Kam Tin

IN 1069, THE CANTON (GUANGZHOU) GOVERNMENT administrator Tan Fu-hip visited Kam Tin and was so enamored with the beauty of the place that he later returned with his family and ancestral graves and settled here. This was the beginning of the Tang clan in Hong Kong, which went on to become the biggest of Hong Kong's "Five Great Clans."

Kam Tin
154 C4

A corner tower at Kat Hing Wai walled village

Subsequent generations of the Tangs built walled villages around Kam Tin and in other parts of Hong Kong as protection against pirates, bandits, and neighbors. Remnants of these villages, and those of other clans, can be found in some parts of the New Territories, but **Kat Hing Wai** (*Bus 51 from Tsuen Wan Ferry Pier, or 64K from Tai Po Market KCR*) is the most popular among visitors. Don't expect a quaint village set among cultivated fields, or a sparkling museum piece. Four hundred members of the Tang clan live here, mostly in homes that have long since replaced the original buildings, and the village and its surroundings have not escaped the gritty urbanization found in many of the villages and towns of the New Territories.

The fine, high-stone walls of the village, with imposing gray-brick corner watchtowers and a chain-iron gate guarding its only entrance, lend the 500-year-old village an impressive air, although the modern pink and purple houses jutting above the wall inside the village compound can take the edge off the experience. At the gate, you'll be asked by one of the wizened old ladies guarding the entrance to slip a HK$1 coin into a hole in the wall.

Inside, the narrow lanes still follow the original geometrical pattern. The main lane, lined with souvenir stands, runs through the center of the village and ends at a small, rather nondescript temple and ancestral hall. Here, and in other places around the temple, more weather-beaten ladies will approach you, happy to don their distinctive wide-brimmed bamboo hats and have their photographs taken for HK$10. After the temple, spend some time wandering through the village lanes, past the open doors of dimly lit homes with

flickering televisions. The village is quite small, so it won't take long.

SHUI TAU TSUEN

From Kat Hing Wai, head west for about 200 yards (180 m) along Kam Tin Road to Mung Yeung Public School and take the lane on the right for a half mile (0.8 km) to the village of Shui Tau Tsuen, set amid fields dotted with water buffalo. The village still retains a splendid row of ornate 17th-century houses, notable for the sweeping, carved timber, boat-prow features along the ridges of their roofs, decorated with sculptured fish and dragons.

Beyond the two restored study halls near the entrance to the village, take the lane that separates them for a few hundred yards to the village's imposing ancestral halls. The largest is the Tang Ching Lok Ancestral Hall *(closed Mon.–Fri.)*, dating back to the late 1700s. Above the entrance to the hall are brightly colored murals of mountains, river scenes, and people, while inside the names of prominent ancestors are listed on the altar. ■

The single entrance at Kat Hing Wa leads to ancient narrow streets.

Hong Kong's clans

The so-called "Five Great Clans" began arriving in Hong Kong from China in the 11th century, settling in the fertile regions of the New Territories, where they built fortified walled villages and farmed the surrounding countryside. The Tang clan was first to arrive, taking up residence in the Kam Tin area, before spreading throughout Hong Kong. They were followed by the Hau, who made their home near the present-day new town of Sheung Shui. Next came the Pangs, who carved out their territory near Fanling. The Liu arrived in the 15th century, followed by the Man a century later. The clans eventually became landlords of the New Territories, Kowloon, and Hong Kong, but the Tangs remained the most powerful. Many ancestors of the Five Great Clans still live in the New Territories. ■

Fanling & Sheung Shui

THESE TWO TOWNS ARE THE LAST STOPS ON THE KCR (Kowloon–Canton Railway) before reaching Lo Wu and the border with mainland China in the northern New Territories. (Lo Wu is closed to visitors unless traveling through to China.) Once traditional rural centers, they have grown into bustling new towns, but still hold a number of attractions reminiscent of the more traditional ways of the New Territories.

Fanling

🗺 154 D4

Both Fanling and Sheung Shui have a series of walled villages and ancestral halls. These were built over the centuries by members of the "Five Great Clans" of Hong Kong (see p. 173), who made their way across from mainland China to settle and farm in the New Territories from about the 11th century onward.

FANLING

In Fanling, the walled village of **Fanling Wai** was built by the Pangs, one of the Five Great Clans, during the Ming dynasty. The village is a ten-minute walk from the Fanling KCR station. From the eastern side of the station, follow the sidewalk north to a traffic circle, then continue north along San Wan

Fredrik Jacobson of Sweden tees off on the 18th hole during the final round of the 2002 Omega Hong Kong Open at world-renowned Hong Kong Golf Club in Fanling.

Sheung Shui
▲ 154 D4

Road to the Pang's ancestral hall. A lane beside it leads to the village.

Follow the lane past a luxuriant banyan tree behind a fence, then bear left for a short distance to a large, murky fishpond, built to provide good *feng shui* to the walled settlement behind.

Three-story modern houses extend behind the walls, replacing the more humble dwellings of old, but the sturdy corner watchtowers hint at how difficult it would have been for bandits or rival clans to capture the village. Fanling still maintains the typical grid system of walled villages, with houses packed tightly together and separated by narrow lanes.

From near Fanling KCR station, Sha Tau Kok Road runs to Lung Yeuk Tau, just outside the town. The area is part of the **Lung Yeuk Tau Heritage Trail,** which incorporates five walled villages and six unwalled ones known as *tsuens,* part of a village network set up by the Tangs. A number of the structures here have been listed as declared monuments and are protected. Among them is the **Tang Chung Ling Ancestral Hall** *(closed Tues.),* dating from 1525. The central chamber of the rear hall, adorned with elaborate dragon's head carvings, holds the ancestral tablets (see sidebar p. 162) of the most important members of the clan. The hall is decorated with fine woodcarvings, moldings, and murals.

Most of the original wall and layout of the village still exists at Lo Wai, whose wall and entrance gate have been restored. Lo Wai was the first settlement built in the area.

Ma Mat Wai entrance tower is worth a look for its chain-ringed gates and red stone lintel, but most of the surrounding wall has been demolished.

More impressive are the fully restored enclosing walls and corner watchtowers at Kun Lung Wai (also known as San Wai). Built in 1744, this village is the most authentic remaining in the area, although most of the original buildings within the walls have been knocked down and replaced.

You can get to some of the villages by Minibus 54K from Fanling KCR station, but the entire trail can be difficult to follow. If you want to try, contact the Antiquities and Monuments Office *(136 Nathan Rd., Tsim Sha Tsui, tel 2721-2326).*

Across the pedestrian bridge over Fanling Highway from the KCR station is Fung Ying Seen Koon, a Taoist temple set amid beautiful lush landscaping, with winding paths, waterfalls, and benches for meditating.

SHEUNG SHUI

One of the finest ancestral halls in Hong Kong is **Liu Man Shek Tong Ancestral Hall** *(Closed Tues. & Fri.)* in the walled village of Sheung Shui Wai, about 15 minutes' walk from the KCR station Sheung Shui. Take exit B1 to San Wan Road and walk north following the train line until you reach San Po Street. Turn right here and cross Po Wan Road into Sheung Shui Tung Hing Road. The first lane on the left enters the village.

Built by the Liu clan in 1751, the exterior of the village hall is enlivened with finely carved timber decorations, exquisite traditional Chinese murals, and pottery figurines on the ridge of its roof. Inside the hall you will find an intricately carved altar holding tablets with the names of the founding ancestors and others who have played important roles in the history of the clan. ■

An elaborate
reconstruction of
a Chinese opera
shed at the Hong
Kong Heritage
Museum in Sha
Tin

Sha Tin

THE SANDY FIELDS FROM WHICH SHA TIN GETS ITS NAME
are nowhere to be seen today. All the sand has gone into making the
concrete to build the huge residential towers that dominate this new
town, one of the first of a series of massive housing projects built in
the New Territories. From a valley of rice fields and small farms in
the late 1960s, it has grown into a thriving city of more than half a
million people.

Sha Tin

A 155 E3

**Sha Tin
Racecourse**

✉ Penfold Park,
Sha Tin

☎ 2966-8345

🚃 KCR East:
Racecourse Station

Sha Tin is probably the most
attractive of the New Territories'
rather drab and often intimidating
new towns. Edging the Shing Mun
River Channel that cuts through the
center of town is a green and shady
ribbon of parkland.

This is one of the few new towns
visited by people from other parts
of Hong Kong. Most come here to
indulge in their favorite pastimes:

shopping at the vast **New Town
Plaza** *(directly connected to the Sha
Tin KCR station)*, one of the largest
and busiest retail centers in Hong
Kong, and gambling on the horses
at the huge **Sha Tin Racecourse.**
If you are in Hong Kong during the
racing season, from mid-September
to June, join 70,000 other betters on
a Saturday (sometimes Sunday) for
a memorable and pulsating day at

Above right: Sha Tin was one of the first new towns—an urban development model for the New Territories.

Hong Kong Heritage Museum

✉ I Man Lam Rd., Sha Tin

☎ 2180-8188

🕐 Closed Tues.

💲 $

🚇 KCR East: Sha Tin, then shuttle bus

the races (see pp. 90–91). The hillside **Ten Thousand Buddhas Monastery** (see pp. 178–79) also attracts the throngs on weekends.

A few attractions are worth visiting before you reach Sha Tin Central. Get off the train at Tai Wai KCR station, then exit its eastern side and head north along Che Kung Miu Road for about 200 yards (180 m) to **Che Kung Temple** on the opposite side of the road. Much less elaborate and ornate than other Taoists temples in Hong Kong, it honors Che Kung, a Song dynasty general.

Inside the temple hall is a 36-foot (11 m) bronze statue of the general, standing with a distinct military air amid plumes of smoke from burning incense. Typical of Taoist temples, legions of fortune-tellers inhabit the grounds. Small paper windmills placed around the temple are said to bring good luck when the wind sets them twirling.

As you continue north on Che Kung Miu Road to the intersection of Lion Rock Tunnel Road, follow the path to the right through a small village and underpass to the old walled village of **Tsang Tai Uk** ("Tsang's big house"), a Tang-clan stronghold built in the mid-19th century. A few clan members still live there. The ancestral hall, with its red timber altar embellished with gilded carvings, lies at the back of a large, rectangular courtyard. The tops of the corner towers in the surrounding wall are shaped like the handles of a wok. Although somewhat faded, it's still possible to get a feeling of how this once thriving village looked in its heyday.

The **Hong Kong Heritage Museum,** a ten-minute walk back along Lion Rock Tunnel Road, over Che Kung Miu Road and the Shing Mun River Channel, sits on the waterfront. The **New Territories Heritage Hall** on the first floor leads you through a series of incisive exhibits highlighting the area's natural environment, prehistory, trade and coastal defense, the life of fishermen and villagers, the advent of British colonization, and the huge new town developments that began in the early 1970s. Next door, the **Cantonese Opera Heritage Hall** reconstructs a shed opera theater with opera models in dazzling costumes. The **T. T. Tsui Gallery of Chinese Art** on the second floor has an extensive and varied range of Chinese artifacts including Tang dynasty terra-cotta figures and porcelain. ∎

Ten Thousand Buddhas Monastery

HIGH IN THE HILLS JUST TO THE NORTHWEST OF SHA TIN, which guarantee excellent *feng shui*, sits the Ten Thousand Buddhas Monastery, the area's biggest attraction after the horse races. Be prepared for a steep climb to the main temple.

The climb starts just beyond the ramshackle village of Pai Tau. You will have to clamber up more than 400 steps to reach the main hall. In some places, the path is wider and the concrete is newer, the result of repairs to the monastery when mud slid down the hillside in July 1997, causing extensive damage. The temple was closed for two and a half years while the repairs were carried out, funded by donations from devotees.

The shelves on the walls of the **main temple** are stacked with almost 13,000 small Buddha statues, each one bearing a slightly different pose and expression and inscribed with the name of the person who donated it to the temple since its founding in the 1950s. Three larger gilded Buddha statues encased in glass stand in the center of the temple.

The **terrace** in front of the temple is lined with fierce-looking, multicolored statues representing Buddha's 18 disciples, or *lohans*. Beyond these are two fantastical bodhisattva images, those midway between enlightenment and the material world; one rides an elephant, while the other rides a wild-looking lion.

In the middle of all this is a statue of another bodhisattva,

Chinese graves

In the New Territories and on some of the outlying islands, you will sometimes notice large horseshoe-shaped graves. These are usually located on a south-facing hill overlooking water to ensure good *feng shui* for the deceased. Hong Kong's urban dwellers are not so lucky. In a city where space is at a premium, cemetery graves are packed tightly together on terraced hillsides. Traditionally, graves are tended in spring during the Ching Ming Festival and in the fall during the Chung Yeung Festival. On these days, families sweep graves and honor their ancestors with offerings of fruit and burning incense. ■

Ten Thousand Buddhas Monastery

🅰 155 E3
☎ 2691-1067
🅢 Donation
🚉 KCR East: Sha Tin

Left: The preferred burial site for Chinese is on the southern side of a hill with water views.

Wei To, who is the protector of monasteries, while a statue of Kwun Yam, the goddess of mercy, stands at his back.

The goddess faces a **red pagoda** which has nine levels, as this is an auspicious number in Buddhism, although it is actually only four stories high. Climb it for great views over Sha Tin.

From here another 69 steps lead to the top level of the temple where you are greeted with the sight of the mummified remains of the monastery's founding abbot, Yuet Kai, sitting upright in a glass case in front of a giant gilded Buddha image.

The abbot, who was a philosophy professor from Kunming in southern China, spent his life devoted to the study of Buddhism.

He arrived in Hong Kong after World War II and set about building the temple.

When Yuet Kai died in 1965 at the age of 87, he was buried in a coffin on the hill. Eight months later, the body was exhumed for reburial and, according to devotees, the abbot not only showed no signs of decomposition, but also emitted a fluorescent glow. He was embalmed, layered in gold leaf, draped in robes, placed in a lotus position, and put on display in his present position as an example of piety.

If you visit on a Sunday or a public holiday, you may find fortune-tellers in the temple hall, but be sure to ask how much it costs before letting them look into your future. ■

Nearly 13,000 gilded ceramic Buddhas, made by Shanghai craftsmen, were donated by worshipers.

Chinese astrology

Behind the image of Hong Kong as a 21st-century city, with its gleaming skyscrapers and booming economy, a more ancient force can sometimes be seen at work. The moon, with its phases and movements, continues to hold sway over the lives of many people in the territory.

Visit Hong Kong during the Lunar New Year, usually in January or February, and you will find that it's the only time of year when the stores are closed. Most open again when the official holiday ends, usually after three days, but some may continue to keep their doors locked. They are waiting for an auspicious day to re-open; a day divined by *feng shui* experts or fortune-tellers according to the lunar calendar. To open earlier could mean poor business for the next 12 months.

Fortune-tellers pore over charts of the movements of the moon to calculate whether days will be good, bad, or average for major events in a person's life. The right day could mean the difference between a good or bad marriage. Young couples will consult the experts for auspicious days on which to tie the knot. To ensure they are among the lucky ones to get married on such a day, they will probably have to get in line for hours outside a marriage registry office three months in advance to reserve their date with destiny.

The moon has been used to divine such important occasions, along with harvests and festivals, for thousands of years in China. And because the lunar month differs in length from those used in the Gregorian calendar, the date for the start of the Lunar New Year changes every year, at least according to calendars in the West.

Each lunar year is governed by one of a dozen animals—rat, ox, tiger, rabbit, dragon (the only mythical beast in the list), snake, horse, goat, monkey, rooster, dog, and pig—creating a 12-year cycle. People are said to take on the characteristics of the animal in whose year they are born.

Both smart and charming, **rats** like to get their own way. They also love a challenge.

The dependable **ox** is able to achieve great things by adopting a careful, methodical approach. Not surprisingly, people born in this animal's year can be stubborn.

A **tiger** is sensitive and likes to be in control, but can also have a bad temper.

Rabbits can be a bit of a pushover with those willing to take advantage, and will handle problems at their own, slow pace.

Clever and powerful **dragons** are said to be lucky in love but lacking in compassion.

Snakes have the ability to charm, are hardworking, and also lucky with money.

Horses are natural-born wanderers and love to travel, but have an impatient streak.

Creative and artistic, **goats** need lots of support and understanding from those around them.

Monkeys love fun and are full of energy. Their devil-may-care attitude, however, can cause them problems.

The truth is all-important to the **rooster,** who likes to be in charge. Strutting is important, with appearance a priority.

The faithful **dog** can make a loyal friend, but can also be stubborn.

And **pigs?** Those born in the last year in the cycle are considered to be polite perfectionists, always willing to see the best in people. ■

Above: A coin depicting a dragon, one of the 12 animals in Chinese astrology
Right: A *tanka* **depicts all 12 animals. In modern Hong Kong, auspicious dates are still determined using the Chinese zodiac.**

Chinese birth signs

Rat: 1900, 1912, 1924, 1936, 1948, 1960, 1972, 1984, 1996

Ox: 1901, 1913, 1925, 1937, 1949, 1961, 1973, 1985, 1997

Tiger: 1902, 1914, 1926, 1938, 1950, 1962, 1974, 1986, 1998

Rabbit: 1903, 1915, 1927, 1939, 1951, 1963, 1975, 1987, 1999

Dragon: 1904, 1916, 1928, 1940, 1952, 1964, 1976, 1988, 2000

Snake: 1905, 1917, 1929, 1941, 1953, 1965, 1977, 1989, 2001

Horse: 1906, 1918, 1930, 1942, 1954, 1966, 1978, 1990, 2002

Goat: 1907, 1919, 1931, 1943, 1955, 1967, 1979, 1991, 2003

Monkey: 1908, 1920, 1932, 1944, 1956, 1968, 1980, 1992, 2004

Rooster: 1909, 1921, 1933, 1945, 1957, 1969, 1981, 1993, 2005

Dog: 1910, 1922, 1934, 1946, 1958, 1970, 1982, 1994, 2006

Pig: 1911, 1923, 1935, 1947, 1959, 1971, 1983, 1995, 2007 ■

Tai Po

TAI PO SITS ON THE LAM TSUEN RIVER WHERE IT FLOWS into Tolo Harbor. Records dating back to the tenth century indicate it was an important market town and a center for pearl diving. The completion of the KCR (Kowloon–Canton Railway) in 1910 opened up the area, but it wasn't until the 1970s that Tai Po began its transformation from a sleepy village into a bustling new town.

Tai Po
🅰 155 E4

**Hong Kong
Railway Museum**
✉ 13 Shun Tak St., Tai
Po Market, Tai Po
☎ 2653-3455
🕐 Closed Tues.
🚆 KCR East: Tai Po
Market KCR station,
then taxi

**Cycleways
reveal the
"other"
Hong Kong.**

The original Tai Po Market railway station, built in Chinese style with a pitched-tiled roof and swirling decorations, was completed in 1913 and now houses the small but fascinating **Hong Kong Railway Museum.** It has a selection of antique steam locomotives and carriages, and lots of wonderful memorabilia including old tickets, posters, and photographs. Information on its Tiffin Train Service, offered before World War II and popular with golfers on their way to the course at Fanling and shooting parties in search of wild boar and barking deer, is a delight.

Opposite the museum lies the entrance to the atmospheric **Tai Po New Market.** The wide pedestrian-only Fu Shing Street is packed with shops selling everything from shoes, bean curd, and bamboo Hakka hats to so-called thousand-year-old eggs. This is a great place to catch the hustle and bustle of New Territories' market life.

In the middle of all the commotion, about half way along Fu Shing Street on the left, is an oasis of calm: the **Man Mo Temple.** Built in the late 19th century, it honors Man, the god of civil servants and literature, and the fierce, red-faced Mo, the god of war and martial arts.

This small temple has a finely carved eaves-board under the roof ledge of its polished granite entranceway. Eight compartments surround a central courtyard, where senior citizens, shaded beneath palm trees, occupy themselves in quiet conversation and games of mahjong and cards.

Cycling

Cycling in Kowloon or on Hong Kong Island is not only inadvisable, it's positively dangerous. However, parts of the New Territories are more cycle friendly, with several of the new towns providing cycleways. The path between Tai Wai, just south of Sha Tin, and Tai Po follows the edges of Shin Min River Channel and Tolo Harbor. Bicycles can be rented from the numerous shops in Tai Wai and Tung Cheung Street in Tai Po. A more pleasant ride is along Bride's Pool Road between the villages of Tai Mei Tuk and Luk Keng in the northeast New Territories. You can rent bicycles at shops in Tai Mei Tuk. Avoid Sundays as the paths get clogged with riders.

There are nine designated areas in Hong Kong's country parks where cycling is allowed, but you need a permit from the Agriculture, Fisheries, and Conservation Department (tel 2708-8885).

The Hong Kong Cyclist Club conducts tours of Hong Kong (tel 2788-3898). ■

TAI PO KAU NATURE RESERVE

Midway between Tai Po and Sha Tin, this 1,138-acre (460 ha) reserve is the oldest in Hong Kong, established in the 1920s to aid the reforestation of the New Territories, much of which had been stripped bare by a combination of village farming, building, and firewood collection. *(Take KCR East to Mai Po Market Station, then a taxi.)*

Five graded and color-coded trails cut through its dense and diverse woodlands; a map board at the entrance indicates their routes. The trails, from a half mile (0.8 km) to 6 miles (10 km) in length, pass under canopied trees, along peaceful, gurgling streams, and over lichen-covered boulders on hillsides thick with ferns. This is a good way to see some of Hong Kong's best subtropical forests without having to clamber up the steep ridges and ravines sometimes found along trails in the territories' country parks. The half-mile (0.8 km) nature trail is the easiest, but none of them is strenuous.

The reserve is rich in birdlife, with over a dozen species recorded, and is also a favorite spot for photographing and watching the numerous butterflies that inhabit the park.

Mammals, including the armadillo-like pangolins, civet cats, and wild boars, live in the dense forests. You will rarely see them along the trails, but you can sometimes hear the odd "barking" call of the barking deer. ■

Chinese bulbuls, Japanese white-eyes, and cuckoos are among the many birds you may see flitting about Tai Po Kau's subtropical foliage.

Plover Cove

THIS AREA OF THE NORTHEASTERN NEW TERRITORIES, just below the border with mainland China, is one of the most sparsely inhabited and isolated areas in Hong Kong. Hakka immigrants from China originally settled here about 300 years ago, but the rugged terrain proved difficult to farm and the few hamlets built here remain isolated and all but deserted.

Plover Cove Reservoir was built to alleviate Hong Kong's chronic water shortages.

Plover Cove

- 🗺️ 155 F4
- ✉️ Plover Cove Country Park Visitor Center, Bride's Pool Rd.
- 🕐 Closed Tues.
- 🚌 Bus: 75K from Tai Po

The area is now home to two country parks, whose sometimes difficult trails reward hikers with stunning panoramas over steep mountain ranges and rolling hills to the waters of Tolo Harbor and Starling Inlet. **Plover Cove Country Park** to the east and **Pat Sin Leng Country Park** to the west are bounded by Plover Cove Reservoir and Starling Inlet, a tidal bay that stretches toward mainland China, and divided by a lush valley.

The gateway to the area is the village of **Tai Mei Tuk** (*Bus 75K from Tai Po Market KCR station*), which sits close to the Plover Cove Reservoir dam wall and is popular with picnickers and day-trippers. The dam was built in the 1960s when drought and a growing

population caused water shortages. Beyond the village, Bride's Pool Road climbs for about 400 yards (360 m) to the **visitor center,** which houses a small exhibition of the area's flora and fauna.

From the visitor center, you can follow the path onto Bride's Pool Road past barbecue sites, often crowded on weekends, but a better option is to head up the hill to the left onto the **Pat Sin Leng Nature Trail.** Along this 2.5-mile (4 km) hike you will have views over Plover Cove Reservoir toward the huge residential towers of the new town of Ma On Shan on the edge of Tolo Harbor, and then across to the peaks of Plover Cove Country Park as you climb to about 1,300 feet (400 m). Farther on, across deep green rolling hills

and past Starling Inlet, the tall apartment buildings of Shau Tau Kok, which edges the border with mainland China, reveal themselves in the distance. The trail then plunges back down to Bride's Pool Road, ending opposite the half-mile-long (0.8 km) **Bride's Pool Nature Trail,** which meanders through a small part of the heavily forested valley floor. The pool is one of Hong Kong's major water catchments, feeding the huge reservoir to its south. Pat Sin Leng Nature Trail starts at the country park's map board by a small green pavilion and winds along a ridge before dropping down to Plover Cove Reservoir.

Another option is to head along Bride's Pool Road north for another 3 miles (5 km) to the hamlet of **Luk Keng,** on the shores of Starling Inlet. The village is a crowded, haphazard mixture of old and new houses, and small temples. Minibuses run from Luk Keng to Tai Mei Tuk, and on to Fanling.

Between late March and August, the village, its ponds, and the remnants of old rice terraces become the biggest breeding area for egrets in Hong Kong. Huge flocks descend and congregate on the small island of **A Chau** to the left of the village.

You can rent bicycles in Tai Mei Tuk and cycle along Bride's Pool Road to Luk Keng. This 6-mile (10 km) ride traverses the valley that splits the two country parks. If you are seeking tranquility, don't cycle on weekends as the route can become extremely crowded. ■

A number of villages around Plover Cove date back hundreds of years.

White-sand beaches filigree Clear Water Bay's hilly coastline.

Sai Kung & Clear Water Bay

The eastern section of the New Territories is Hong Kong's playground. This is a strikingly scenic area of hiking trails cutting along verdant hillsides that plunge down to isolated beaches, coves, bays, dozens of deserted islands, and tiny villages nestled in steep valleys. In some of these surprisingly pristine and beautiful places, it's hard to believe you are only 40 minutes away from the crowds, noise, and high-rises of Kowloon.

Much of this area is under the ordinance of Hong Kong's Country Parks, and there are numerous opportunities for recreation. You can hike, camp, and swim; rent windsurfers and canoes; and charter boats—from small *kaidos* (motorized boats) to luxury launches—to reach isolated beaches and islands. Come in the week to best enjoy the splendors of the countryside. On weekends, especially Sundays, beaches and hiking trails fill with people, which can take the edge off the experience.

The pleasant fishing town of Sai Kung is the launch pad for visits to the country parks, and an ideal place to relax after a long hike or a day on the beach. At windswept Clear Water Bay peninsula, on the southeastern tip of the New Territories, the spectacular golf course at the posh Clear Water Bay Country Club edges the South China Sea. Here you will also find numerous hiking trails, less demanding than the often rigorous treks farther north. Beaches nearby are easily accessible. ■

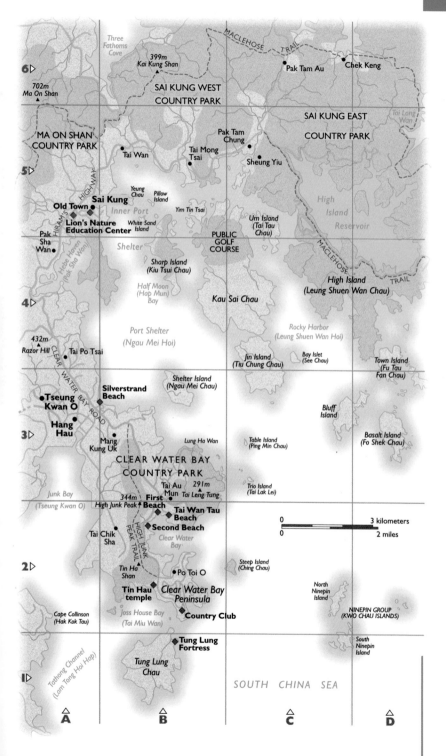

Three Fathoms Cove

MACLEHOSE TRAIL

6▷

399m
Kai Kung Shan

Pak Tam Au

Chek Keng

702m
Ma On Shan

SAI KUNG WEST
COUNTRY PARK

SAI KUNG EAST
COUNTRY PARK

Tai Long Wan

MA ON SHAN
COUNTRY PARK

Pak Tam
Chung

Tai Wan

Tai Mong
Tsai

Sheung Yiu

5▷

Yeung
Chau

Pillow
Island

High
Island
Reservoir

Old Town **Sai Kung**

**Lion's Nature
Education Center**

Inner Port

Yim Tin Tsai

White Sand
Island

Um Island
(Tai Tau
Chau)

PUBLIC
GOLF
COURSE

Pak
Sha
Wan

Shelter

Sharp Island
(Kiu Tsui Chau)

MACLEHOSE

*High Island
(Leung Shuen Wan Chau)*

TRAIL

Half Moon
(Hap Mun)
Bay

Kau Sai Chau

4▷

Port Shelter
(Ngau Mei Hoi)

Rocky Harbor
(Leung Shuen Wan Hoi)

432m
Razor Hill

Tai Po Tsai

Jin Island
(Tiu Chung Chau)

Bay Islet
(See Chau)

Town Island
(Fu Tau
Fan Chau)

Shelter Island
(Ngau Mei Chau)

**Silverstrand
Beach**

**Tseung
Kwan O**

Bluff
Island

**Hang
Hau**

3▷

Mang
Kung Uk

Lung Ha Wan

Table Island
(Ping Min Chau)

Basalt Island
(Fo Shek Chau)

Junk Bay
(Tseung Kwan O)

CLEAR WATER BAY
COUNTRY PARK

Tai Au
Mun

291m
Tai Leng Tung

Trio Island
(Tai Lak Lei)

344m
High Junk Peak

**First
Beach**

**Tai Wan Tau
Beach**

Second Beach

Tai Chik
Sha

Clear Water
Bay

0   3 kilometers

0   2 miles

2▷

Tin Ha
Shan

Po Toi O

Steep Island
(Ching Chau)

North
Ninepin
Island

NINEPIN GROUP
(KWO CHAU ISLANDS)

**Tin Hau
temple**

*Clear Water Bay
Peninsula*

Cape Collinson
(Hak Kok Tau)

Joss House Bay
(Tai Miu Wan)

Country Club

South
Ninepin
Island

**Tung Lung
Fortress**

1▷

Tathong Channel
(Lam Tong Hoi Hap)

*Tung Lung
Chau*

SOUTH CHINA SEA

△   △   △   △
A   B   C   D

Clear Water Bay

AT THE SOUTHEASTERN CORNER OF THE NEW TERRITORIES is Clear Water Bay, an almost untamed section of the area with a rugged coastline, bare hills, whitewashed villas, and exceptional panoramas of the South China Sea. The beaches and country park here are popular on the weekends, so it's best to visit during the week.

Most people come to the area for its two main beaches—**Clear Water Bay First Beach** and **Clear Water Bay Second Beach**—curving around deeply indented Clear Water Bay. These clean, white-sand, easily accessible beaches sit at the bottom of a jagged cliff face and can be reached by steps. Another, smaller beach, **Tai Wan Tau,** lies in the northern corner of the bay.

There are other beaches off Clear Water Bay Road before you reach these popular stretches of sand; the pretty **Silverstrand Beach,** backed by cliffside mansions and apartments, is the most accessible. You will have to descend some steep steps to get there from the parking lot. The beach gained notoriety in the early 1990s after a number of fatal shark attacks, but shark nets have since been installed.

The headland from the northern border of Clear Water Bay forms the eastern section of **Clear Water Bay Country Park.** At the park's entrance is a visitor center, barbecue area, and the start of the circular **Tree Walk** track, a pleasant, short amble that takes you through a cool, heavily forested section of the park. Near the start of the walk, a lookout offers splendid views of the Ninepins Islands group (Kwo Chau), Tung Lung Chau (see p. 214), other offshore islands, and to the fairways of the golf course of the exclusive Clear Water Bay Country Club across the bay.

From the parking lot at the entrance to the country park, you can take a well-marked track to the top of 955-foot (290 m) **Tai Leng Tung** for exceptional panoramas of islands and sea, then continue to Lung Ha Wan on the northern side of the headland.

A scenic coastal road with very little traffic, ideal for walking, winds south from the Clear Water Bay beaches for about 2.5 miles (4 km) to the entrance of the Clear Water Bay Country Club. About a half mile (0.8 km) before the entrance, a road drops down to **Po Toi O,** a fishing village scenically located on the edge of an inlet and a favorite spot for weekend junk cruises (see p. 129). At the entrance to the country club, a sign indicates the start of the High Junk Peak Country Trail.

Left: The main beaches at Clear Water Bay are easily accessible, but crowded on weekends.

Clear Water Bay

- 🅰 187 B3
- ✉ Clear Water Bay Country Park Visitor Center
- ☎ 2719-0032
- 🕒 Closed Tues.
- 🚌 Bus: 91 from Choi Hung MTR

Above: Fish farms at Po Toi O. The hamlet still maintains its traditional fishing village character.

TIN HAU TEMPLE

East of the sign and to the right of the entrance to Clear Water Bay Country Club, a series of steps takes you down to the **Tin Hau temple** which looks over Joss House Bay. The temple site dates back to 1266, making it one of the oldest in Hong Kong. Rock carvings there indicate the visit of a Song dynasty official in 1274. The present temple, built in 1878, was seriously damaged by Typhoon Wanda in 1962, but has since been renovated.

The main altar has three images of Tin Hau, the Queen of Heaven and protector of fisherfolk. In the intriguing goddess "bedroom" is a bed for each image, along with a washstand, basin, and mirror. The main hall features an 18th-century model junk, crewed with a deck full of carved sailors. A large plaza and pier have been built in front of the temple for the crowds arriving by ferry during the annual Tin Hau festival in April (see p. 48). At most other times, the temple is deserted. The large offshore island of Tung Lung Chau, with its old Chinese fortress, sits at the entrance to rocky Joss House Bay.

If you are feeling energetic, you can return to the Clear Water Bay beaches via the 2.5-mile (4 km) **High Junk Peak Country Trail** which takes you up the barren hills of Tin Ha Shan for excellent views across the bay. A signposted side trail takes you back down to the beaches just before the steep ascent to **High Junk Peak** (Tu Tue Yung). ■

Sai Kung

Boats, including sampans and junks, crowd the fishing harbor at Sai Kung.

THIS BUSTLING FISHING TOWN IS THE STARTING POINT for hiking and beach trips to the surrounding countryside (see pp. 192–193). Many people also visit from Hong Kong's crowded districts to soak up the atmosphere of this agreeable town, breathe some fresh air, and dine at the renowned seafood restaurants lining the quayside. The town of Sai Kung makes for a pleasant day's outing, but avoid Sundays when crowds and traffic clog the place.

Kau Sai Chau Public Golf Course

- 🅰 187 B4
- ✉ Kau Sai Chau
- ☎ 2791-3380
- 💲 $$$
- 🚇 MTR: Choi Hung, then Minibus 1

Start with a stroll along the **quay** at the end of Fuk Man Road, the town's main street, for a dose of fishing village atmosphere. The **harbor** buzzes with activity. A few fishing boats tie up alongside the wharf delivering their catch to the seafood restaurants, and junks take on passengers for pleasure cruises to the splendid nearby islands, beaches, and pristine scenery around Shelter and Rocky harbors. Smaller boats *(kaidos)* ferry people to the scattering of islands and island beaches in the inner harbor, or take them for tours around the harbor. Peer into the huge fish tanks outside the restaurants for a staggering variety of sea life. Choose your fish—ask the price first—then take it to a quayside restaurant to be cooked for you.

During your amble along the quay, you are likely to be offered a pleasure trip on a kaido. Charter one for an hour's jaunt around the inner harbor or take the regular services to the white sandy beach at **Half Moon (Hap Mun) Bay** on Sharp Island (Kiu Tsui Chau). Less frequent services also run to beaches on Pak Sha Chau (White Sand Island) and Cham Tau Chau (Pillow Island).

Farther west along the quay, behind a small Tin Hau temple off Yi Chun Street, is Sai Kung's **old town,** a maze of alleyways brimming with activity and Chinese herbalist stores, noodle shops, convenience stores selling Chinese goods, and small family homes. This is an excellent area to get a look at a traditional village way of life.

GOLFING

If you are a golf fan, head across to the inner harbor's biggest island, **Kau Sai Chau,** and Hong Kong's only public **golf course.** Ferries leave from the course's private pier at the quay every 20 minutes. The golf course, a gift from the benevolent Hong Kong Jockey Club, is one of the most scenic in Asia, with constant and spectacular views of the South China Sea, nearby islands, and the jagged hills of Sai Kung Country Park. The two 18-hole courses were designed by Gary Player, and there is a 72-bay floodlit driving range and indoor

and outdoor practice pitching and putting facilities.

You can rent clubs and shoes at the clubhouse. Reservations are essential and you will need a handicap certificate. The course is not particularly cheap by U.S. standards; a round of 18 holes will cost between US$85 and $115 depending on the day (weekends are more expensive) and the course. Visitors pay up to twice as much as Hong Kong residents.

NORTH OF TOWN

Back on the waterfront, backtrack past Fuk Man Road along the waterfront promenade that runs north for about a half mile (0.8 km). The beach here is not a particularly good one for swimming (although this does not deter the crowds of people who flock in on Sundays), but you can rent windsurfers or relax at one of the restaurants or bars that look out over the beach. Just to the west, at the waterside village of **Tai Wan,** it's possible to canoe around Inner Shelter Harbor.

Unfortunately, the fringes of Sai Kung Town are undergoing extensive development, which is likely to destroy much of what is left of the town's character and village atmosphere. High-rise residential towers are planned for the area north of town, while Hiram's Highway, the road that runs down from Clear Water Bay Road into Sai Kung, is in the process of being widened and rerouted to accommodate the growth of the area. ■

Live seafood is selected from quayside fish tanks before being carted off to nearby restaurants.

Sai Kung Country Parks

SAI KUNG PENINSULA HAS SOME OF HONG KONG'S FINEST and wildest countryside. The area has long been an isolated part of Hong Kong, characterized by tall peaks, an exposed, convoluted coastline, and small remote Hakka villages—features that now draw many hikers to the area. It's a splendid place for walking, with well-marked and well-maintained trails. And here you will find Hong Kong's best beaches.

Sai Kung Country Parks
- 🗺 187 B6
- ✉ Sai Kung Country Park Visitor Center, Pak Tam Chung
- ☎ 2792-7365
- 🕐 Closed Tues.
- 🚌 Bus: 94 from Sai Kung Town

Pak Tam Chung is as far as you can go into the park by private car, although public buses travel to Wong Shek Pier and, on weekends and public holidays, Hoi Ha. Taxis are also allowed to enter the park. Pak Tam Chung is the place most people begin their hikes. The village has a visitor center where you can pick up information on hiking routes.

Four parks make up the 25,950 acres (10,500 ha) of the peninsula; Sai Kung East, Sai Kung West, Hoi Ha Wan Marine Park, and Wan Tsai. The largest and most popular is **Sai Kung East,** which contains High Island Reservoir—one of Hong Kong's main water sources—and trails leading to outstanding

viewpoints and glorious beaches.

From Pak Tam Chung, head east along the road into the park to where the road forks at the top and the reservoir begins. It's about a 5-mile (8 km) trip to where the dam meets the South China Sea in awesome fashion. Though long, it's not a particularly strenuous walk, but if the 10-mile (16 km) return trip sounds too far, catch a taxi from Pak Tam Chung to the end of the reservoir and walk back.

The road begins by winding up hills, with the expansive High Island Reservoir spread out below. Farther into the walk, at the first dam wall, there are views of sheer headlands plunging into the jagged shoreline

and whaleback islands scattered out to sea. At the end of the walk, you pass over the second dam wall and down to its base at the reservoir's eastern end. Here, the dam's main wall towers behind you spectacularly as you look out to sea. From the eastern end of the dam wall, a track runs down over a hilly pass to **Long Ke Wan,** a horseshoe-shaped bay with a wide, white, sandy beach.

Hong Kong's best beach, **Tai Long Wan,** is about a 40-minute walk from Pak Tam Au, farther into the country park on the road to Wong Shek Pier. The track, just off the main road, winds down through the cool, heavily forested Ngau Wu Tun hill past stunning panoramas of Long Harbor to the tiny deserted village of **Chek Keng,** one of a number in the area left abandoned. After Chek Keng, you climb along a concrete path up the Tai Mun Shan overpass to Tai Long Au and views to the white sand and rumbling surf of Tai Long Wan (Big Wave Bay), before descending down to the beach. A small village just before the beach sells noodles, water, and soft drinks. The return walk is about 6 miles (10 km).

A shorter 3-mile (5 km) hike through **Hoi Ha Wan Marine Park,** one of the few remaining areas in Hong Kong where coral can be found, takes you past small ravines and old rice paddy terraces, looking out across the Hoi Ha Bay.

From Hoi Ha village, head east along the beach to a coastal path that skirts Ho Ha Bay. The track leads across a neck of land to Wan Tsai and heads north past stands of paperbacks, acacias, and casuarinas. At the bluff on the tip of the promontory, you see out to Mirs Bay and a couple of small islands marking the marine park's boundary. To the southeast, across the deeply indented Long Bay, the peninsula's highest point, Sharp Peak (1,535 feet/468 m), rears dramatically. Return to Hoi Ha along the track running down the promontory's eastern side.

A warning: Dogs, both domestic and stray, are sometimes found along country park trails. Some can be a bit vicious but can be deterred with the threatening wave of a sizable stick, a useful aid when hiking. ■

Tai Long Wan— "big wave way"— ranks as Hong Kong's best beach.

A drive along the Sai Kung Peninsula

The drive starts from where Clear Water Bay Road, running northeast from Kowloon, meets Hiram's Highway and dips down into the town of Sai Kung. This winding, scenic route follows the coast and into Sai Kung Country Park. You can return to Kowloon via the hilly Sai Sha Road that cuts through countryside, villages, and the massive Ma On Shan New Town to Sha Tin.

Stunning views of the lush, jagged coast of the Sai Kung Peninsula open up, with villages dotting the shoreline and islands scattering the channel beyond.

The green, looming 2,303-foot (702 m) peak of Ma On Shan, one of the highest in the New Territories, dominates the view as you turn left onto Hiram's Highway from Clear Water Bay Road. Notice the whitewashed villas and luxury developments built into the hills that edge the coast.

Hiram's Highway dips down to the coastal area of Sai Kung, and winds 1.2 miles (2 km) to the massive **Marina Cove ❶**, with its hundreds of villas wrapped around a boat marina. Continue along Hiram's Highway for another 1.2 miles (2 km) to the point

where the road opens to views of the wide bay at **Pak Sha Wan ❷**, also called Hebe Haven. Here, dozens of bobbing pleasure craft shelter in the bay, which is almost totally enclosed by a narrow, curved peninsula. You can park here and sit on the deck of the Hebe Haven Yacht Club *(10½ Miles, Hiram's Hwy., tel 2719-8300)* for a drink and to enjoy views across the bay.

The highway winds its way past villages, wooded areas, and garden nurseries for another 1.8 miles (3 km) to the town of **Sai Kung ❸** (see pp. 190–91), the main

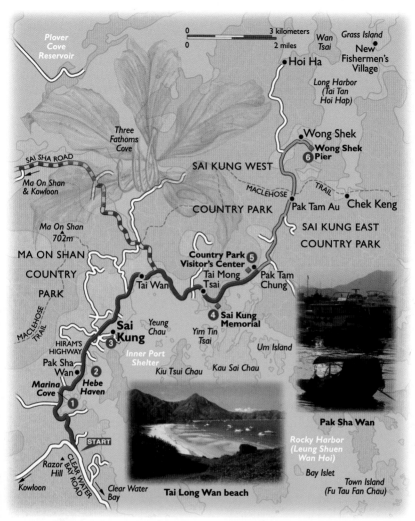

Pak Sha Wan

Tai Long Wan beach

community in the area. Here, the road name changes to Po Tung Road for a short distance before becoming Tai Mong Tsai Road, and continues past the town about a half mile (0.8 km) to a small beach and seaside restaurants.

The road now hugs the contours of Inner Port Shelter, offering sea glimpses through the eucalyptus trees and grassy picnic areas that line the bay to the traffic circle at Shi Sha Road, which winds its way over the hills to the new town of Ma On Shan, near Sha Tin (see p. 176).

Past the traffic circle, views to the bay open up to the numerous islets of Inner Port

🗺 See area map p. 155

▶ Hiram's Hwy. at Clear Water Bay Rd.

↔ 10.5 miles (17 km); 15.5 miles (25 km) including Wong Shek Pier

🕑 1.5 hours; 2 hours including Wong Shek Pier

▶ Wong Shek Pier

NOT TO BE MISSED

- Sai Kung
- Sai Kung Memorial
- Wong Shek Pier

Pleasure boats fill the calm bay at Pak Sha Wan.

Shelter and the larger islands of Sharp Island and Kau Sai Chau as the road dips, rises, and runs along the coast at the most scenic section along the route.

On one rise, about 3.5 miles (6 km) from Sai Kung Town, an obelisk overlooking the water at the **Sai Kung Memorial** ❹ pays tribute to the guerrillas and Sai Kung villagers who died during the Japanese occupation between 1941 and 1945. An impressive and finely cast bronze statue with a tableau of figures of villagers and fighters stands at the edge of the road.

A further 1.2 miles (2 km) brings you to the guarded entrance of Sai Kung Country Park at Pak Tam Chung (see pp. 192–193). Park and head to the **Country Park Visitor Center** ❺ *(Pak Tam Chung, Sai Kung, tel 2792-7365, closed Tues.)*, which houses a small but entertaining museum containing displays of coral found off the coast at Hoi Ha Marine Park (see p. 193), geographic and topographic features of the park, typical park flora and fauna, and traditional village, fishing, and rural life in the area.

Hikers make their way up Ma On Shan, one of the highest peaks in the New Territories.

The only private cars allowed into the park are those that belong to the people who live there or their guests. But you can take a taxi, or, better still, catch the hourly No. 94 double-decker bus that slowly grinds its way up the steep hills to the village of Pak Tam Au, before swooping down through forests and small villages to **Wong Shek Pier** ❻, at the southern end of Long Harbor. If you can, take the front seat on the top deck for the best views of the sheer peaks that dominate the park. The 5-mile (8 km) ride takes about 10 to 15 minutes.

You can rent windsurfers and dinghies at the **Wong Shek Water Sports Center** *(Tel 2328-2311)*, take a walk along the waterfront, or relax at the picnic area on the water's edge.

If you want to return to Kowloon, you could take the alternate route along Sai Sha Road, which passes more villages and gives occasional sweeping panoramas of Three Fathoms Cove and Tolo Harbor, before coming to Ma On Shan. This new town, with its residential towers, is a classic example of Hong Kong-style development, rising from what was a cluster of small villages just over ten years ago. From here, follow the expressway signs back to Kowloon. ∎

Tap Mun Chau

TAP MUN CHAU (GRASS ISLAND) GUARDS THE ENTRANCE to Long Harbor at the northeastern extremity of the Sai Kung Peninsula, where the narrow Tolo Channel runs into Mirs Bay and the nearby mainland China border. In the 1980s and early 1990s, it was a favorite dropping-off point for illegal immigrants arriving from the mainland, until Hong Kong's marine police got wise.

The island, with its busy fishing village, offers the agreeable combination of isolation and easy access and is worth visiting if you have time. On weekends, ferries meet the hourly bus from Sai Kung. During the week, they run just three times a day, so it may be best to rent a *kaido* (small boat) at the pier to make the 20-minute trip through the sheltered waters of Long Harbor to the island's pier,

tiny village, and **Tin Hau temple.** The temple is notable for its well-crafted porcelain roof figurines and location. It's the last Tin Hau temple in Hong Kong before the open sea; fishermen traditionally visit these temples before sailing, to pray for a safe voyage (see sidebar p. 93).

Tap Mun is named after the grassy and windswept hills that roll over the island. Plenty of trails crisscross these hills, making for pleasant walking. The northern half of the island is uninhabited and intensely quiet. Climb the track behind the village—there is a map board near the pier showing walking trails—to view the pounding surf on the island's east coast. The track then runs down to Tap Mun's only **beach** at Chung Wai, before climbing up and heading south to the **Balanced Rock,** a weird rock formation just off the island near its southeastern tip. It then continues around the southern tip of the island, past the newer houses of New Fishermen's Village and a Christian chapel, to the pier and main settlement.

There are a couple of restaurants at the village. New Hon Kee Seafood Restaurant (*tel 2328-2428*), set on stilts above the water, is a good place to have a meal and watch for the ferry returning to Wong Shek Pier. Again, avoid visiting the island on Sundays, when crowds of people converge. The last ferry from the island leaves at 6 p.m. on weekends and 4:40 p.m. on weekdays. ■

Intricate porcelain figures grace the entrance to Tap Mun's Tin Hau temple.

More places to visit in the New Territories

Colorful offerings hang from the Lam Tsuen Spirit Trees; they are flung onto branches by those seeking good fortune.

CHINESE UNIVERSITY OF HONG KONG

The university's art museum houses an excellent collection of paintings and calligraphy by Guangdong artists from the Ming period to modern times, and other artists from the Yuan, Ming, and Qing dynasties. There are also bronze seals dating from pre-Qing to modern times, and period collections of jade flower carvings, as well as other designs and ceramics.
🅰 155 E3 ✉ Ma Liu Sui ☎ 2609-7416
🚉 KCR East to Chinese University Station, then shuttle bus

LAM TSUEN SPIRIT TREES (WISHING TREES)

People tie bundles of colorful paper and an orange to either end of a red cord and launch it into one of two trees here—a bauhinia and a banyan—while making a wish. If the bundle catches a tree branch, then the wish will be granted. Anyone who manages to do it on the first attempt is considered a very fortunate person. According to legend, a fisherman was miraculously cured of illness by an earth god when he prayed at the trees, and since then they have been considered lucky. Hundreds of these colorful offerings dangle from the branches. Further offerings are burned at the two earth god shrines at the base of the trees. You can buy these offerings for about HK$20. The trees are situated outside Lam Tsuen Tin Hau Temple, which was built in 1768. Inside there's a shrine dedicated to those killed in an intervillage incident in the 19th century.
🅰 154 D4 ✉ Lam Kam Rd., Lam Tseun, Tai Po 🚉 KCR East to Tai Po Market, then bus 64K

LIONS NATURE EDUCATION CENTER

Nestled in a pretty valley a few miles from Sai Kung, the center is a less grand version of the Kadoorie Farm & Botanical Garden (see p. 163). It was originally a government farm, but later developed into a center for conservation and education. Scattered among its 40 acres (16 ha) are a specimen orchard with over 30 different types of fruit trees, herbal gardens, vegetable fields, a bamboo grove, and a fernery, along with ponds full of aquatic plants, an arboretum, and a nature trail. A series of halls contain an insectarium, a huge display of seashells collected from Hong Kong's coastline, a fishery exhibition highlighting Hong Kong's dwindling marine resources, exhibits featuring the life, methods, and tools of Hong Kong's minute farming community, and an explanation of the territories' country parks.

🅰 155 F2 ✉ Hiram's Hwy., Sai Kung ☎ 2792-2234 🕐 Closed Tues. 🚇 MTR: Choi Hung, Minibus 1: Sai Kung, then taxi

MACLEHOSE TRAIL

This 60-mile (100 km) trail meanders over rugged ridges and through remote villages, skirting sandy beaches as it traverses eight New Territory country parks from Sai Kung in the east to Tuen Mun in the west. It climbs near the peaks of two of Hong Kong's highest mountains, Tai Mo Shan and Ma On Shan, along the way. The trail has ten sections, each graded by its degree of difficulty, some for serious hikers only, others relatively easy. The views along the entire route are outstanding. Every November, an arduous team race called

Hong Kong's longest hike, the 60-mile MacLehose Trail traverses the length of the New Territories.

the Trailwalker takes place. Thousands take part, with some superfit teams taking only 13 hours to complete the journey.

Country Parks Management Office
🅰 155 G3 ✉ 303 Cheung Sha Wan Rd., Kowloon ☎ 2150-6868 🚇 MTR: Tsim Sha Tsui

SHEUNG YIU VILLAGE

The fortified village of Sheung Yiu was built about 150 years ago by a Hakka clan named Wong and has been partly restored to serve as a museum, containing Hakka furniture and a collection of cooking and farming implements. It lies a pleasant 20-minute walk along the Pak Tam Chung Nature Trail from the gates of Sai Kung East Country Park (see pp. 192–93). Follow the signs from the Country Park Visitor Center.

🅰 155 G3 ✉ Sheung Yiu Village, Pak Tam Chung Nature Trail ☎ 2792-6365 🕐 Closed Tues. 🚇 MTR: Choi Hung, Minibus 1 to Sai Kung Town, then bus 94

TAI FU TAI MANSION

Tai Fu Tai Mansion is an excellent, fully restored example of a traditional Chinese dwelling of the scholar-gentry class, built by Man clan member Man Chung-luen around 1865. The elegant facade is built on a granite-block base with a green brick wall, and is richly embellished by ceramic figurines and moldings on the niches. Above the framed entrance is a red wood board inscribed with gilded Chinese characters heralding the name of the mansion. A boat-prow ridge on the roof of the entrance hall has more moldings and exquisite ceramic figurines.

Inside, two side chambers frame the central courtyard, with three bedrooms at the front of the dwelling. Various other rooms are set against the mansion's outside wall, with the main hall at the rear of the courtyard. The rooms are decorated with plaster moldings, woodcarvings, and motifs on the walls.

The main hall retains some of its original black wood furniture, and under its eaves are two "honorific" boards engraved with gilded Chinese and Manchu characters. Portraits of Man Chung-luen and other clan members can be found at the back of the hall.

Nearby, the **Man Fung Lung Ancestral Hall,** thought to have been built at the end of the 17th century, has also been restored. While not nearly as ornate as Tai Fu Tai Mansion, it's worth a look for its imposing stone columns and beautifully carved supporting brackets.

🅰 154 C4 ✉ Tung ChanWai, San Tin 🕐 Closed Tues. 🚇 KCR East to Sheung Shui, then bus 76K ■

Rural charm, bustling waterfronts, glorious seafood, deserted beaches, and, in many cases, splendid isolation greet visitors who take the time to visit Hong Kong's many islands.

Outlying islands

At Pak Tai Temple, Cheung Chau

Outlying islands

HONG KONG'S WATERS ARE LITTERED WITH 234 ISLANDS—FROM TINY SCRAPS of rock jutting out of the sea to substantial slices of land taking in mountain peaks, long, lonely beaches, and communities of fisherman and farmers. The islands maintain a more isolated and rural feel than the New Territories, and pockets of a traditional way of life can still be found. Spend at least a day on one of the outlying islands.

Cheung Chau's bustling harbor: The island relies on fishing for much of its income.

Lung Kwu Chau

NEW TERRITORIES
p. 153

**Sha Chau &
Lung Kwu Chau
Marine Park**

3▷

Sha Chau

Kap Sui Mun

The Brothers
(Mo To Chau)

9

Central Ferry Piers

**Hong Kong
Disneyland**

Chek Lap Kok

✈ International
Airport

Benny's Bay

Discovery
Bay

Discovery
Bay

**Tung Chung
Fort**

9

*Lantau
Island*

Tung Chung
Sunset Peak
(Tai Tung Shan)

Finger Hill

**Silvermine
Beach**

Peng Chau

2▷

Po Lin **Ngong**
Monastery **Ping 360**
Ngong Ping

869m

Mui Wo

Sunshine Island
(Chau Kung To)

HON

Tai O

LANTAU COUNTRY PARK

Hei Ling
Chau

East Lamma Channel
(Tung Pok Liu Hoi Hap)

LANTAU TRAIL

934m
Lantau Peak
(Fung Wong Shan)

Cheung
Sha

West Lamma Channel
(Sai Pok Liu Hoi Hap)

**Tin Hau
temple**

Yung Shue
Wan

466m

Shek Pik
Res.

**Cheung Sha
Beach**

**Hung Shing
Ye Beach**

Chinese Pavilio

Tai Hom Sham

Shek
Pik

Ha Mei Wan

Sok Kwu Wa

Tai Long
Wan

**Tung Wan
Beach**

Lo So Shing Beach

353m

Tung O
Wan

Fan Lau Kok

Cheung Chau

Mt. Stenhouse

Shek Kwu Chau

Lamma Island

SOKO ISLANDS

0 — 5 kilometers
0 — 3 miles

△
A

△
B

△
C

△
D

1▷

About 100,000 people live in the outlying islands, less than 2 percent of the whole of Hong Kong. Over the past three decades, many people have abandoned their island homes and drifted across to the main urban areas of Hong Kong seeking their fortunes. Left behind are the older people, some still clinging to traditional ways. Ironically, a number of bedroom communities have sprung up on the bigger and more central islands for people seeking relief from Hong Kong's clamorous ways, including many Western expatriates.

Hong Kong's major islands are less than an hour away from Central District's Outlying Islands Ferry Terminal, an easy jaunt made more convenient by regular ferry services. On weekends and holidays, people pile onto these ferries and head for the beaches and seafood restaurants lining the quaysides of villages, or take to the innumerable hiking trails that ramble over hills and along sparkling coastlines.

One of the most popular islands is Lantau with its precipitous peaks, peaceful hillside monasteries, fishing villages, and string of white-sand beaches. At Chek Lap Kok, on the north shore, stands Hong Kong's massive international airport and the latest of its new towns, Tung Chung. Surprisingly, these developments have had little effect on other areas of the island. Near the airport, at the northeastern tip, a huge Disneyland theme park opened in 2005.

People head to Cheung Chau for its crowded

Glazed figurines adorn Cheung Chau's Pak Tai Temple.

harbor, bustling waterfront, watersports, and easy hiking, while Lamma is favored for its seafood restaurants, splendid beaches, relaxed atmosphere, and great hiking.

Few people venture to the other outlying islands because of the time and effort involved, but if you can put up with a little legwork and irregular ferry schedules, they are worth the visit. A trip on the weekend to isolated Ping Chau in Mirs Bay in the Northeastern New Territories carries with it a splendid ferry ride through the Tolo Channel, while windswept Tap Mun Chau (see p. 198) offers some wonderful solitude during the week. ■

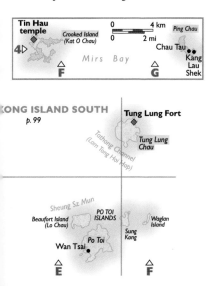

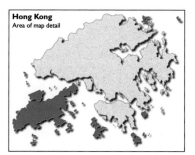

Hong Kong
Area of map detail

Lamma

LAMMA IS THE CLOSEST OF THE BIG OUTLYING ISLANDS TO
Hong Kong Island and the third biggest after Lantau and Hong Kong
Island itself. This peaceful community of fishermen, farmers, and
Western expatriates carries a distinct rural ambience. With villas and
apartments clinging to green hills and overlooking the sea and waterfront restaurants, it almost conjures up a Mediterranean feel. There
are frequent ferries to Lamma, a mere 30 minutes away.

Lamma

202 D1
New World First
Ferry: 2131-8181
Ferry: Outlying
Islands Ferry Pier 5,
Central District,
Hong Kong Island

Yung Shue Wan, at the northern
end of Lamma, is one of only two
small villages on the island and the
ferry gateway to the island. It's home
to a large number of expatriates who
prefer the rustic surroundings and
cheaper rents to the noise, crowds,
and expense of Hong Kong Island.

You can easily walk from Yung
Shue Wan to the second village of
Sok Kwu Wan along a well-marked
concrete path. The 1.5-mile (2.4
km) trail, which opens up to fantastic views along some sections, can

be walked in about 75 minutes.
From Sok Kwu Wan, ferries run
back to the Outlying Islands Ferry
Pier in Central District on Hong
Kong Island.

Yung Shue Wan sits prettily at
the edge of a small bay, with houses
spilling along its lowlands and up
to the surrounding hills. Like much
of Hong Kong, it is suffering at the
hands of development. Most of the
farmland that partly enclosed the
village now sports three-story
houses, and part of the bay has

pleasant stretch of sand, although you'll have to put up with the looming presence of the chimneys of Lamma's giant power plant.

At the beach, Lamma's highest peak, 1,076-foot (353 m) Mount Stenhouse, rears to the south. The path then leads north along bare hills to a tile-roofed **Chinese pavilion,** where you can pause to take in the fabulous views of the imposing mount and the bays and coves that dent the island's coast. On weekends and holidays, the coast is dotted with pleasure boats.

Down the road, **Sok Kwu Wan** comes into view over the hills. It sits on a deep, fjordlike inlet clustered with fish farms. The scarred hills of a quarry across the bay from the village dampen the view, but it is abandoned and parts have already grown back. The trail then drops to delightful **Lo So Shing Beach**—nestled in a cove just before the village.

Sok Kwu Wan nuzzles the bay at the foot of a sheer hill. The colorful bay brims with pleasure craft and fishing boats dropping off their catch to fill the bubbling fish tanks outside the seafood restaurants lining the quayside. Take a seat along with the groups of gregarious diners for a seafood meal before hopping on a ferry back to Hong Kong Island. ■

A dim sum vendor at Yung Shue Wan: Weekenders flock to the island to dine at waterside restaurants.

been reclaimed, with the construction of a breakwater and seawall. Despite this, the village still manages to cling to its charm.

Running from the end of the ferry pier, Yung Shue Wan Main Street is lined with small shops, fresh seafood stands, restaurants, and a few bars. It takes only a few minutes to walk through the village. A side path just past the main intersection takes you to a hundred-year-old Tin Hau temple, dedicated to the Queen of Heaven and guardian of fishermen (see sidebar p. 93). Two stone lions guard the entrance, and inside are images of the veiled Tin Hau, complete with bridal headdress.

On the outskirts of the village take the concrete path that wends its way past fields of tall grass, banana groves, acacia trees, and clusters of brightly painted homes to sandy **Hung Shing Ye Beach** (no shark nets). Here you'll find a

Chinese white dolphins

When construction work began in the waters off Chek Lap Kok to create the enormous new airport in the early 1990s, Hong Kong rediscovered one of its lost natural treasures, the Chinese white dolphin, also known as the Indo-Pacific humpback dolphin or, more popularly, the pink dolphin.

The creatures make their homes along coastlines, often at river mouths, or near mangrove forests. They are one of 80 cetacean species of dolphin that are found in small populations as far apart as Australia, South Africa, and along the Chinese coast up to the Yangtze River. Mention of them has been found in Chinese literature dating back to the Tang dynasty (618–907).

Chinese white dolphins *(Sousa chinensis)* are unique in color. Almost black at birth, maturing dolphins turn a light gray, eventually changing to their distinctive pale pink color. They grow to about 10 feet (3 m) and can live for up to 40 years. Although young males tend to stray from their groups, scientists say the dolphins are territorial, so very unlikely to leave their habitat, which puts them at great risk of extinction.

Marine scientists in Hong Kong estimate the number of Chinese white dolphins living in the Pearl River Delta, whose brackish waters provide an ideal environment for them, at about 1,000, with up to 163 living in Hong Kong waters, mainly in the waters north of Lantau Island.

The plight of these dolphins captured public attention during the construction of the airport, a project that involved flattening the island of Chek Lap Kok near Lantau and reclaiming a large amount of land around it. Land reclamation during this project destroyed much of the dolphins' inshore feeding areas, while boat traffic continues to cause underwater disturbance, injury, and death. Water pollution—mainly sewage from Hong Kong and chemicals from Pearl River tributaries—and overfishing have added to their troubles.

The storm of media attention sparked scientific studies into the dolphins and their habitat and put pressure on the authorities, which eventually led to serious attempts to preserve them and create safer habitats. The Hong Kong government created artificial reefs to attract fish to feed the dolphins, established a 4.5-square-mile (12 sq km) marine park, and put restrictions on land reclamation and other public works in areas where they are seen.

Dolphin-watching is becoming an increasingly popular pastime in Hong Kong, where they are often spotted in the waters near the airport. One company, **Hong Kong Dolphinwatch** (see p. 129), organizes regular dolphin-watching trips (the company will take you out again free of charge if none are spotted). ∎

Top: Pollution and boat traffic threaten the estimated 200 Chinese white dolphins living at the mouth of the Pearl River Estuary near Lantau Island.
Bottom: Dolphin-watching has helped increase the awareness of the plight of the mammals.

Lantau

📍 202 B2

🚢 Ferry: Outlying
Islands Ferry Pier,
Central District,
Hong Kong Island

Lantau

LANTAU, THE LARGEST OF HONG KONG'S ISLANDS, AT TWICE
the size of Hong Kong Island, was little touched by development until
the completion of the international airport on its northeastern coast
in 1998. Its size has allowed it to absorb this massive project and, on
the whole, still preserve a peaceful, bucolic atmosphere.

**A fish vendor at
Tai O village. Fish
processing is now
the town's major
industry, replacing
smuggling.**

A 50-minute boat ride from the
Outlying Islands Ferry Pier in
Central District on Hong Kong
Island brings you to **Mui Wo**
(also called Silvermine Bay because
of the silver mines that once skirted
the settlement). It lies at the edge of
a deep bay carved out of the southeast coast. The village's slightly
unkempt appearance is improved
by scenic views to the island's
rugged interior and a well-tended
and generous sweep of sand at
Silvermine Beach, popular
with day-trippers during summer.

Mui Wo is the starting point for
the 44-mile-long (70 km) **Lantau
Trail,** which is divided into
12 sections of varying degrees of
difficulty. There's a lot of steep
climbing in some sections, but
views along the trail are endlessly

spectacular, and camping is
allowed. The trail reaches Hong
Kong's second highest peak, the
towering 3,064-foot (934 m)
Lantau Peak (known as Fung
Wong Shan in Chinese, or "phoenix
mountain"), and Sunset Peak
(2,851 feet/869 m).

From the ferry pier at Mui Wo,
buses regularly head off beyond
the bay along South Lantau Road
and the southern coastline, passing
the village houses, restaurants,
and vacation apartments that line
the eastern sections of the long,
narrow stretch of sand at **Cheung
Sha Beach.**

Midway, Tung Chung Road cuts
north across the island toward
Tung Chung, Hong Kong's latest
new town, opposite the airport at
Chek Lap Kok.

About a mile (1.6 km) beyond
Tung Chung is **Tung Chung
Fort.** Built in 1832, it is enclosed
by a granite block wall, its three
arched entrances engraved with
Chinese character inscriptions.
The six muzzle-loading cannon
on the fort's ramparts once pointed
out over the sea, ready to fire at
marauding pirates.

If you are visiting Lantau just
for the day, forget the fort and
continue along South Lantau Road
as it cuts inland, skirting Shek Pik
Reservoir, passing the road to **Po
Lin Monastery** and its gigantic
Buddha (see p. 210), before winding its way down to the stilt houses
perched over a tidal creek at the
fishing village of **Tai O.** The
village, partly built on Lantau

Island and connected to a tiny island by a 50-foot (15 m) bridge, was once Lantau's biggest; its Tanka boat people make a living from fishing and trading salt with China.

During the late 1980s and early 1990s, Tai O earned some notoriety as a smuggling port. Televisions and other electronic equipment were loaded onto creaking timber barges for the short haul to Chinese waters.

Despite the construction of concrete homes, the village still manages to maintain some of its ramshackle charm, along with the powerful odors of its fish-processing industry. You can bargain for a short *kaido* (small motorboat) trip along the canal for a closer look at the rickety stilt houses, and on to the harbor, dotted with houseboats and junks.

In contrast, on the east coast of Lantau is **Discovery Bay,** commonly referred to as DB or Disco Bay, a modern, planned dormitory community that successfully manages to expunge any feeling of being in Asia. Complete with marina, golf course, restaurants, and beach (the sand had to be shipped in), it is more interesting for its concept than anything else. Residents riding around in whirring golf buggies give it a slightly surreal atmosphere. High-speed ferries next to the Star Ferry Pier in Central District whisk residents and visitors to Discovery Bay in about 20 minutes.

North of Discovery Bay is Penny's Bay, the site of a huge Disneyland theme park that opened in 2005. ■

The fishing village of Tai O, on Lantau's western tip, features houses built on stilts in the water.

Po Lin Monastery

THE GIANT BRONZE BUDDHA STATUE AT PO LIN
("precious lotus") Monastery—the biggest seated, outdoor image of
its kind in the world—is Lantau's number-one attraction. Despite the
crowds who flock there and the often theme-park atmosphere, it's
difficult not to be impressed by the grandeur of the place.

Po Lin Monastery

🅰 202 B2
✉ Lantau Island
💲 $
🚌 Ferry to Mui Wo,
Lantau, then bus
2 from Mui Wo

Before the 85-foot (26 m) Tian Tau
Buddha statue was built at the end
of the 1980s, Po Lin was a peaceful
and serene religious retreat sitting
in splendid isolation high up on the
Ngong Ping plateau in the shadow
of the towering Lantau peak. When
it was completed, the number of
visitors were naturally restricted by
the narrow roads up the mountain.

The Buddha image, cast in 202
pieces at a factory in Nanjing, cost
more than HK$60 million and took
three years to build. It sits on a hill
above the monastery, at the end of
a steep stairway. On the large platform encircling the statue are six
bronze bodhisattva statues, offering
gifts to the Buddha.

The monastery grounds are
about 150 yards (140 m) from the
steps leading to the big Buddha.

The main temple that holds the
finely carved gilded images of the
historical Buddha, Shakyamuni,
flanked by the Healing Buddha on
the right and Amitabha on the left,
is riotously ornate, filled with
carved timber features, swirling
colorful frescoes running above the
doorways and windows, and tiered
bulb-shaped lanterns dangling
from the high, beamed ceilings.

To the left of the main temple
are large dining rooms where
you can enjoy a vegetarian meal
*(purchase meal tickets from a
booth at foot of steps to the big
Buddha)*. Avoid weekends,
especially Sundays, when it's
crowded. You can stay overnight
at the monastery's dormitories
and wander the temple grounds
early next morning. ∎

Hong Kong Disneyland

HONG KONG DISNEYLAND IS AN AMERICAN THEME PARK with Chinese characteristics. The compact park, built on reclaimed land near Hong Kong Airport and opened in September 2005, contains all the iconic Disney attractions, but concessions have been made, especially in regards to Chinese superstitions (no clocks on Main Street, U.S.A.) and food, which is distinctly Asian.

Inside the main gate you'll come to **Main Street, U.S.A.,** with shops—their shelves clogged with fluffy toys and other souvenirs—as well as cafés, restaurants, and an information center at the City Hall on Town Square. At the center, you can make dining reservations, exchange currency, leave messages, and obtain park maps.

A trip on the **Hong Kong Disneyland Railroad,** which circles the park from Main Street, is a good way to become oriented with the park's attractions and layout. The railway's steam train makes one stop as it rumbles around the park perimeter—at Fantasyland, located at the park's opposite end.

Watery rides in **Adventure-land** take you down Jungle Rivers and to Tarzan's Island and Treehouse by raft, while the familiar Disney icons of Sleeping Beauty Castle and the indoor roller coaster, Space Mountain, dominate **Fantasyland** and **Tomorrowland.**

Mickey's PhilharMagic movie theater features a huge 3-D screen showing such staples as "The Little Mermaid," "The Lion King," and "Beauty and the Beast" mixed in with some stunning special effects.

There are two hotels adjoining the park—Hong Kong Disneyland Hotel, with its over-the-top "Victorian elegance," and the enormous glitz-in-over-drive Disney's Hollywood Hotel (see p. 256). Both are rendered with enough whimsy to qualify as theme park destinations in themselves. ∎

The Sleeping Beauty Castle at Hong Kong Disneyland

Hong Kong Disneyland
- 202 C1
- Penny's Bay, Lantau Island
- 1-830-830
- MTR: Hong Kong Resort Station
- $$$$$

Cheung Chau walk

Lying 7.5 miles (12 km) southwest of Hong Kong Island, the fishing island of Cheung Chau measures just under a square mile (2.4 sq km). Because of its small size and relatively tame topography, most of Cheung Chau's attractions can be visited on foot in less than two hours. This walk takes you through the bustling heart of the island to tranquil temples and appealing countryside.

Start on busy **Praya Street,** facing the harbor, with its jumble of shops, restaurants, and apartment blocks. Head north until the wall of shops and restaurants finishes. To the right, beyond a playing field, is the flamboyantly decorated **Pak Tai Temple ①**. It features vibrantly colored glazed dragons and other figurines crowning its roof, carved granite pillars, gilded-wood carvings at its altar, and wall murals inside. Cheung Chau's Bun Festival is celebrated here each May.

Follow Pak She Street to the right past a mishmash of houses and shops until it crosses Kwok Man Street. It now becomes **San Hing Street.** Vegetable stalls, herbal medicine and incense shops, and clothes and bag outlets spill onto the lane, while on the balconies above washing airs in the breeze. Life here is lived at close quarters, but it is surprisingly peaceful.

The lane opens into a small square; turn left and take Tung Wan Road down to the **Tung Wan Beach ②,** a generous sweep of sand with a verdant headland at its southeastern corner. Follow the Cheung Chau Beach Road left along the beachfront for a short distance to a small park where an abstract sculpture honors Cheung Chau's most famous daughter, Lee Lai-san, who won Hong Kong's first-ever gold medal, for mistral sailing, at the Atlanta Olympics in 1996.

Back at the square, walk south on Hing Lung Main Street, which abruptly changes into Tai San Street, and in places becomes so narrow that shop awnings on either side of the lane almost touch.

A block before Tai San Street ends, turn right and take the first alley on the left to its end. Go up some steps and to the right and you will see the **Hung Shing Temple ③**, built to honor a sea god. Inside, colored fairy lights flicker over the wood flower carvings on the main altar. The temple looks out toward the harbor.

Take Tai Hing Tai Road left and continue heading south. As the path curves round to the right, magnificent views of the hundreds of junks in the harbor, backed by the green peaks of nearby Lantau Island, open up in spectacular style. A little farther on the left, colorful figurines decorate the roof at a Tin Hau temple.

Tai San Street now hugs the coastline and becomes Cheung Chau Sai Tai Road. At its

A maze of lanes wanders behind Cheung Chau's waterfront promenade.

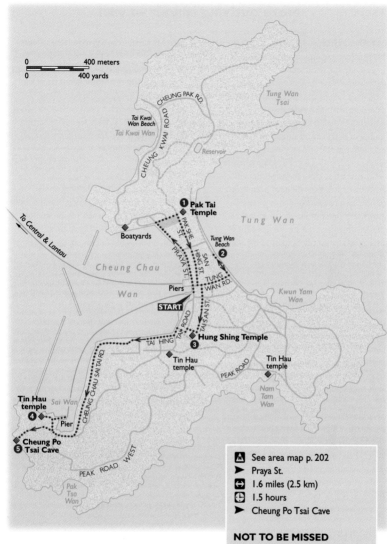

0 | 400 meters
0 | 400 yards

CHEUNG PAK RD

Tung Wan Tsai

Tai Kwai Wan Beach
Tai Kwai Wan

CHEUNG KWAI ROAD

Reservoir

To Central & Lantau

1 Pak Tai Temple

Tung Wan

Boatyards

Tung Wan Beach
2

Cheung Chau

PAK SHE ST.

SAN HING ST.

PRAYA ST.

Piers

TUNG WAN RD.

Wan

START

Kwun Yam Wan

TAI SAN ST.

TAI SHAN ST.

Hung Shing Temple
3

TAI HING

TAI HING ROAD

CHEUNG CHAU SAI TAI RD

Tin Hau temple

PEAK ROAD

Tin Hau temple

Nam Tam Wan

Tin Hau temple
4

Sai Wan

Pier

5 Cheung Po Tsai Cave

PEAK ROAD WEST

Pak Tso Wan

> ⛰ See area map p. 202
> ➤ Praya St.
> ↔ 1.6 miles (2.5 km)
> 🕐 1.5 hours
> ➤ Cheung Po Tsai Cave

NOT TO BE MISSED
- Praya Street
- Pak Tai Temple
- Tin Hau temple

end, a wooded path to the right winds up a hill to a tranquil **Tin Hau temple 4**, with its fine porcelain roof figurines, overlooking the sea at the southern end of the island.

Follow the path back to a short trail heading toward the **Cheung Po Tsai Cave 5**. According to legend, this is where notorious pirate Cheung Po Tsai once stored his booty. Cheung is said to have commanded a fleet of more than 700 vessels in the early 1800s before being defeated by the combined navies of China, Britain, and Portugal. Return along the trail to Sai Wan Bay near the Tin Hau temple, where you can head back to Cheung Chau village by taking a *kaido* (small motorboat) from its pier at Sai Wan Bay. The boat trip gives close-up views of the harbor's fleet of fishing junks. ∎

More outlying islands to visit

KAT O CHAU

This isolated, ungainly island spreads between Plover Cove and the Chinese border in the northeastern New Territories. Its small population spends its time catching, drying, and selling fish. Steep cliffs hold caves where pirates once used to hide their booty. A number of temples and shrines near where boats arrive at Kat O Wan ("crooked island") include a well-preserved **Tin Hau temple.**

Because it's so close to the border with mainland China, you will need permission to visit the island as part of a tour group. The Hong Kong Tourism Board *(tel 2508-1234)* can help organize permits and has a list of travel agents that conduct tours to the island.
△ 203 F4 ㊂ KCR East: Sheung Shui, bus 78K to Shau Tau Kok Ferry Pier, then boat

PENG CHAU

Horseshoe-shaped Peng Chau lies just to the east of Lantau. Its 8,000 people are jammed into just over half a square mile (1.3 sq km) of land, and its narrow lanes are packed with homes, shops, and restaurants, giving it a lively Chinese character. Short walks include a climb to the island's highest point—**Finger Hill** at 311 feet (95m)—and some excellent views; check the map board at the pier. An 18th-century **Tin Hau temple** stands on Wing On Street facing the ferry pier. Day-trippers head here on weekends to visit the seafood restaurants, but the beach at Tung Wan is not particularly inviting.
△ 202 C2 ㊂ Ferry: Outlying Islands Ferry Pier, Central District, Hong Kong Island

PING CHAU

The island of Ping Chau lies in Mirs Bay in the northeastern New Territories near the Chinese border and is part of the Plover Cove Country Park (see pp. 184–85). Most of the people who once lived here are long gone, but the island is a popular place for day-trippers. It has long, pretty beaches and a trail that follows the coastline past strange rock formations and a couple of waterfalls in a loop around the island. It's worth taking the trip to Ping Chau for the ferry ride, which passes through the wide, fjordlike Tolo Channel and

on to Mirs Bay, stopping at isolated villages along the way. You can stay overnight at the camping ground at **Kang Lau Shek** ("drum tower rock") on the southeastern tip of the island or rent a room, or bed, in Chau Tau, near the ferry pier.
△ 203 G4 ㊂ KCR East University Station, then ferry from Mai Liu Shui Ferry Pier Sat., Sun., & public holidays

PO TOI

Po Toi is a group of islands lying on the southern fringes of Hong Kong, about 3 miles (5 km) southeast of Stanley on the south of Hong Kong Island. The rugged main island, Po Toi, is threaded with hiking trails leading to interesting landmarks and fantastic sea and island views from the top of the hills. Only a handful of people live there, running a few seafood restaurants overlooking Tai Wan Bay, near the island's only settlement.

At the ferry pier take the path south through **Wan Tsai,** past vegetable gardens and banana trees to some steps on the right. Head down these to a series of prehistoric rock carvings of stylized animals and fish and interlocking spirals. Continue along the path to the island's southern tip and the weird rock formations. The island is very popular with day-trippers on Sundays.
△ 203 E1 ㊂ *Kaidos* (small motorboats) from St. Stephen's Beach, Stanley, on Sat., Sun., & public holidays. From Aberdeen on Tues., Thurs., Sat., Sun., & public holidays

TUNG LUNG CHAU

This rocky island sits just off the southern tip of the Clear Water Bay Peninsula (see p. 188), at the eastern entrance to Victoria Harbor. Follow the path from the small hamlet at the ferry pier to the well-preserved **Tung Lung Fort** sitting on a rocky headland in the island's northeast. The walk takes about an hour from the pier and offers spectacular coastal views along the way. A path in the opposite direction takes you to a prehistoric rock carving believed to be the image of a dragon on sea cliffs.
△ 203 F2 ㊂ MTR: Sai Wan Ho, then ferry from Sai Wan Ho Ferry Pier Sat., Sun., & public holidays ■

The cobblestone streets and Old World charm of Macau contrast with the frantic pace of modern China exemplified in Guangzhou. Both cities are within easy reach of Hong Kong.

Excursions

Ma Kok Mui Temple, Macau

Macau

Up until December 20, 1999, when the Portuguese handed it back to China, Macau was Asia's oldest European enclave. The few visitors to Hong Kong who bother with the side trip to this city—it's only one hour by ferry—are pleasantly surprised by its charm and character. The mood is changing, however, with the coming of big casinos.

Portugal was the first European nation to try its luck trading with China. Persistence—and more than the odd threat—earned it a little piece of Chinese land on a tiny peninsula at the mouth of the Pearl River Delta in 1557. Over the centuries, Macau's influence waned as other European nations jostled for lucrative trade privileges. By the time Hong Kong was colonized in 1841, Macau was in terminal decline.

In 1966, China's Cultural Revolution fermented in the enclave and rioting and killings ensued. Portugal threatened to abandon Macau because of the violence and, fearing a loss of trade, China backed down. Again in

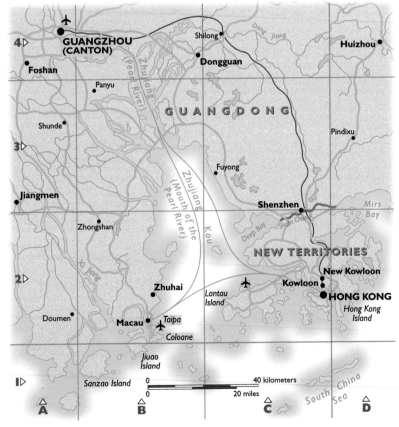

Above: The popular Casino Lisboa is a fascinating way to experience Hong Kong's gambling obsession. **Left:** A-Ma Temple, dedicated to the Queen of Heaven, is Hong Kong's oldest temple.

1974, when Portugal began divesting itself of its colonies, it offered to hand Macau back to China, but this was rejected. It wasn't till after China reached a handover agreement with Britain in the 1984 Joint Declaration that a similar arrangement was made with Portugal. Under the 1987 Sino-Portuguese Pact, Macau, like Hong Kong, would enjoy a high degree of autonomy for 50 years beyond its handover.

Tiny Macau—just 9 square miles (23.5 sq. km), including the islands of Taipa and Coloane—has ten million visitors a year, almost exclusively from Hong Kong and mainland China.

The ending of a gambling monopoly of Macau's shabby casinos has heralded an enormous change to the enclave's gambling industry. If the result matches the hype, Macau will be transformed into the "Las Vegas of the East." A huge gambling complex is being built on the Cotai Strip, a section of reclaimed land between Taipa and Coloane islands. Led by the U.S.-based Las Vegas Sands, the strip will consist of up to 20 casinos resorts. The first of the hotels, the 1,690-room Regal Galleria, is scheduled to open in late 2007.

Macau Fisherman's Wharf, being constructed in the city's outer harbor, is another of Macau's ambitious tourist projects. It will combine entertainment, retail, food, hotel, marina, and convention facilities, plus such over-the-top artifice as an enormous volcano, complete with pyrotechnics and flowing lava, that visitors enter on mining carts.

Macau has been left with a wealth of colonial heritage, making strolling a pleasure. In 2005, this compact part of the city was awarded a World Heritage site listing.

Getting to Macau is simple. Fast and comfortable Jetfoils leave the Macau Ferry Terminal in Hong Kong's Western District every 15 minutes. You will need to pass through immigration in both Hong Kong and Macau, so bring your passport. ■

Macau Peninsula

MACAU HAS NEVER EXPERIENCED THE SPURTS OF unbridled growth characteristic of Hong Kong, a situation that is manifest in both its architecture and attitude. Its winding cobblestone streets, pastel-colored colonial buildings, restored early 20th-century mansions, baroque churches, fine parks, and slow pace effect a pleasant, leisurely atmosphere, evoking a Mediterranean air, a world away from the manic pace of Hong Kong.

PENINSULA EAST

A ten-minute walk from the Macau Ferry Terminal is the Tourism Activities Center in Rua Luis Gonzaga Gomes, which houses two museums. The **Macau Grand Prix Museum** is a delight for car enthusiasts, displaying gleaming Formula 3 and other racing cars and motorbikes that have thundered around the streets of the city during the annual Macau Grand Prix (held every November) since 1954.

Next door to the Grand Prix Museum, in the same building, is the **Macau Wine Museum,** which neatly presents varieties of wine from the different regions of Portugal, along with a collection of winemaking utensils and a mock-up of a cellar. The admission price includes a glass of wine.

The Tourism Activities Center is part of a larger complex called the **Forum.** Head around the corner to the main entrance on Avenida de Marciano Baptista to an exhibition hall which houses a remarkable array of gifts presented by China's provinces after Macau was handed back to the mainland in December 1999.

Gifts include an extraordinary jade ball carving resting on crystal fashioned into a lotus flower; a screen framed with engraved rosewood and finished with an astonishing 78,000 precious stones including pearls, agate, and jade; and a magnificent sundial resting

upon nine dragons, carved from a single piece of jade and weighing 1,100 pounds (500 kg). You can't help being impressed.

Two blocks southeast of the Forum lies Avenida de Amizade, the main thoroughfare running from the ferry terminal toward the center of the city. The avenue once lined the waterfront before a huge slab of reclaimed land was added. On the waterfront at the southeast corner of the reclaimed land is Macau Cultural Center, which houses the **Macau Museum of Art.** Its five floors of permanent and temporary exhibits contain the city's most comprehensive collections of Chinese calligraphy and ceramics, along with paintings by Western artists.

Avenida de Amizade ends at the mustard-colored, barrel-shaped main tower of the **Lisboa** hotel (see p. 257). The ostentatious design of the hotel—the upper sections of its facade resemble a giant roulette wheel—is a local landmark, and the hotel houses Macau's most popular casino in its huge basement. Head there to see the Chinese obsession with gambling at its grittiest—but be prepared to witness all the vices associated with such scenes.

Near the Hotel Lisboa on the artificial Nan Van Lakes is the **Cybernetic Fountain.** It has 86 water spouts, the most energetic shooting plumes of water 250 feet

Macau Grand Prix Museum & Macau Wine Museum
- 🅰 Map p. 224
- ✉ Tourism Activities Center, 431 Rua Luis Gonzaga
- ☎ 798-4108
- 🕐 Closed Tues.
- 💲 $
- 🚌 Bus: 1A, 3, 3A, 10A, 10B, 12, 17, 23, 28A, 28B, 28C, 32

Forum
- 🅰 Map p. 225
- ✉ Avenida de Marciano Baptista
- ☎ 853/988-4117

(80 m) into the air. Every night, except Friday, between 6:30 and 7:30, and again between 9:30 and 10:30, the fountain erupts into an entertaining and watery sound and light show.

PENINSULA SOUTH

The cobblestone square of Largo de Santo Agostinho, on Rua Central, opposite the Largo do Senado (Senate Square, see p. 222), is set with a number of old buildings. Included is **São Agostinho** (St. Augustine's Church), which was built by Augustinian friars in 1856, although the present structure dates back to 1814.

This baroque-style church, built in cream-washed stone with white columns and motifs surrounding its windows, is notable for its spacious interior, and an altar dressed in marble, topped with a statue of Christ carrying the cross.

Opposite the church and next to the renovated **Dom Pedro V Theater,** the first European theater in southern China and still hosting performances, is **São Jose** (Chapel of St. Joseph), part of a seminary set up in 1728 to train Chinese priests. The chapel was built 30 years later. It is laid out in a cruciform shape, with a three-tiered whitewashed facade topped with twin brick-roofed towers. A door next to the elaborate main altar leads to a beautiful cloistered garden and plant nursery.

Back on Rua Central, head south along Rua de São Lourenço to yet another of the city's impressive ecclesiastical sites. Dating back

The ramparts of Fortaleza do Monte overlook Macau.

Macau Museum of Art
- ▲ Map p. 225
- ✉ Avenida Xian Xing Hai
- ☎ 853/791-9814, 9800, 9802
- 🕐 Closed Mon.
- 💲 $
- 🚍 Bus: 1A, 23

Dom Pedro V Theater
- ▲ Map p. 224
- ✉ Largo de Santo Agostinho

to the 1560s—its facade is a 19th-century addition—the imposing **São Lourenço** (St. Lawrence's Church) is fronted by a staircase and an ornamental gate.

The church's cream-and-white facade features square twin towers and a Chinese tile roof. Inside, gold and white beams along its magnificent high, timbered ceiling support chandeliers. A statue of St. Lawrence sits on the richly adorned main altar, dressed in multicolored vestments.

As you head south from St. Lawrence's Church, Rua Padre Antonio becomes Calcada da Barra when it reaches another square, Largo Lilau, and winds around to the **A-Ma Temple.** Dedicated to A-Ma, the Queen of Heaven (known as Tin Hau in Hong Kong), it is Macau's oldest temple, pre-dating Portuguese settlement. The name "Macau" is derived from A-Ma Gau, the "bay of A-Ma."

The temple is a collection of prayer halls, pavilions, and court-yards winding up past boulders, through moon gates and past old ladies with begging bowls to the heavily wooded slopes of Penha Hill. The main shrine, to the right of the entrance, has statues of A-Ma and a model of a war junk complete with little cannon.

The **Macau Maritime Museum** lies opposite A-Ma temple. It juts from the entrance to the inner harbor with walls rising to evoke sails and windows fashioned into portholes. The highlight of a visit here is the dozens of scale replica boats, some of which are superbly crafted. Particularly impressive is the 1:40 scale model of the Portuguese naval training boat, the *Sagres,* under full sail.

From the museum, head east along Rua se São Tiago da Barra until it curves to become Avenida da Republica at the southern tip of the Macau Peninsula and start of

Macau's second artificial lake, Sai Van. South, across the lake on the harborfront, you'll notice the huge, arched, black granite **Gate of Understanding,** built in 1993 to cement Macau's relationship with China. Farther east is the needle-shaped **Macau Tower,** soaring 1,110 feet (338 m), and by far Macau's tallest structure. The outdoor observation deck on the 61st floor allows stunning views of Macau, China, and, on clear days, Hong Kong, about 40 miles (65 km) away. Below the observation deck is a revolving restaurant.

The Macau Tower is part of the Macau Convention and Entertainment Center. At the entrance to the convention center, which sits next door to the tower, are several restaurants and cafés that open onto an expansive plaza with more cafés, fountains, a children's playground, and seating areas, while a timber boardwalk runs along the waterfront.

If all that isn't exciting enough, try the **Macau Tower Sky Jump,** in which you plummet earthward at 45 mph (75 kmh) from the top of the tower before being eased down to earth as the cable-car breaks click in just before ground level. Another adrenalin-rush is **Skywalk X,** were you get to stroll along a tower ledge (attached to a harness), about 800 feet (230m) above the ground.

Avenida da Republica winds around the northern shore of Sai Van Lake and makes for a pleasant amble, with shady trees, stone retaining walls, cobblestone footpaths, and small parks and benches giving a European feel.

The avenue ends near the **Residence of the Portuguese Consul** built atop a small hill. The residence is the former Bela Vista Hotel, once one of Asia's most famous hotels. The colonial, castle-

Macau Maritime Museum
- Map p. 224
- ✉ Largo do Pagode da Barra
- ☎ 595-481
- ⏱ Closed Tues.
- 💲 $
- 🚌 Bus: 1, 1A, 2, 5, 6, 7, 9, 10, 10A, 11, 18, 21, 21A, 34

style building was constructed in the 19th century and has served variously as a boarding school, hostel for refugees, and hotel.

PENINSULA NORTH

The goddess of mercy, Kun Iam (known as Kwum Yam in Hong Kong), is honored at the large and elaborate **Kun Iam Tong Temple** on Avenida do Coronel Mesquita. The temple was established in the 13th century and its present structures date from 1627. A huge entrance gate featuring a myriad porcelain figures clustered along its roof ridges provides a suitably grand introduction to this lovely temple. In the main hall an image of Kun Iam—attended by 18 *arhats* (Chinese sages) on either side—is lavishly clothed in embroidered silk. Behind the temple, terraced gardens feature fountains fashioned into Chinese landscapes.

Walk north down Avenida do Coronel Mesquita and turn right on Avenida do Almirante Lacerda to **Lin Fong Miu** (Temple of the Lotus), with a bas-relief tableau of Chinese historical and mythological figures carved in the 19th century embellishing its facade. The first hall through the entrance—guarded by stone lions—is dedicated to A-Ma. Beyond this, you will find a courtyard decorated with a frieze of writhing dragons and a lotus pond.

Head north from here down Istmo Ferreira do Amaral to the 19th-century **Barrier Gate** (Portas do Cerco or "gate of siege"), constructed in grand style to mark the Macau–China border. ∎

A junk carved into a boulder at A-Ma Temple symbolizes the deity's relationship with the sea.

Colorful colonial buildings, including the Igreja de São Domingos, edge the Largo do Senado.

Macau walk

This walk begins in central Macau and wends its way north and then to the east past some of Macau's best-known attractions, ending with sweeping views of the city and harbor.

Start your walk at **Largo do Senado** (Senate Square), at the heart of old Macau. The square—with black-and-white mosaic stones laid in wave patterns and a lively spurting fountain—is lined with a fine array of restored colonial buildings. The **Leal Senado** ❶ ("loyal Senate"), now the municipal council building, faces the square on the opposite side of Avenida Almeida Riberio. Originally completed in 1784, with its imposing facade of white plaster and green-shuttered windows added a century later, the building earned the name "loyal" because of Macau's resolute refusal to recognize Spain's occupation of Portugal in the 17th century. From its grand foyer, a stone staircase embellished with blue-and-white tiles leads to a delightful garden. Farther up the stairs are the wood-paneled senate chamber and library.

Standing out among the colonnaded and lively pastel-colored buildings around the square is the startling white facade of **Santa Casa da Misericordia** ❷ ("holy house of mercy"), a mission set up in 1568 and one of the oldest in Asia.

Continue through to the northern end of the square to **Igreja de São Domingos** ❸ (St. Dominic's Church), one of the city's best examples of Portuguese colonial baroque architecture, which infused local elements into 18th-century baroque style. Its classical design is married with Chinese roof tiles, extensive use of timber, and large shuttered windows. The church's facade rises on three tiers of cream-washed stone adorned with white stucco motifs, iconic columns, carved teak doors, and windows protected by green louvered shutters, with a bronze cross rising from the triangular roof-top pediment.

Inside, the church is no less impressive, especially the cream-colored stone altar, decorated with white-stucco moldings and twisting columns, which climbs to the ceiling. The centerpiece of the altar is a 17th-century image of Our Lady of the Rosary, flanked by statues of St. Dominic and St. Catherine of Sienna.

The cross below Our Lady is that of the Dominican order.

Next to St. Dominic's is the **Museum of St. Dominic's** ❹ *(Largo de São Domingos).* In addition to a room on its first floor devoted to pictures of the renovation of the church, the three-level museum carries about 300 works of sacred art, made unusual because many of the images and religious regalia were crafted in former Portuguese colonies in Africa, Malaya, India, and Macau using tropical woods and ivory, along with vestments made from Chinese silks.

Take a left turn at the museum along the narrow and cobblestone-paved Rua da Pahla, which soon becomes Rua São Paulo. It winds past a collection of small colonial buildings and balconied Chinese shop-houses to the grand stone stairway and magnificent facade of the **Ruinas de São Paulo** ❺ (Ruins of St. Paul; see p. 226), Macau's most enduring symbol and recognized as one of the finest monuments to Christianity in Asia.

Just to the right of the church, at the top of the stairway, head right a short distance and take the escalators to the **Macau Museum** ❻ *(Monte Fort, tel 357-9111, closed Mon., $).* Built into the side of **Fortaleza do Monte** ❼ (Monte Fort), this excellent museum's three floors guide you through Macau's lively history and works hard to emphasize the role played by both the Portuguese and Chinese in its development.

The top floor of the museum leads out to the grounds—now pleasant gardens— of Monte Fort, where you can get sweeping views of Macau and check out the emplacements housing the original guardrooms and cannon. The fort was built by Jesuits between 1617 and 1626. The cannon were used only once, when the Dutch invaded in 1622. A cannonball fired by a priest hit a powder keg on one of the invading ships creating panic and allowing the Portuguese to drive back the invaders.

Return through the museum to the Ruins of St. Paul, down the stairway, and turn right to follow Rua de Santo Antonio, a street famous for its Chinese antiques and reproductions (this is where many antique retailers from Hong Kong come to pick up bargains to resell in their shops) to **Igreja de Santo**

American and British citizens lie buried at the tranquil Protestant Cemetery.

Antonio ❽ (St. Anthony's Church), which stands on the site of Macau's first chapel, built in 1558. The church has burnt down three times, the last time in 1930. The current facade, with its gray, bulky presence, was built in 1940, and gives the church an intimidating, rather than an aesthetic presence.

Opposite St. Anthony's Church, behind a solid wall, is the **Macau Protestant Chapel and Cemetery** ❾. The tiny, whitewashed chapel fronts a small, well-tended cemetery with tombs and gravestones set amid green lawns and frangipani trees. This is where Macau's mainly British and American citizens were laid to rest in the 18th and 19th centuries. Gravestones tell tales of shipboard accidents, shipwrecks, fever, and disease. Among those buried in the cemetery are George Chinnery (1774–1852), known for his paintings of Macau, and Robert Morrison (1782–1834), a Protestant missionary to China, who translated much of the Bible into Chinese.

Adjacent to the cemetery is the **Camoes Grotto and Garden** ❿ *(Praca Luis de Camoes)* a lush park of winding paths, boulders, shady banyan trees, ferns, and bamboo groves climbing to a lookout and views to the Inner Harbor and mainland China. The park is dedicated to Luis de Camoes, a 16th-century Portuguese poet who penned the epic poem *Os Lusiada.* A bronze bust of the poet sits in a grotto inside the entrance to the park.

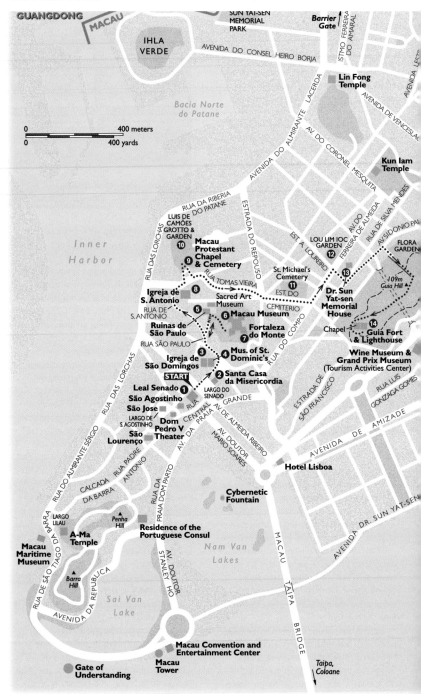

GUANGDONG MACAU

IHLA VERDE

SUN YAT-SEN MEMORIAL PARK

Barrier Gate

AVENIDA DO CONSEL HEIRO BORJA

Bacia Norte do Patane

Lin Fong Temple

AVENIDA DE VENCESLAC

Kun Iam Temple

0   400 meters
0   400 yards

Inner Harbor

RUA DA RIBERIA DO PATANE

LUIS DE CAMÕES GROTTO & GARDEN ⑩

Macau Protestant Chapel & Cemetery ⑨

LOU LIM IOC GARDEN ⑫

FLORA GARDEN

109m Guia Hill

RUA TOMAS VIEIRA

St. Michael's Cemetery

⑪

⑬

Igreja de S. Antonio ⑧

Sacred Art Museum

RUA DE S. ANTONIO

⑤

Ruinas de São Paulo

RUA SÃO PAULO

④

Macau Museum ⑥

⑦ Fortaleza do Monte

Dr. Sun Yat-sen Memorial House

Chapel

Guia Fort & Lighthouse ⑭

Igreja de São Domingos

START

Mus. of St. Dominic's ③

② Santa Casa da Misericordia

Wine Museum & Grand Prix Museum (Tourism Activities Center)

RUA LUIS GONZAGA GOMES

Leal Senado ①

LARGO DO SENADO

São Agostinho
São Jose

LARGO DE S. AGOSTINHO

São Lourenço

Dom Pedro V Theater

RUA CENTRAL

AV. DE ALMEIDA RIBEIRO

ESTRADA DE SÃO FRANCISCO

AVENIDA DE AMIZADE

Hotel Lisboa

AV. DOUTOR MARIO SOARES

CALCADA DA BARRA

LARGO LILAU

Penha Hill

Residence of the Portuguese Consul

Cybernetic Fountain

A-Ma Temple

Nam Van Lakes

MACAU TAIPA BRIDGE

AVENIDA DR. SUN YAT-SEN

Macau Maritime Museum

Barra Hill

Sai Van Lake

AVENIDA DA REPUBLICA

AV. DOUTOR STANLEY HO

Gate of Understanding

Macau Tower

Macau Convention and Entertainment Center

Taipa, Coloane

From the entrance to the park head to the rear of St. Anthony's Church, east along Rua Tomas Vieira, to a small traffic circle. On the other side of the circle take Estrada do Cemiterio and continue east to the hillside **St. Michael's Cemetery** ⓫. This Catholic cemetery is crowded with extravagant gravestones adorned with large statues of the Virgin Mary, harp-playing angels, and various saints.

Continue east along Estrada do Cemiterio and turn left at Avenida do Conselheiro Ferreira de Almeida. Here you'll pass some lovely restored 1920s buildings, painted in bold browns and yellows, now housing government departments, before reaching the walled **Lou Lim loc Garden** ⓬ at the junction of Estrada Adolfo Loureiro. These beautifully landscaped gardens are modeled on the famed gardens of Suzhou. The gardens are heavily wooded, with a large pond sitting in front of a flamboyant colonial home (now an art gallery). Paths wind around the park, over zigzagging bridges, through bamboo groves, grottoes and to pagoda-style pavilions, and past ponds full of lotus plants.

From the gardens, continue along Estrada Adolfo Loureiro and cross Avenida do Conselheiro Ferreira one block to Avenida Sidonio Pais. Turn right and walk a short distance to Rua de Silva Mendes and the **Dr. Sun Yat-sen Memorial House** ⓭ *(Av. Sidonio Pais, tel 574-064, closed Tues.)*, the Moorish-style home built by Sun's family in the 1930s, replacing the original, more modest dwelling in which he lived during his visits to Macau. Inside you'll find memorabilia and photographs outlying Sun's four-decade struggle to overthrow the Qing dynasty and establish the Chinese Republic (see p. 33).

Keep heading north along Avenida Sidonio Pais to Flora Garden, where you can hop on a cable car *(closed 6 p.m., $)* for an 80-second ride to Guia Hill, at 360 feet (109 m), the highest point in Macau. From here, take the path to 17th-century **Guia Fort** ⓮ and have a look at the first lighthouse built (in 1865) on the China coast and still operating, inspect the ruins of the fort, and admire the sweeping views of Macau from the cannon platform. Next to the lighthouse is a simple chapel containing a fine image of the Virgin Mary holding the Baby Jesus. ■

Ruinas de São Paulo

Ruinas de São Paulo

🗺 Map p. 224

OF ALL THE CHURCHES IN MACAU, THE MOST IMPRESSIVE by far is São Paulo (St. Paul's), even though all that now remains is its remarkably well-restored tiered stone facade. Built in the early 17th century by members of the Jesuit Order, this towering facade is an example of ecclesiastical architecture at its most magnificent. When it was first completed, St. Paul's was hailed as the greatest monument to Christianity in Asia.

Although São Paulo's facade is all that's left of the once spectacular structure, the church remains Macau's symbol.

In 1762, when the liberal-minded Jesuits were expelled from Macau by the Portuguese government, the church became a military barracks and gradually fell into disrepair. A fire erupted in the barracks' kitchen in 1835, destroying the basilica's buildings and church—except for the stone facade. It was left to crumble slowly, and by the 1980s it looked as if it was about to tumble over. Thankfully, the government began restoration work in 1991, which was completed in 1995.

The tiered facade is richly embellished with carvings and statues. The triangular section at the top holds a bronze dove symbolizing the Holy Spirit. The surrounding stars, sun, and moon represent "the place of divinity." Directly below, in an alcove in the second tier, implements of crucifixion flank the Infant Jesus, while angels carry a cross and a scourging pillar.

The third tier holds a large statue of Our Lady of Assumption, again in an alcove, surrounded by angels celebrating her ascension to Heaven. To the left, the Virgin Mary hovers above a Portuguese galleon, guiding it safely across the "Sea of Torments of Sin," while to the right, a similar image tops a seven-headed hydra. Chinese characters here proclaim the legend: "The Holy Mother tramples the heads of a dragon."

The fourth tier contains statues of four Jesuit notables including, on the far left, the beatified Francisco de Borja. Next to him is the Jesuit founder, St. Ignatius, while farther to the right are the Apostle of the Orient, St. Francis Xavier, and the beatified Luis Gonzaga. Above the main entrance on the bottom tier are inscribed the words *Mater Dei* (Mother of God).

Behind the facade, excavations have revealed the crypt of the church's founder, father Alessandro Valignano, which now forms part of the **Museum of Sacred Art.** Next to his tomb are the bones, including a few skulls, of various Catholic martyrs from Japan and Vietnam, displayed in glass cases. The one-room museum holds a collection of sculptures, paintings, and religious regalia recovered from various churches in Macau. ∎

Macau's islands

MACAU'S TWO ISLANDS OF TAIPA AND COLOANE ARE EASILY accessible via two long, arching bridges (to Taipa) and a causeway (from Taipa to Coloane). Much of 2.4 square-mile (6.2 sq km) Taipa has taken on the identity of one of Hong Kong's new towns, with dozens of towering apartment blocks and a rather soulless atmosphere, while marginally bigger Coloane is much less developed. Both have their share of attractions that can easily be covered in half a day.

Avenida da Praia Residences

✉ Avenida da Praia, Taipa

☎ 853/827-103, 527

🕐 Closed Mon.

🚌 Bus: 11, 22, 28A, 30, 33, 34

TAIPA

Charming **Taipa Village** is at the island's southern end. Here, narrow lanes are lined with quaint Chinese shop-houses, open-air restaurants, and pastel-colored colonial buildings. To the east of the village, **Our Lady of Carmel Church** stands in a cobblestone square atop a small hill. From here, take the garden path down to the small, banyan-shaded **Avenida da Praia,** with its restored mansions dating back to the 1920s, called the **Avenida da Praia Residences.** The first of these is the **Macanese House,** a museum with louvered shutters and deep verandas, fashioned into a Macanese family home of the 1920s with period furniture. The other four residences, similar in architectural design, house an exhibition gallery, displays on the regions of Portugal and the history of Taipa and Coloane, and a reception room and restaurant.

COLOANE

A long causeway near Taipa Village links the two islands. Buses to the island stop at the small, pretty main square, **Largo Presidente A.R. Eanes,** at Coloane Village, but the rest of the village is mostly pretty shabby. Head left at the waterfront to the **Chapel of St. Francis Xavier.** The church, with its cream-and-white facade and blue timber doors, is a late addition to Macau's surfeit of churches, built in 1928.

Keep heading south along Ave-

nida Cinco Outubro to **Tam Kong Temple,** dedicated to a Taoist god of seafarers. Porcelain figures decorate the temple's tiled roof. Inside, a 4-foot-long (1.2 m) carved whalebone dragon boat, filled with a crew of wooden men in red coats and yellow hats, adds interest.

From the village square you can hop on a bus for the short ride to **Ha Sa Beach.** The long curving beach gets its name from the color of its sand—Black Sand Beach.

The world's largest A-Ma statue crowns **Coloane Peak,** with the adjacent **A-Ma Cultural Village** *(closed Mon.)* adding more tributes to the Goddess of the Sea. The village comprises a number of buildings dating from the Qing Dynasty, including an A-Ma "palace," a dressing hall, and a museum. ■

Boys on the rocks at Ha Sa Beach, a popular recreational spot

Taipa
🗺 Map p. 225

GETTING THERE

Buses run frequently from the Macau Peninsula to both Taipa and Coloane. From here, buses to Taipa village include Nos. 11, 22, 28A, and 33. Buses to Coloane Village include Nos. 21A, 25, 26A. These continue to Hac Sa Beach. ■

Guangzhou

This sprawling metropolis of ten million people is the engine that has driven China's emergence as an economic power. It has used its proximity and relationship with Hong Kong to power its way to prosperity. The city is the face of modern China, with its gleaming high-rise towers, a relatively well-off population, and a vitality close to matching that of Hong Kong, just 75 miles (120 km) southeast.

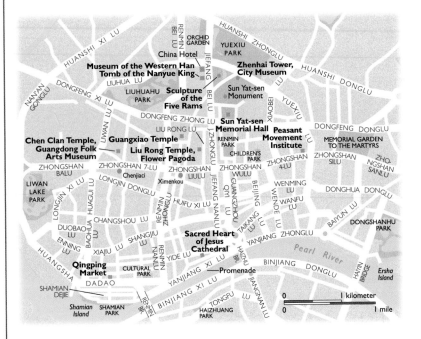

This vitality is not surprising. Most Hong Kong people—the Cantonese—originally hail from Guangzhou and its province, Guangdong. Over the past two decades, they have transformed the city into the most modern and vibrant in China.

Guangzhou is easily accessible from Hong Kong, just a few hours by train or high-speed ferry. For those wanting a quick glimpse into the changing complexion of modern China, it is an ideal excursion.

Guangzhou is not an attractive city, nor one that leans heavily on tourism. It exhibits all the characteristics of a modern Asian city hell-bent on growth. Its heavy traffic, sprawl, and constant din are intimidating, but despite this, there are still a number of attractions—temples, parks, and museums—that make it

worth the visit, at least for a day or two. These attractions are relatively close together and not hard to find. Taxis are everywhere and their fares are cheap. A modern subway system, although limited, also runs between some of these sites.

Most visitors limit themselves to old Guangzhou, which spreads back from the banks of the meandering Pearl River. Much of this area, with its riverfront promenades, colonnaded 1920s shop-houses, mazes of narrow, winding laneways, impromptu markets, and mercantile bustle, is amenable to walking.

Charming Shamian Island, once a British and French concession, retains nearly all of its colonial character. From there, amble east along the shaded riverfront promenade taking in the busy river traffic before heading north

through the city's side streets to the imposing Gothic spires of the 19th-century Scared Heart of Jesus Cathedral. Farther north into the heart of the city are the ancient temple compounds of Guangxiao and Lui Rong, and to the west, the riotously ornate Chen Chan Temple.

Near the landmark China Hotel is the impressive Museum of the Western Han Tomb of the Nanyue King, with its fascinating collection of relics buried with Wen Di (137–122 B.C.), the second emperor of the short-lived

Guangzhou's Ozhong Interchange at night exemplifies China's growing modernity.

Nanyue dynasty. Opposite, the expansive Yuexi Park has a number of attractions worth visiting. Nearby, the Sun Yat-sen Memorial Hall honors the founder of modern China, while to the west, a snippet into the life of China's other great leader Mao Zedong can be found at the quirky Peasant Movement Institute, housed inside a 14th-century Confucian temple. ■

Shamian Island & around

THE NORTH BANK OF THE PEARL RIVER IS AMONG Guangzhou's oldest and most interesting areas, mixing hints of colonialism with a vibrant street life. Beside the riverbank, parts of which are given over to generous promenades, you can join the locals strolling and catching river breezes, then head into the city's winding laneways to catch the excitement of everyday street life.

Shamian Island
🅼 Map p. 228
(SW corner)

Live turtles at Guangzhou's famous Qingping market

A relic of Guangzhou's concessions to colonialism is found on **Shamian Island,** a small slice of land on the northern banks of the Pearl River and divided from the city by a narrow canal. This was once the British and French Concession granted by China in 1859. It was here the Europeans built grand buildings, laid cobblestone streets, and planted rows of banyan trees and hedged gardens. Surprisingly, the place was left alone during Guangzhou's mad development scramble of the 1990s.

Over the last few years, the colonial buildings have been restored, and are now occupied by offices, restaurants, and boutiques. The main boulevard, **Shamian Dejie,** running through the center of the island east to west, has rows of neatly trimmed hedges, trees, and brick-paved plazas with seating areas. The island has very little traffic, making it a delightful place to stroll. Along its waterfront, outdoor restaurants occupy space in shaded **Shamian Park.** You can sit here and watch boats chug their way along the Pearl River while you sip on a beer, a pleasing experience. Shamian's quaintness and gentility sits in stark contrast to the manic pace of the rest of the city.

Across Shamian Island's canal is the colonnaded colonial facade of the city's most famous market, **Qingping.** The market was one of the first of its kind in China and came into being soon after the introduction of free market economics to China in the late 1970s. Stores in the front arcades of the market sell the usual collection of dried medicinal herbs including mushrooms, spices, sea horses, anise, bark, deer antlers, and so on. As you move farther into the market, stands along the warren of side streets offer the more mundane

fish, fresh fruit and vegetables, flowers, potted plants, and goldfish. But as you go deeper, it gets a bit more bizarre. Here, sections are devoted to the diverse culinary habits of the Cantonese: a take-away menagerie of monkeys, dogs, civet cats, deer, scary live scorpions, horrible writhing centipedes, cockroaches, trays of huddled toads, lamely hopping frogs, and crawling tortoises, all destined for the pot. Even more disturbing are the occasional sights of tiger paws and rhino horns laid out on mats on the ground.

Back on peaceful Shamian Island, beyond Shamian Park, head east along the banyan-tree-shaded wide waterfront boulevard past people playing badminton, practicing *tai chi,* and sitting and chatting on park benches. You'll leave the island across a small bridge and onto Yangjian Xi Lu (Yangjian Road West). After a couple of hundred yards, the street opens up to the waterfront and a generous **promenade,** with the branches of shady banyan trees arching over the sidewalk, a favorite spot for strolling lovers in the evenings and tai chi practitioners in the early morning.

A few blocks back from the waterfront on Yide Lu (Yide Road) is China's oldest Catholic church, the imposing **Sacred Heart of Jesus Cathedral,** known as *shi shi jiaotang* or "stone house" in Chinese. This Gothic-inspired edifice, with its twin spires, heavy timber doors, flowered window lattices, and colored-glass features, is a surprising find in area of balconied shop-houses, rundown tenements, and bustling narrow laneways. Construction began in 1863, and it was consecrated in 1888. Notice the carved Chinese-style lions jutting out from its walls.

Just to northeast of Shamian Island on Huangsha Avenue is the **Cultural Park,** an odd and faded mixture of attractions, including a roller-skating rink, a sad-looking Dolphin Performance Hall, a Fishing Exhibition full of empty fish tanks, an amusement park with wonderfully antiquated rides, and a mildly interesting Hang Dynasty Hall. ∎

Picturesque Shamian Island has a more relaxed air than the rest of the city.

Old Guangzhou

ALTHOUGH GUANGZHOU IS A HUGE, SPRAWLING CITY,
many of its main attractions are within a relatively easy distance from
one another and can be reached by short taxi rides. In between these
attractions, you'll see Chinese city life at its most vibrant; from wide
avenues lined with shiny high-rise office towers and clogged with
traffic, to bustling side streets with colonnaded shop-houses and
narrow lanes brimming with people and activity.

Guangzhou
 Map p. 228

**Chen Clan Temple
& Guangdong Folk
Arts Museum**
Map p. 228
Zhongshan 7-Lu
8181-7371
$
Subway: Chenjiaci

Start your tour at Zhongshan 7-Lu
(Zhongshan Road, Section 7) at the
Chen Clan Temple, next to the
Chenjiaci subway station. It is one
of the most beautiful and ornate
ancestral halls in China and one of
the very few to survive the Cultural
Revolution of the 1960s and 1970s.

This expansive temple
comprises 19 buildings interspersed
with garden courtyards and linked
by a network of long verandas. The
roof ridges and eaves of the halls
are lined with thousands of brilliantly colorful and expressive
porcelain figurines depicting a
confusion of mythological scenes,
while intricate stone bas-reliefs,
featuring similar scenarios, are
sculptured above the doorways.

The sturdy main doors, decorated
with paintings of Chinese
guardians Qin Qiong and Wei
Chigong, open to the vaulted ceiling
supported by carved timber beams,
while sublimely decorated lanterns
hang from above. Timber panels
crafted into beautiful patterns
screen the entrance hall from the
first courtyard. From there, verandas embellished with timber
latticework and topped with more
porcelain figurines, lead to the
complex's other halls, each featuring
similar exquisite detailing.

A number of the halls have been
given over to the **Guangdong
Folk Arts Museum,** which
displays arts and handicrafts from
all over China, but especially from

Guangdong Province. The collection, dating mainly from the Qing period up until recent times, comprises some magnificent examples of embroidery, porcelain work, enamelware, ceramics, papercuts, stained-etched glass, shell patchwork, basketwork, and lacquerwork. Carvings have been fashioned from jade, stone, ivory, ox-horn, shell, and wood.

Particularly impressive are the two gilded shrines—fashioned into sedan chairs—for holding ancestral tablets, flanking the altar in the main hall. These exquisite pieces feature Taoist religious tableaus (there is also one of dozens of clambering crabs!) sculptured in wood and with extraordinary detail. Also worth a lot closer inspection are the miniature ivory carvings—less than half an inch in size. They are so small a magnifying glass has been set up to view them.

Hop back on the subway for one station (Xinemkou) to the **Guangxiao Temple** on Hongshu Lu (Hongshu Road). It is one of Guangzhou's oldest temples, dating back to the 4th century. Past the pot-bellied Laughing Buddha at the entrance, its neatly trimmed hedges and shady banyan trees make for pleasant strolling. The restored buildings feature an ingenious multibracketing timber roof system, supporting broad and sweeping multi-eave roofs, with ridges lined with porcelain figurines. Inside the spacious main hall are three large gilded Buddha images side by side. Behind them sits a serene-looking goddess of mercy, Kwun Yam, flanked by *lohans* and backed by a colorful mural that features mythological scenes.

Nearby to the east, on Liu Rong Lu (Liu Rong Road), stands the 197-foot (60 m) **Flower Pagoda,** with nine external and 17 internal floors, the impressive centerpiece of **Liu Rong Temple** ("temple of the six banyan trees"), dating from around the sixth century. You can climb to the top of this octagonal structure for outstanding views of sprawling Guangzhou. Behind the pagoda, the main shrine, rebuilt in 1984, holds three large gilded Buddhas.

In 1983, bulldozers accidentally unearthed the tomb of Wen Di, the second emperor of Nanyue (137–122 B.C.), a localized dynasty of five kings, which lasted less than a century. The tomb was excavated and turned into the **Museum of the Western Han Tomb of the Nanyue King,** just east of the China Hotel on Jeifang Bei Lu (Jeifang Road North). The museum re-creates the setting of the tomb; you walk down some stairs from a grassy knoll into the tomb chambers, where the king, along with an accompaniment of human sacrifices, including his concubines, cooks, guards, and musicians, were buried. The museum houses the remains of Wen and the others along with the thousands of jade, gold, bronze, iron, crystal, and fabric funerary objects buried with them, including Wen's burial shroud, made from a thousand pieces of jade.

Across from the museum, also on Jeifang Bei Lu, is the biggest of Guangzhou's parks, the 232-acre (93 ha), hilly and heavily wooded **Yuexiu Park.** On one of its hills, near the entrance to the south gate, sits one of the city's main attractions: the **Sculpture of the Five Rams,** a rather unattractive concrete rendering of goats climbing a hill, although after viewing it, you are left to wonder why. Erected in 1959, it is the symbol of Guangzhou, whose name means "city of rams" (or Goat City). Myth holds that

Buddha image at Liu Rong Temple, one of a number of ancient temples in the city

Museum of the Western Han Tomb of the Nanyue King

🅰 Map p. 228

✉ 867 Jiefang Bei Rd.

☎ 8666-4920

💲 $

Sun Yat-sen Memorial Hall

⚑ Map p. 228
✉ Donfeng Zhong Lu
☎ 3428-1366
💲 $

Museum of National Institute of Peasant Movement

⚑ Map p. 228
✉ 42 Zhongshan 4-Lu.
☎ 8333-3936
🕐 Closed Mon.
💲 $

hundreds of years ago, five celestial beings riding five rams through the air arrived in the city, presenting stalks of rice to the locals as an indication that the region would forever remain free from famine.

Take the path to the right of the goats down the hill to pretty Nanxui Lake, cross a bridge, and head right up the hill to **Zhenhai Tower.** The tower was built in 1380 (today's version dates from 1928) and was used by the French and British troops during the Opium Wars (see pp. 29–32) because of its lofty position overlooking the south of the city. It now houses the **Guangzhou City Museum,** with mildly interesting exhibits tracing the history of the city from neolithic times to the present. The fifth floor has a balcony with views over the city.

At Liuhau Park, rowboats can be hired for a paddle around the lake.

To the right of the tower, on another hill, stands a marble and granite obelisk commemorating the revolutionary, Sun Yat-sen (see p. 33), who mastered the overthrow of the Qing dynasty in 1912. The monument was built in 1929, four years after his death. The obelisk overlooks the gigantic **Sun Yat-sen Memorial Hall,** set behind a broad expanse of manicured

lawns and entered at Dongfeng Zhong Lu (Dongfeng Road Central). Built in 1931 on the site of the Qing governor's residence, the huge building, measuring 154 feet (47 m) high and 233 feet (71 m) long, is done in heavily ornate, traditional style, with sweeping roofs topped with blue tiles. Inside, a domed ceiling rises above a 3,200-seat theater.

Next to the hall is a small exhibition hall with a collection of historical photographs; unfortunately for foreign visitors, captions are only in Chinese.

To the west of the memorial hall, on Renmin Bei Lu (Renmin Road North), is pretty **Liuhau Park.** Here, you can rent rowboats and paddle around the city's largest artificial lake.

Guangzhou has a number of revolutionary museums. Among the best of these is the **Museum of National Institute of Peasant Movement,** housed inside a Confucian temple dating back to 1370. Outstanding temple architecture, consisting of garden courtyards, swooping tiled roofs adorned with porcelain figurines along ship brow ridges, and finely carved ceiling beams and latticework mixes with more prosaic examples of peasant movement studies in the temple's rooms.

Established in 1924, the institute is famed as the place Communist Party leaders Mao Zedong and Zhou Enlai lectured young party members. The temple's halls are turned over to a museum with much of the original institutes' furnishings still in place, including classrooms, dormitories, offices, library, doctor's room, and Mao's quarters. One small room is dedicated to Mao with plenty of photographs, posters, badges, statues, busts, and other paraphernalia dedicated to him. ∎

Travelwise

**Tram driver,
Hong Kong Island**

PLANNING YOUR TRIP

TRAVELWISE INFORMATION

PLANNING YOUR TRIP

WHEN TO GO

CLIMATE

Hong Kong sits on the South China Sea, just south of the Tropic of Cancer, and has a subtropical climate. Winter (Dec.–Feb.) can see temperature fluctuations between 50°F (10°C) and 76°F (25°C). At this time, cool Arctic winds blow across the Asian continent. The temperature can drop to zero on some peaks in the New Territories, but rarely sinks below 45°F (7°C) in urban areas. There is little rain and humidity is relatively low. Spring is marked by a sharp increase in humidity. Summer (June–Aug.) is hot, with humidity reaching 90 percent and over, and is subject to bouts of heavy rain. Best times to visit are March to April and late September to November, when humidity drops and there's little or no rainfall.

Hong Kong lies within a typhoon region and may be buffeted by severe rainstorms and fierce winds, which can occasionally force the complete shutdown of businesses and public services for 24 hours or more. The typhoon season is May to November, but August is the most prone. The suspension of transportation and other services is governed by a series of numbered signals (1 for caution, 3 for worsening, 8 for take immediate shelter, etc.), which are posted widely and repeated on TV and radio. During a number 8 signal, shops and offices close and most public transportation shuts down after people head home.

The average temperatures for Hong Kong are:

Spring March to May 72°F (22°C)

Summer June to August 85°F (30°C)

Fall   September to November 74°F (24°C)

Winter December to February 63°F (17°C)

WHAT TO TAKE

Winter and spring can be cool, especially after sunset, so a sweater or jacket is advisable. In summer, air-conditioning in restaurants, bars, movie theaters, offices, and on public transportation can be cool enough to warrant a light jacket.

An umbrella is a must in summer. Also bring a light waterproof jacket. Some of the top restaurants expect men to wear a jacket, if not a tie, but most settle for neat, casual attire.

From mid-spring to late fall, lightweight, loose, cotton clothing is advisable. T-shirts and neat shorts are acceptable streetwear, especially during the oppressively hot and humid summer months. A lot of your time will be spent on foot, so bring comfortable walking shoes. Sandals—not flip-flops—are acceptable. If you plan on hiking in Hong Kong's country parks, bring a sturdy pair of hiking boots.

No matter what you wear dress neatly, as people in Hong Kong often measure you by your appearance. Although it is a cosmopolitan city, women should refrain from wearing revealing clothing.

INSURANCE

Arrange adequate medical and travel insurance to cover worst-case possibilities before leaving your home country. Only third-party cover is provided in car rental agreements.

Theft or loss of property covered by personal insurance should be reported as soon as possible to the Hong Kong police. You will need to go in person to a police station where you will be given a stolen-property form to fill in. The process is efficient and police are dutifully polite to visitors.

ENTRY FORMALITIES

VISAS

Citizens from the United States, Canada, Australia, and Europe can stay up to three months without a visa, provided they have a passport valid for at least three months beyond their departure date. British citizens can stay up to six months visa free. Visitors may need to prove to immigration officers on arrival that they have sufficient funds and an onward ticket before being allowed to enter, although this is a rare occurrence.

If you wish to stay longer than the visa-free period, you will need to apply for a visa at an SAR counter of a Republic of China embassy, consulate, or visa office before arrival.

Visitors are not allowed to enter employment (paid or unpaid) or establish or join any business.

The Hong Kong Immigration Department is at 2/F, Hong Kong Immigration Tower, 7 Gloucester Rd., Wan Chai, tel 2824-6111, www.info.gov.hk/immd/.

Hong Kong citizens are required by law to carry their identity cards at all times. Visitors must also carry some form of identity with a photograph. Police have the right to stop you and ask for ID, although this happens very rarely to foreigners. A driver's license with photograph is adequate.

Macau

Residents from the United States, Canada, Australia, Europe, and a number of other countries can stay in Macau for up to one month without a visa. Passports need to be valid three months beyond the length of visit.

Guangzhou

Hong Kong is the easiest place to obtain visas for China. All visitors to China need a visa. Exceptions are for those visiting Shenzhen Special Economic Zone (on the border with Hong Kong). Visitors from certain countries including the United States, Canada, Australia, and Europe are allowed a 72-hour stay.

Single or multiple entry visas—each stay is for 30 days— to China can be obtained in Hong Kong from travel agents or from China Travel Services (tel 2789-5401). Agents charge a commission on top of the normal visa costs, which range between HK$100–700 depending on the number of entries and how quickly you want the visa, but the service is well worth it. You will need one passport-size photograph. Obtaining a visa from the Visa Office of the Ministry of Foreign Affairs of the People's Republic of China (5th Floor, Low Block, China Resources Bldg., 26 Harbor Rd., Wan Chai, tel 2983-9812) is cheaper, but it is often crowded and can be frustratingly slow. Visas are usually issued within two to three days. You can have an express visa in 24 hours but will need to pay extra. U.S. citizens are required to pay more for their visas than other nationalities.

CUSTOMS

Although Hong Kong remains a duty-free port, there are restrictions on the amount of alcohol, cigarettes, and perfumes you can bring into the country. Adults (18 and over) can import duty-free a maximum of 200 cigarettes or 50 cigars or 250 g of tobacco, plus a liter bottle of wine or spirits, 60 ml of perfume, and 250 ml of eau de toilette.

The import of animals or animal parts is strictly controlled. Firearms, narcotics, copyright-infringed goods, and products deriving from endangered animals, such as ivory or tiger skins, are prohibited. Firearms must be declared and handed into custody until departure.

Cars can be brought in for personal use without payment of duty.

There are no currency restrictions.

DRUGS & NARCOTICS

Although penalties for importation of drugs are not as harsh as some countries in Asia, they are still severe. You should clearly label medicines for personal use and obtain a statement from your doctor if you are bringing in a large amount of pharmaceuticals. For smaller amounts, bring a doctor's prescription.

HOW TO GET TO HONG KONG

AIRLINES

Hong Kong is a key regional hub for east Asia and is connected to all parts of the world by numerous airlines. The territory's chief airline is Cathay Pacific, which operates daily flights from London, Australia, Canada, Europe, and a few major U.S. cities—Los Angeles, New York JFK, and San Francisco. Hong Kong's second airline, Dragonair, has daily flights to numerous Chinese cities. From the United States, Continental and United are among the airlines offering regular scheduled flights. Qantas flies daily between Australia and Hong Kong.

The flight time from New York is 18 hours, from Los Angeles 15 hours, from London 13 hours, from Sydney 8 hours.

Useful numbers in Hong Kong

British Airways, tel 2822-9000 or 800-AIRWAYS
Cathay Pacific, tel 2747-1234 or 800-233-2742
Continental, tel 3198-5777
Qantas, tel 2842-1438 or 800-227-4500
United, tel 2810-4888 or 800-538-2929

AIRPORT

Hong Kong is served by Hong Kong International Airport at Chek Lap Kok, which opened on Lantau Island in 1998. It is 28 miles (45 km) from Central District on Hong Kong Island. About three-quarters of the

airport site was constructed on land reclaimed from the sea. The terminal building, designed by British architect Sir Norman Foster, is Hong Kong's single largest building. Its winglike roof and glass walls have been critically acclaimed as a landmark in modern architecture.

The fastest airport-to-city link is the Airport Express high-speed train, which runs at 15-minute intervals between 5:50 a.m. and 1:15 a.m. and takes under 25 minutes to the Central interchange on Hong Kong Island, where it connects directly with Hong Kong's subway system or Mass Transit Railway (MTR) at Hong Kong Station. Outside the station is a taxi rank. There is also a stop at Kowloon. You can check in your baggage at airline counters at Hong Kong station before boarding the train to the airport. One-way tickets cost HK$100 ($13) for adults and HK$50 ($6.40) for children. Return tickets, valid for a month, cost HK$180 ($23).

An airport bus operates every 15 minutes. It takes one hour to Central and costs HK$40 ($5).

Airport money exchange bureaus are open between 6 a.m. and 11 p.m. daily, but the exchange rates are on the low side. There are ATMs in the arrivals hall.

Departure tax, often included in airline fares, is HK$120 ($15). Security tax and fuel surcharges are also usually included in the air fares.

Because of the distance from the airport to the city, taxis are expensive and take longer than the train. Expect to pay HK$350 ($45) to Central District and HK$280 ($36) to Tsim Sha Tsui.

HOW TO GET TO MACAU

The **TurboJet Company** runs fast ferries from the Macau Ferry Terminal at the Shun Tak Center, 200 Connaught Road Central— above the Sheung Wan MTR station in Hong Kong's Western

District. Ferries run every 15 minutes from 7 a.m. to 1:45 a.m., Between 2:30 a.m. and 6 a.m., departures vary from 45 to 90 minutes. The trip takes about one hour and immigration procedures are efficient and speedy. You can buy tickets at the terminal just before your trip, although it is advisable to book on weekends. For inquiries tel 2859-3333, for reservations tel 2921-6688.

HeliExpress (tel 2108-4838) runs a half-hourly helicopter service between Hong Kong and Macau from 9 a.m. to 11 p.m. daily, departing from its helipad at the Shun Tak Center. It costs HK$1,700 ($219), including tax and insurance surcharge, one way and takes about 16 minutes.

HOW TO GET TO GUANGZHOU

Guangzhou is easily reached from Hong Kong in less than two hours by through-trains departing from Hong Kong KCR (Kowloon–Canton Railway) station in Kowloon. There are seven services a day and immigration procedures are efficient. Fares are HK$230 ($30) for premium class, HK$190 ($25) for first class, and HK$180 ($23) for standard class. For reservations and inquiries tel 2947-7888. Tickets can also be purchased from China Travel Services (tel 2789-5401) and travel agents.

GETTING AROUND

TRAVELING IN HONG KONG

BY CAR

Because of the limited opportunities for driving, car rental is not as common here as other major tourist destinations and is not a popular choice of transportation among visitors. It is also expensive. Renting a car for the day could cost you well over $100.

Visitors with a driver's license from their own country are permitted to rent and drive cars. Driving is on the left. Three road toll tunnels connect Hong Kong Island to Kowloon. Street parking in busy areas such as Central, Causeway Bay, and Kowloon can be very difficult, if not impossible, and traffic police are very vigilant in enforcing restrictions, but you can usually find room in the city's underground and covered parking lots.

Cars are banned on Lamma, Cheung Chau, and most other outlying islands, and movement restrictions operate on Lantau Island, where a bridge connects only with the airport.

It's against the law to drive or travel in a car, front or back, without wearing a safety belt. Hong Kong has a large number of motorcycle traffic police who diligently stop cars with unbelted occupants.

The police frequently set up road blocks to check for illegal immigrants, so you should carry your driver's license and passport at all times.

Drink-driving laws are enforced. As a rule, don't drive if you have drunk more than one pint of normal strength (5 percent alcohol by volume) draft beer, or two 200 ml glasses of wine, or one single measure of spirits.

Road atlases are widely available in bookstores.

Renting a car

The agent for Avis and Hertz car rental is: Tiglion Travel Services Limited, Yue Xiu Building, 160–174 Lockhart Rd., Wan Chai, Hong Kong
Tel (852) 2511-7189
Fax (852) 2519-7296
E-mail: travel@tiglion.com
Website: www.tiglion.com

BY PUBLIC TRANSPORTATION

Hong Kong has a highly efficient, inexpensive, and integrated public transportation system, combining government and private companies. Most times, you never have to wait more than a few minutes between rides.

Timetable information

Bus, train, and subway (known as the MTR—Mass Transit Railway) maps and timetables are available at Hong Kong Tourism Board (HKTB) offices (see p. 242) and bookstores.

Bus

Hong Kong has one of the world's largest fleets of double-decker buses in the world. On some roads in Central in the rush hours, traffic jams are caused solely by continuous walls of buses. Elsewhere they are often the quickest, cleanest, and most comfortable means of getting about.

All of the buses are air-conditioned—even in winter—so you should take a lightweight jacket for journeys of 20 minutes or more.

Double-decker services generally operate daily between 6 a.m. and midnight. Fares are posted on the counter beside the driver. You put the exact fare into a box, also beside the driver (no change is given) or wave your "Octopus" card (see p. 239) over a small electronic device. Many drivers speak little English.

In addition, fleets of 16-seater minibuses (called maxicabs in some areas) ply the main routes. Red minibuses run prescribed routes on Hong Kong Island and Kowloon. Green minibuses take the roads in the New Territories. They do not run to any timetable and they pick up and drop off passengers along the route— you have to shout to the driver when you want to get off. Some services between Hong Kong Island and Kowloon run all night.

The payment system varies. Change is given on red minibuses—you pay when leaving—while you are required to put the exact fare into a box next to the driver when you board a green minibus.

Trams

Hong Kong is one of only two places in the world still operating double-decker trams (the other place is the British seaside town of Blackpool). A journey on a tram is something every visitor should experience. Try to get a seat upstairs at the front. Tracks run from Kennedy Town in Western District to Shau Kei Wan at the eastern end of Hong Kong Island. Trams also run every few minutes to the racetrack at Happy Valley, from 6 a.m. to 1 a.m. daily. There is a flat fare of HK$2 for any distance. You enter at the rear of the tram and pay on leaving at the front by placing HK$2 in a box next to the driver. No change is given. Tours by open-top tram run twice daily, tel 2548-7102.

Peak Tram

A funicular tram, built in 1888, carries passengers up the steep mountainside to the Peak. The service operates daily from 7 a.m. to midnight at 15-minute intervals, and takes 12 minutes. You can return to the city by bus 15 to the Star Ferry terminus. A free shuttle bus connects the Star Ferry with the lower funicular tram station in Garden Road, Central.

Harbor ferries

Fleets of ferries crisscross Hong Kong's harbor, linking both Hong Kong Island and Kowloon with the outlying islands and satellite towns along the New Territories' coast.

The most famous ferry is the Star Ferry, which operates between the "Star" piers in Central District and Wan Chai on Hong Kong Island, and Tsim Sha Tsui and Hung Hom on Kowloon. The familiar olive-green-and-cream ferries, with burnished-wood interiors, run every five to ten minutes between 6:30 a.m. and 11:30 p.m. daily, and the trip takes eight minutes. A similar service runs between Tsim Sha Tsui and Wan Chai, and Central and Hung Hom at less regular intervals.

Ferries and hydrofoils operate regular services daily to the islands of Lamma, Lantau, Peng Chau, and Cheung Chau.

Journeys take up to an hour. A regular fast hydrofoil takes 25 minutes between Hong Kong Island and Discovery Bay on Lantau Island. All these ferries run from the Outlying Islands Ferry piers in front of the ifc building. For timetable information details of daily harbor tours, tel 2508-1234.

Mass Transit Railway (MTR)

This subway system has a number of routes linking Hong Kong Island and the Kowloon peninsula. The island line runs most of the length under the urban sprawl along the harborside of Hong Kong Island from Sheung Wan in the west to Wan Chai in the east. You can change to Kowloon lines at Admiralty and North Point stations. Services operate every few minutes from about 6 a.m. to about 1 a.m. daily. The system is fast, safe, and spotlessly clean.

Ticket-vending machines, with fare information, give change for coins, or you can change notes at station booths.

Trains

The Kowloon–Canton Railway (KCR) operates a service to the Hong Kong Special Administrative Region (SAR) border with China at Lo Wu from Hung Hom in Kowloon, a distance of 21 miles (34 km).

Trains run between five and ten minutes and more frequently during rush hours in each direction from about 6 a.m. until midnight. Tel 2947-7888.

Light Rail Transit (LTR)

This service runs along five routes in the western New Territories, connecting suburban areas between the new towns of Yuen Long and Tuen Mun between 5:30 a.m. to 12:30 a.m. A ferry service to Central District connects with the LTR at Yuen Long.

Ticket Information

Electronic "Octopus" stored-value, multiple-journey cards are interchangeable on the MTR, KCR, LTR, City Bus, Kowloon Motor Bus buses, and outlying islands ferries. You can purchase them in different denominations from booths at MTR and KCR stations. Pass the card over electronic processors to pay the fare.

Try to avoid rush hours (8 a.m.–10 a.m. and 5 p.m.–7 p.m.) as it can get very crowded, especially on the MTR and KCR.

Taxis

There are around 18,000 metered taxis in Hong Kong. Fares are low compared with most Western cities.

Red taxis operate on Hong Kong Island and Kowloon, but beyond the urban areas and on other islands they are green.

There's a surcharge of HK$20 for crossing the harbor via one of the tunnels. Taxis are not permitted to pick up or drop passengers where there is a yellow line along the roadside, usually in congested locations.

Most drivers speak a little English and will know the location of the major hotels and other destinations.

Taxi numbers are displayed on the dashboard. To lodge a complaint against a driver, tel 2527-7177.

To trace lost property, tel 2385-8288.

PRACTICAL ADVICE

COMMUNICATIONS

POST OFFICES

There are numerous post offices and smaller sub post offices, but these are sometimes hard to find and can be crowded. The main offices are adjacent to the Star Ferry Pier on Hong Kong Island and in Kowloon at 10 Middle Road. Both are open 8 a.m. to 6 p.m. Monday to Saturday and 8 a.m. to 2 p.m. on Sunday. Smaller offices close at 5 p.m. Monday to Friday and at 1 p.m. on Saturday, and are closed on Sunday and public holidays. For the locations of other offices, tel 2921-2222.

TELEPHONES

There is a large variety of public phones. They cost HK$1 for a five-minute local call. Some are coin only or card only, Others take both phone cards and credit cards. Stored-value phone cards for HK$50, HK$150, and HK$200 can be bought at convenience stores.

Local calls from private phones (not cellular) are free and Hong Kong people see it as their inalienable right to use phones in restaurants, bars, and stores free of charge for local use. Businesses will often put their phones in a convenient place for customers—and passersby—to use. Check with your supplier for cellphone compatibility. All Hong Kong phones numbers are eight digits and there are no area codes. To call Hong Kong from overseas, dial the international access code, then the country code 852 before the number.

To make collect calls, dial 10010. Directory inquiries, 1081. Overseas IDD and phone card inquiries: 10013.

CONVERSIONS

Although the British Imperial system still remains, Hong Kong uses the metric system for weights and measures.

Speed and distances are in kilometers:
1 mile = 1.6 km

Weights are in kilograms and tonnes:
1 kg = 2.2 lbs
1 tonne = 0.98 ton

Volumes are in liters:
1 liter = 1.75 pints

Temperatures are in centigrade:
0°C = 32°F

ELECTRICITY

All appliances operate at 220 volts. The standard plug connection is the British-style square three-pin, now used by all major hotels. Older buildings still use a mix of round two- and three-pin plugs. Adaptor plugs are widely available in stores and electrical goods shops.

HOLIDAYS

Banks, post offices, government offices, and most commercial offices close on Sundays and public holidays. Most shops, restaurants, and bars remain open, except during a few days over Chinese New Year—Hong Kong's quietest time of the year when many locals travel abroad. Dates vary from year to year, but usually fall mid-January to mid-February. Several other annual Chinese holidays are linked to the lunar calendar. Many Chinese shops operate as normal on Christmas Day.

The following are also established holidays:

January 1
    (New Year's Day)
January/February
    (Chinese New Year)
Late March/Early April
    (Good Friday, Easter
    Saturday, Easter Monday)
Early April
    (Ching Ming)
April/May
    (Buddha's Birthday)
May 1
    (Labor Day)
July 1
    (Hong Kong Establishment
    Day, marking the end of
    British colonial rule)
August 17
    (Sino-Japanese War
    Victory Day)
September
    (Mid-Autumn Festival)
October 1
    (China's National Day)
December 25
    (Christmas Day)
December 26
    (2nd Christmas Day)

LIQUOR LAWS

Hong Kong has very liberal rules. Alcohol can be bought virtually anywhere, from street stands and convenience stores to harbor ferries. It's possible to get a drink around the clock seven days a week. Many bars open from late morning until 3 a.m. the next day. It's illegal to sell alcohol to anyone under 18.

MEDIA

NEWSPAPERS

Hong Kong has a free and open media. There are two local English language daily newspapers, the *South China Morning Post* and *The Standard*. They carry local and international news and features, including sections devoted to English and European soccer and U.S. baseball, football, basketball, and hockey. The *Asian Wall Street Journal* is also published here. *The Post* gives special emphasis to events in mainland China. Several weekly free *What's On* guides are also widely distributed in bars and restaurants. There are numerous Chinese-language daily newspapers. Several regional weekly news magazines are based in Hong Kong, notably the *Far Eastern Economic Review*, *Time Asis*, and *Asiaweek*. International newspapers and magazines, including *U.S. Today* and the *International Herald Tribune*, can be found in bookstores and newsstands. Newsstands at the Star Ferry concourse in Tsim Sha Tsui have a huge selection of British, U.S., Australian, Canadian, Asian, and European newspapers.

RADIO

Thirteen stations offer music, news, and other entertainment on FM and AM bands. Most are Cantonese, but several have English services. The shortwave BBC World Service, with international news every hour on the hour, is retransmitted on a local medium wave frequency to provide excellent reception.

TELEVISION

There are two English-language free-access terrestrial television stations. Most hotels also provide numerous cable and satellite channels featuring CNN, CNBC, and BBC World, plus movie and sports channels.

MONEY MATTERS

The Hong Kong dollar is the unit of currency, pegged to the U.S. dollar (around HK$7.79 to US$1). The Hong Kong dollar is divided into 100 cents. Coins come in denominations of 10, 20, and 50 cents, and $1, $2, $5, and $10. Notes are in denominations of $10, $20, $50, $100, $500, and $1,000.

The notes come in three different types for each denomination and bear the names of three different banks: the Standard Chartered Banking Corporation, the Bank of China and the biggest, the Hong Kong and Shanghai Banking Corporation (HSBC).

Large bank branches, especially in the Hong Kong Island central business district, offer exchange services for travelers' checks and cash. There are currency exchange bureaus at the airport and in the main shopping districts frequented by foreign visitors, and their exchange rates are usually lower than banks. Both banks and exchange bureaus charge a commission. Ask what it is before exchanging.

Hotels will also exchange cash and travelers' checks for guests, and offer even lower rates than banks or exchange bureaus. However, you may have difficulty cashing the old US$50 and US$100 bills.

Local people increasingly do their personal banking via Automatic Teller Machines (ATMs) attached to banks. HSBC "Electronic Money" machines provide 24-hour cash withdrawal in local currency for Visa and MasterCard holders. American Express cardholders have access to Jetco (network

of Hong Kong banks) ATMs and can withdraw local currency and travelers' checks at the "Express Cash" ATMs.

A growing number of ATMs now belong to the Maestro and Cirrus networks.

OPENING TIMES

In many respects, Hong Kong is a 24-hour city. Shops and department stores open seven days. Most big stores will open about 10 a.m. and close at about 8 p.m. or 9 p.m. Smaller shops, especially in Kowloon and Causeway Bay, open until 11 p.m. or later. Some of the night markets are open until 11 p.m.

Major banks open 9 a.m. to 4:30 p.m. Monday to Friday and 9 a.m. to 12:30 p.m. on Saturday. Business hours are generally 9 a.m to 5 p.m. Monday to Friday and Saturday mornings.

Government offices open at 9 a.m. and close at 5 p.m Monday to Friday and at noon or 1 p.m. on Saturday. Some close from 1 to 2 p.m.

Most shops and stores open on weekends and public holidays, except for a few days at Chinese New Year, but banks, post offices, and government offices close.

RELIGION

The main religions in Hong Kong are Buddhism and Taoism, but there is also a sizable number of Christians. Muslims count for around 80,000, while there are smaller groups of Hindus, Sikhs, and Jews.

PLACES OF WORSHIP

Catholic Cathedral of the Immaculate Conception, 16 Caine Rd., Mid Levels, Hong Kong Island, tel 2522-8212

Anglican Dioceses of Hong Kong, 1 Lower Albert Rd., Central, tel 2526-5335

Islam Union of Hong Kong, Osman Ramju Sadick Islamic Center, 40 Oi Kwan Rd., Wan Chai, tel 2575-2218

Jewish Cultural Center and Synagogue 1 Robinson Place, 70 Robinson Road, Mid Levels, tel 2801-5440

TIME DIFFERENCES

The difference from Greenwich Mean Time (GMT) is +8 hours in winter and +7 in summer.

From New York the time difference is +13 hours.

From Los Angeles the time difference is +16 hours.

Hong Kong does not observe daytime saving.

TIPPING

Hong Kong is not a tipping town. Most hotels and upscale restaurants add a 10 percent service charge to their bills, so tipping is redundant. In places that don't, a tip of less than 10 percent can be left at your discretion, depending on the level of service given. In small cafés and bars, leaving a few coins in the check tray is normal practice. In taxis, simply round up the fare to the nearest dollar.

TOURS

The Hong Kong Tourism Board (see p. 242), in conjunction with a number of tour operators, offers excellent tours, and it's worth joining a few if time is limited. The Land Between tour offers a snapshot of the New Territories. A heritage tour will take you to temples, walled villages, and ancestral halls. There's also a trip to Lantau and its beaches, a fishing village, and the Po Lin Monastery. You can choose from a variety of day and nighttime harbor cruises, a quick flight over Hong Kong in a helicopter, or even hire a stretch limo with chauffeur to guide you to the sights in style.

TRAVELERS WITH DISABILITIES

Many modern buildings provide wheelchair access, but older buildings can be more difficult.

Most of the top hotels have facilities for people with disabilities, but it's a good idea to give them advance notice. Getting around Hong Kong's crowded streets in a wheelchair can be a nightmare. Some taxi drivers are helpful, but forget public transportation.

VISITOR INFORMATION

The Hong Kong Tourism Board (HKTB) has three visitor centers, as well as an English-language telephone information service (tel 2508-1234), which operates from 8 a.m. to 6 p.m. daily. The offices have plenty of travel brochures and will arrange tours, as will hotels.

Airport
In the arrival halls and transfer section. Literature available 24 hours. Face-to-face inquiries between 7 a.m. and 10 p.m. daily.

Kowloon
At the Star Ferry terminal, 8 a.m. to 6 p.m. daily.

Hong Kong Island
The Center, 1st floor, 99 Queen's Rd. Central. Open 8 a.m. to 6 p.m. daily.

TOURIST OFFICES ABROAD
The HKTB has offices in a number of countries. Some main addresses:

United States
115 East 54th St.
New York, NY 10022
Tel 212/421-3382
Fax 212/421-8428

10940 Wilshire Blvd.
Suite 2050
Los Angeles, CA 90024
Tel 310/208-4582
Fax 310/208-1869

United Kingdom
6 Grafton St.
London W1S 4EQ
Tel 020/7533-7100
Fax 020/7533-7111

EMERGENCIES IN HONG KONG

CONSULATES

United States
26 Garden Rd., Hong Kong Island, tel 2523-9011

Canada
14th floor, One Exchange Sq., Central, Hong Kong Island, tel 2810-4321

United Kingdom
1 Supreme Court Rd., (opposite the Conrad International Hotel), Hong Kong Island, tel 2901-3000

Australia
23rd–24th floors, Harbor Center, 25 Harbor Rd., Wan Chai, tel 2827-8881

EMERGENCY PHONE NUMBERS

For police, fire, or ambulance services, tel 999

MEDICAL SERVICES
On Hong Kong Island:
Queen Mary Hospital, Pokfulam Rd., tel 2855-3838

In Kowloon: Queen Elizabeth Hospital, 30 Gascoigne Rd., tel 2958-8888

The following hospitals have 24-hour services:

Caritas Medical Center, 111 Wing Hung St., Sham Shui Po, Kowloon, tel 3408--7911

Prince of Wales Hospital, 30–32 Ngan Shing St., Sha Tin, New Territories, tel 2645-1222

Queen Mary Hospital, 102 Pokfulam Rd., Hong Kong, tel 2855-3111

LOST OR STOLEN CREDIT CARDS AND TRAVELERS' CHECKS
American Express, tel 2811-6122
Diners Card, tel 2860-1888
MasterCard, tel 800-966677
Visa, tel 800-900 782

HEALTH

No special precautions or inoculations are necessary before visiting. Tap water and iced water in hotels is considered safe, but visitors may choose to drink only bottled water.

Visitors are not covered by the government health service and are advised to obtain medical insurance before traveling. Most government hospitals provide 24-hour emergency outpatient treatment services for a modest charge, but they can be crowded. Most large hotels can summon a doctor at short notice.

If you need to take quantities of prescribed drugs for medical reasons you should carry a letter from your doctor at home to verify that they are for your own use only. This can be presented to customs or immigration authorities if necessary.

Hong Kong's outlying islands and nature trails are plagued with mosquitoes, especially during the hot, humid summer months. They are most active at dusk, and although nonmalarial, can cause severe itching to sensitive skin. It's advisable to cover up as much as possible or use a roll-on or spray repellent.

In hot, humid weather, drink plenty of bottled water if you are walking or hiking. Also wear a sunscreen (SPF 15 and above), as the subtropical sun can burn skin very quickly, even in cloudy conditions.

SAFETY

Hong Kong is a very safe city, and there is usually no problem walking in most parts of the city at any time of night and day—even for women. Violent crime against visitors is virtually non-existent. Because of its small size and large police force, cops on the beat are seen regularly, and if you get into trouble, it should not be difficult to find one. As anywhere, don't leave bags or luggage unattended in public places. Pickpockets sometimes haunt the MTR and crowded night markets.

HOTELS & RESTAURANTS

Hong Kong hotels used to be among the most expensive in the world. Thankfully, those days are gone and now there are some great deals to be had. Of course, you can always spend a small fortune and be treated like royalty at some, but the bulk offer efficient service and quality facilities for a reasonable price.

Hong Kong is famed throughout Asia for its restaurants, notably its Cantonese cuisine. Being a cosmopolitan place, there are also hundreds of other excellent dining options from around the world. But don't expect to find too many bargains—when it comes to restaurants, Hong Kong is expensive.

HOTELS

A few years back, some Hong Kong establishments with little more than basic facilities were not afraid to ask US$200 or more a night. A glut of rooms and the fall off in visitor numbers after the 1997 handover to China forced many mid-range hotels to drop their prices substantially. This, coupled with the increasing numbers of tourists from mainland China, who simply couldn't afford the prices being asked, brought room rates down even further. While no means the bargain center of Asia for hotels, Hong Kong offers some pretty good deals if you shop around.

Expect exceptional service and quality in the best hotels, but be prepared to pay for it. These are often found in the Central and Admiralty Districts on Hong Kong Island, and along the waterfront across the harbor in Tsim Sha Tsui.

Less expensive and budget-priced hotels—many of which offer excellent service and accommodations—tend to be in districts such as Western, Causeway Bay, farther up the Kowloon Peninsula and in the New Territories. Because of Hong Kong's excellent transportation system, all are within easy reach of the main tourist areas.

As a general rule, don't expect big guest rooms in mid-range and budget hotels. Like Hong Kong apartments, they are often small and some are downright pokey.

Start your search for a hotel before you visit. The Hong Kong Hotel Association has an excellent and comprehensive website at www.hkta.org/hkha/. It lists all its member hotels and provides links to their websites. Making reservations online will bring substantial savings with some hotels and many give big discounts for stays of seven days or longer, but you will need to ask for them. Most hotels will add a 10 percent service charge and a 3 percent government tax to the bill.

There are some excellent-value accommodations in neighboring Macau, where prices for food and lodging can be as much as a third less than in Hong Kong.

Most big hotels have decent restaurants; ones that are worth a special trip (and their own entry) have been noted with a restaurant icon beneath the hotel icon.

RESTAURANTS

Hong Kong has the highest per capita ratio of restaurants in the world. Many visitors come to Hong Kong primarily to savor Chinese cuisine, which is overwhelmingly Cantonese, but they will also find a wealth of other cooking styles—from within Southeast and east Asia and from other parts of the world.

Hong Kong is not a particularly cheap place to eat out. Food is of a consistently high standard, but don't expect bargain prices, although many have daily lunch and dinner specials that can cut a decent slice off your bill. Annoyingly, Hong Kong restaurants and bars seem to make little distinction in price between alcoholic and nonalcoholic drinks, so don't look too surprised if a watered-down glass of cola sets you back

PRICES

HOTELS
An indication of the cost of a double room without breakfast in U.S. dollars is given by $ signs.

$$$$$	Over $400
$$$$	$300–$400
$$$	$200–$300
$$	$100–$200
$	Under $100

RESTAURANTS
An indication of the cost of a three-course dinner without drinks in U.S. dollars is given by $ signs.

$$$$$	Over $90
$$$$	$60–$90
$$$	$35–$60
$$	$20–$35
$	Under $20

US$7–8 at some establishments. The mark-up on wine can be astounding, especially in the upscale places.

Macau is a special treat, offering not only Portuguese dishes but also the unique Macanese style—a fusion of cuisines evolved over the past 400 years from Portugal's colonial empire. It incorporates elements of Cantonese, Portuguese, Indian, Malaccan, and African.

Cantonese cuisine emphasizes freshness, and menus often reflect what was bought that day from the numerous markets. Fish and other seafood is often kept alive and on view in the restaurants to be cooked to order.

Restaurants typically open for lunch about 11:30 a.m. and close about 3 p.m. They reopen again about 6 p.m. for dinner and close about 11 p.m. A 10 percent service charge added to the bill means you don't need to leave a tip.

Many of the restaurants listed in the following pages are well patronized, especially during lunch from 1–2 p.m. and in the evening, so make reservations.

HOTELS & RESTAURANTS

ADDITIONAL INFORMATION

Many hotels and restaurants accept all major credit cards. Smaller ones may accept only some, as indicated in each entry. Abbreviations used are: AE American Express, DC Diners Club, D Discover, MC MasterCard, and V Visa.

L = lunch
D = dinner

The hotels and restaurants have been arranged alphabetically by price range within each district.

HONG KONG ISLAND NORTH

CENTRAL

🏨 MANDARIN ORIENTAL
$$$$$
5 CONNAUGHT RD.
TEL 2522-0111
FAX 2810-6190
Service and room quality are what you would expect from one of the very top hotels in Hong Kong. It has 40 suites, four bars—notably the wood-paneled Chinnery—and four restaurants, including the renowned Vong, which serves French-Asian fusion cuisine. The indoor swimming pool resembles Roman baths.
🛏 542 P 🔁 🚫 🔲
🗱 🖋 🅰 All major cards

🏨 RITZ-CARLTON
🍴 $$$$$
3 CONNAUGHT RD.
TEL 2877-6666
FAX 2877-6778
Luxury and outstanding service combine with a prime position amid the gleaming banking towers and skyscrapers of Central. Some rooms have views of Victoria Harbor, while heavy mahogany and walnut furnishings blend with fine Asian artifacts. There are two bars and five restaurants, including the intriguing **Shanghai Shanghai** (see this page).

🛏 216 P 🔁 🚫 🔲
🗱 🖋 🅰 All major cards

🏨 BISHOP LEI INTERNATIONAL
$$
4 ROBINSON RD.
TEL 2868-0828
FAX 2868-1551
Bishop Lei is a quiet hotel in the residential district above Central with excellent views of the downtown skyline and harbor. More than one-third of the accommodations are suites. The Terrace Room restaurant has a large open-air terrace. Free shuttle services run to the main tourist areas.
🛏 203 🔁 🚫 🔲 🗱
🖋 🅰 All major cards

🍴 VONG
$$$$$
MANDARIN ORIENTAL
5 CONNAUGHT RD.
TEL 2825-4028
Both food and decor are part of a bold attempt to blend Asian and French styles. Seafood dominates. Lobster in Thai herbs and crab spring rolls with a tamarind dip are favorites. Ask about the "black plate"—a selection of richly sauced appetizers. Emphasis is placed on stylish presentation, but portions can be small for the price. Attractive separate menu for vegetarians.
🍴 120 P Central Station
🚫 🔲 🅰 All major cards

🍴 LE TIRE BOUCHON
$$$$
45 GRAHAM ST.
TEL 2523-5459
This stand-alone French restaurant on a steep quiet street away from the line of rival eateries has a spacious yet romantic setting. House specialties include baked goat cheese salad, pan-fried duck liver with apple and calvados, and a tender chateaubriand. Vintage French wines complement the food.
🍴 60 🚫 🔲 🅰 All major cards

🍴 SHANGHAI SHANGHAI
$$$$
RITZ-CARLTON
3 CONNAUGHT RD.
TEL 2869-0328
A serious attempt to replicate a club-restaurant of the decadent 1920s era in Shanghai can be found in the basement of the Ritz-Carlton. The menu has Cantonese elements as much as Shanghainese. One of the house specialties is drunken chicken, made to a Cantonese recipe with a generous dash of chardonnay. Shanghainese dishes include fish tail in brown sauce and braised noodles with chicken. The nightly musical show begins at 9:30 p.m., best accompanied by a dessert of lotus roots in fragrant osmanthus honey.
🍴 90 P 🚫 🔲 🅰 All major cards

🍴 SOHO SOHO
$$$$
43 LYNDHUST TER.
TEL 2147-2618
Soho Soho's owners seek to persuade the world the British can cook more than fish and chips and soggy vegetables. So-called Modern British is offered—a fusion of traditionally solid English dishes with lighter Mediterranean touches, such as roast lamb in pepper and spinach, and calves' liver and bacon with tomato relish. British desserts include toffee pudding and treacle tart, to name just two.
🍴 55 🚫 🔲 🅰 All major cards

🍴 HUNAN GARDEN
$$$
THE FORUM, 3RD FLOOR
EXCHANGE SQ.
TEL 2868-2880
It may be in a modern glass-and-concrete tower block, but the indoor waterfall, bright marble decor, and musicians playing the traditional pipa and erdu (at dinner only) all help to transport diners back to the home province of the

late Chairman Mao. Hunan cuisine, which is richer and in some cases more spicy than Cantonese, is not so common in Hong Kong. House specialties include Hunan ham with a hint of sweetness, mashed chicken in bamboo soup, eels in garlic sauce, and spicy vegetable rolls. Chinese rice wine is available.
🔲 80 🆂 Central Station
💱 📶 All major cards

JIMMY'S KITCHEN
$$$
SOUTH CHINA BUILDING
1–3 WYNDHAM ST.
TEL 2526-5293
Jimmy's is an essential part of Hong Kong for many residents, and it's been around for 70 years. Its English pub-like ambience and decor, such as mock Elizabethan beams and gleaming brasses, belie the excellent British-oriented cooking, with Chinese touches. Regular dishes include oysters kilpatrick and black pepper steak. A specialty is the noted seafood mixed grill. Regulars usually leave room for the solidly English bread-and-butter pudding. Good wine selection from Europe and elsewhere. It's best to make reservations, especially at lunch time.
🔲 46 🆂 💱 📶 All major cards

KIKU
$$$
13 BASEMENT
THE LANDMARK
TEL 2521-3344
A business haunt in the heart of Hong Kong's financial district, hence the privacy screens between tables. The problem of attracting service is overcome by the use of summon-buttons on each table. Benkay is noted for its fresh and very fishy sushi, beef shabu shabu, and clear clam soup. Ginseng wine is available.
🔲 120 🆂 Central Station
💱 📶 Citibank

🔲 LUK YU TEA HOUSE
No modern reproductions here: The early 20th-century art deco, stained glass, wood paneling, and ceiling fans are genuine. The ambience is busy and loud, but customers seeking some privacy can reserve a partitioned booth. Cantonese cuisine includes shark's fin and bird's-nest soups, and prawns stir-fried with Chinese mushrooms and bamboo shoots. Dim sum is also served. Wine is very limited, but most customers drink beer or tea.
$$$
LUK TEA BUILDING
24 STANLEY ST.
TEL 2523-1970
🔲 76 🆂 💱 📶 All major cards

🔲 M AT THE FRINGE
$$$
2 Lower Albret Road
Central
TEL 0852 2813-6262
Michelle Garnaut's restaurant has been delighting Hong Kong patrons for almost 15 years. The restaurants' gorgeous design naturally complements a delicious European menu, one of the highlights of which is the slowly baked salt-encased leg of lamb with grilled aubergine, roasted pumpkin, beans, and potatoes.
🔲 tk 🕐 tk 🆂 tk 💱 tk 📶 tk

🔲 ORANGE TREE
$$$
17 SHELLEY ST.
TEL 2838-9352
Dutch owner-chef Pieter Onderwater cooks up an interesting range of European and Oriental dishes, served in a small clubby setting alongside Hong Kong Island's Mid-Levels escalator. Most fish and the smoked eel are imported from Onderwater's homeland, while smoked duck with

mango suggests a more exotic origin than the Netherlands. Vegetarians are well catered for with dishes such as globe artichoke stuffed with asparagus. In spring or fall, try to reserve one of the two tables on the tiny balcony overlooking the escalator.
🔲 50 🆂 Central Station
💱 📶 All major cards

🔲 WYNDHAM STREET THAI
$$$
60 WYNDHAM ST.
TEL 2869-6216
Upscale Thai restaurant where concern for fresh ingredients is underlined by the daily changing blackboard menu. The practice of importing Thai herbs, fresh peppers, and chilis by air is reflected in the prices. Salad of pomelo fruit and herbs is a tangy starter. Cast aside the heavier coconut-based curries and order lightly steamed red emperor fish in sweet and sour sauce.
🔲 36 🕐 Closed Sun. L 🆂 💱 📶 All major cards

🔲 YUNG KEE
$$$
32–40 WELLINGTON ST.
TEL 2522-1624
This boisterous institution in Cantonese cooking was established in the 1940s. Roast goose is such a renowned specialty that the Yung Kee sells 300 birds every day. There's a constantly changing large menu that also caters for vegetarians. Dim sum served in the afternoon.
🔲 120 🆂 💱 📶 All major cards

🔲 STAUNTON'S WINE BAR & CAFÉ
$$
10–12 STAUNTON ST.
TEL 2973-6611
This hip restaurant, bar, and meeting place, nestling alongside the Mid-Levels escalator, is a perfect place to see Hong Kong and be seen. Popular with expats and trendy local

Chinese, expect reasonably priced fine wines and nouveau cuisine—without the small portions.

🛏 60 ⬛ 🅢 🅢 All major cards

🍽 2 SARDINES
$$
43 ELGIN ST.
TEL 2973-6618
A Mediterranean air pervades this small, friendly bistro in SoHo, beside the Mid-Level escalator. Sardines and other fish are the mainstay here, together with crisp vegetables and salads with the rich flavors of olive oil, capers, and thyme. Small selection of reasonably priced European wines.

🛏 25 🅢 🅢 🅢 All major cards

🍽 GREENLANDS
$
64–66 WELLINGTON ST.
CENTRAL
TEL 2893-0587
Rich sauces and tangy flavors are the bedrock at this small, popular Indian restaurant. In addition to the menu choices, the chefs produce excellent-value buffet lunches and dinners every weekday. It gets busy here, so reservations are recommended.

🛏 35 🅢 🅢 🅢 All major cards

ADMIRALTY

🏨 CONRAD
🍽 INTERNATIONAL
$$$$$
PACIFIC PLACE
TEL 2521-3838
FAX 2521-3888
The 61-story Conrad towers above the Pacific Place shopping mall. Rooms are large and tastefully decorated in neutral colors. The hotel has five restaurants, including the Brasserie On The Eighth and the highly regarded **Nicholini's** (see opposite).

🛏 513 🅟 🔄 🅢 🅢
🌊 🍷 🅢 All major cards

🏨 ISLAND SHANGRI-LA
The Shangri-la is one of Hong Kong's most luxurious hotels, providing stunning views over the city and the harbor while ideally located above the Pacific Place shopping mall. The rooms are among the largest in Hong Kong and many open onto a dramatic interior atrium rising 17 floors through the heart of the hotel. There are 34 suites, four bars, and seven restaurants, including a lobster bar. The Cyrano Bar, on the 56th floor, offers live music and cocktails with sunset views.

$$$$$
PACIFIC PLACE
SUPREME COURT RD.
TEL 2877-3838
FAX 2521-8742

🛏 565 🅟 🔄 🅢 🅢
🌊 🍷 🅢 All major cards

🏨 JW MARRIOTT
🍽 $$$$
1 PACIFIC PLACE
TEL 2810-8366
FAX 2845-0737
Located above the Pacific Place shopping mall, the Marriott offers views across Victoria Harbor to Kowloon from most of its spacious, well-appointed rooms. The Cigar Bar is a haunt of leading Hong Kong businessmen. Five restaurants, including **Man Ho** (see opposite), serve everything from Californian-Asian fusion cuisine to sushi.

🛏 602 🅟 🔄 🅢 🅢
🌊 🍷 🅢 All major cards

🍽 BRASSERIE ON THE EIGHTH
$$$$$
CONRAD INTERNATIONAL
PACIFIC PLACE
TEL 2521-3838
The high-class French cuisine here mixes traditional dishes such as braised oxtail stew or French fish soup, and new lighter creations such as scallops with sesame seeds.

Save space for *oeufs à la neige*—poached meringue. The ambience is formal but warm.

🛏 76 🅟 🕐 Closed Sat. L
🅢 🅢 🅢 All major cards

🍽 NICHOLINI'S
$$$$$
CONRAD INTERNATIONAL
PACIFIC PLACE
TEL 2521-3838
An elegant Italian restaurant with panoramic views across the harbor and Kowloon Peninsula. Dishes reflect top chef Giovanni Greggio's home region of Verona, but with slightly more extravagance— try the panfried goose liver in a caviar and champagne sauce, for example. Fish dishes are prominent, such as Venetian-style calamari and baked sea bass with eggplants and olives. The pasta is freshly made on the premises and the cheeses and wines are mostly Italian. Service is impeccable.

🛏 110 🅟 🅢 🅢 🅢 All major cards

🍽 MAN HO
$$$$
JW MARRIOTT
1 PACIFIC PLACE

TEL 2841-3853
It's worth visiting just for the renowned tea-smoked pigeon, but the braised duck with lotus roots in a rich sauce equally reflects a high-quality Chinese menu. The restaurant is busy at lunchtime, but good table spacing and a decor dominated by the color gold help create a relaxed atmosphere most of the time.
🔁 80 🚭 ❄ 🅲 All major cards

🍴 ZEN
$$$
THE MALL, LOWER GROUND FLOOR
PACIFIC PLACE
TEL 2845-4555
Very much Westernized Cantonese, the Zen is modeled on its namesake founded in London many years ago. It's extremely busy at lunchtime when lines form just to buy takeouts. Specialties include sliced pork rolls and deep fried boneless chicken wings stuffed with vegetables and served with a lemon sauce. Dim sum is cooked to order.
🔁 86 🚭 ❄ 🅲 All major cards

🍴 CHIU CHOW GARDEN
$$
GROUND FLOOR
LIPPO CENTER
TEL 2845-4151
The best Chinese restaurants are noisy, frenetic places, and here the clatter is accompanied by bright decor and swinging red lanterns. Specialties include poached cold crab, sliced soy goose with bean curd, and minced pork wrapped in olive leaves with fried green beans. Chiu Chow boasts some of the cheapest restaurant wines. Ask for a window table overlooking busy Queensway, where even the old trams seem to be in a hurry.
🔁 140 🚭 ❄ 🅲 All major cards

🍴 DUBLIN JACK
$$
37 COCHRANE ST.
TEL 2543-0081
This authentic Irish bar offers more than just a wide selection of premium Scotches and whiskeys, and beers on tap. Expect lush stew, bangers and mash, and the undisputed best fry-up in town.
🔁 68 🚭 🅲 All major cards

🍴 LA CITE
$$
LOWER GROUND FLOOR
PACIFIC PLACE
TEL 2522-8830
Great people-watching location if you secure a table "outside" in the so-called courtyard of the airy but covered shopping mall. This French-style bistro is ideal for a shopping expedition lunch, with a large selection of sandwiches, salads, soups, and desserts.
🔁 70 🚭 ❄ 🅲 All major cards

LAN KWAI FONG

🍴 VA BENE
$$$$
58 D'AGUILAR ST.
TEL 2845-5577
One of Hong Kong's very best Italian restaurants, matched by an extensive Italian wine cellar. Fish dishes are prominent— pan-roasted garoupa in white wine and garlic, for example— but meat lovers and vegetarians are also well catered for. Beef tenderloin carpaccio is a house specialty and one of chef Pino Piano's personal favorites.
🔁 60 🚭 ❄ 🅲 All major cards

🍴 CAFÉ DES ARTISTES
$$$
30–32 D'AGUILAR ST.
TEL 2526-3880
Wicker furniture adds to the relaxed atmosphere in this Parisian-style café. The menu changes with the seasons. Try

the pumpkin and carrot soup, pan-roasted duck breasts in brandy, or matador-grilled beef with wild mushrooms.
🔁 40 🚭 ❄ 🅲 All major cards

🍴 INDOCHINE 1929
$$$
CALIFORNIA TOWER,
2ND FLOOR
D'AGUILAR ST.
TEL 2869-7399
The mock French colonial style belies the top-quality Vietnamese cuisine. Dishes range from the more French-influenced Hanoi style, to the spicier offerings of Ho Chi Minh City. Fish is prominent, but the beef noodle soup is highly recommended. Try the house specialty—soft shell crab cooked in garlic. French wines dominate.
🔁 60 🚭 ❄ 🅲 All major cards

🍴 POST 97
$$$
COSMOS BUILDING
9–11 LAN KWAI FONG
TEL 2186-1816
Taking its name from the British handover of Hong Kong to China in 1997, this haunt of trendy youthful Westerners and Chinese serves British-style food, but enlivened with Mediterranean and Southeast Asian influences. Rack of lamb with homemade ravioli and wild mushrooms, breasts of quail with artichokes, and cheesecake made with Baileys creamed whiskey are just a few specialties.
🔁 48 🚭 ❄ 🅲 All major cards

🍴 RED PEPPER
$$$
7 LAN FONG RD.
TEL 2577-3811
Spicy Sichuan cuisine that caters as much to vegetarians as meat-eaters. A popular choice is sizzling fried prawns in chili sauce delivered in a hot pan. Fragrant lychee tea complements the food.

HOTELS & RESTAURANTS

🛏️50 🔲 🔲 All major cards

🍴 THAI LEMON GRASS

$$$
BASEMENT
30–32 D'AGUILAR ST.
TEL 2905-1688

More subtle Thai food, less fiery than elsewhere, is served in an elegant, warm atmosphere. The emphasis here is on seafood—whole fish such as mullet gently simmered in ginger and herbs. Other specialties include crayfish coconut salad and steamed prawns with lemon grass.

🛏️46 🔲 🔲 All major cards

🍴 BEIRUT

$$
27 D'AGUILAR ST.
TEL 2804-6611

A crowded but cheerful Lebanese restaurant specializing in meze dishes (small servings similar to Spanish tapas, including minced eggplant, hummus and falafel), making it a popular haunt of vegetarians. Try one of the legume-loaded dips as a main course. Meat-eaters can tuck into generous portions of spicy shawarma lamb. There's a Lebanese vintage wine list.

🛏️48 🕐 Closed Sun. from 4 p.m. 🔲 🔲 All major cards

VICTORIA PEAK

🍴 THE PEAK LOOKOUT

$$$$
121 PEAK RD.
TEL 2849-1000

This restaurant with a view features a seafood and oyster bar as well as an open-air barbecue. Expect regional specialties such as satay and Hunan chicken rice as well as Western fare, like Sunday roast. There is also a children's menu. Expect, however, to pay the price of high-rent realty.

🛏️90 🔲 🔲 All major cards

WESTERN DISTRICT

🏨 HARBOR PLAZA RESORT CITY

$
18 TIN YAN RD.
TIN SHUI WAI
TEL 2180-6688
FAX 2180-6333

Large and somewhat anonymous hotel that compensates with spacious accommodations. Self-sufficiency facilities available. There are 38 suites and several bars and restaurants. Good connections to downtown Tsim Sha Tsui by road and subway.

🛏️1,102 🅿️ 🔲 🔲 🔲 All major cards

🏨 ISLAND PACIFIC

$
152 CONNAUGHT RD. WEST
TEL 2131-1188
FAX 2131-1212

One of Hong Kong's newest waterfront hotels lies in an old and fascinating part of town, full of Chinese dried food stores. Rooms have a modern feel and full-length windows treat guests to outstanding harbor views. The tram line runs by and there's a free shuttle bus service. Island Pacific has an all-day café-bar.

🛏️346 🅿️ 🔲 🔲 🔲 All major cards

WAN CHAI

🏨 GRAND HYATT

🍴 $$$$
1 HARBOR RD.
TEL 2588-1234
FAX 2802-0677

The Grand Hyatt lies in a prime location adjoining the harborfront Hong Kong Convention and Exhibition Center. It's worth a visit just for the art deco opulence in its lobby. Sumptuous rooms and suites have feather down duvets covered in Egyptian cotton bed linen. There are seven different dining choices, from Grissini—serving fine Italian cuisine—to the Japanese **Kaetsu** (see this page).

🛏️570 🅿️ 🔲 🔲 🔲 🔲 🔲 🔲 All major cards

🏨 RENAISSANCE HARBOR VIEW

$$$
1 HARBOR RD.
TEL 2802-8888
FAX 2802-8833

This large non-descript Marriott-group hotel stands on the Wan Chai waterfront, linked to the Hong Kong Convention and Exhibition Center. It offers excellent service, modern, well-appointed rooms, and fantastic harbor views, as well as landscaped gardens with rock gardens and waterfalls. Dining choices include Italian at the Scala restaurant and Cantonese at the Dynasty.

🛏️860 🅿️ 🔲 🔲 🔲 🔲 🔲 All major cards

🏨 CENTURY HONG 🍴 KONG

$$
238 JAFFE RD.
TEL 2598-8888
FAX 2598-8866

The Century is an international standard hotel located close to the main shopping and nightlife areas., popular among business travelers and convention delegates. It has 24 suites, two bars, and two restaurants, most notably, **Lao Ching Hing** (see this page). Causeway Bay is only minutes away on foot, while the nightlife scene of Wan Chai is even closer.

🛏️516 🅿️ 🔲 🔲 🔲 🔲 🔲 All major cards

🏨 EMPIRE HONG KONG

$$
33 HENNESSEY RD.
TEL 2866-9111
FAX 2861-3121

Situated in the heart of the vibrant Wan Chai nightlife district and close to shopping and business areas, this well-appointed property is popular, with 36 suites and two restaurants, one of them serving Shanghainese. The Empire Brew Pub serves a wide selection of bottled and draft beers.

(i) 345 **P** 🛗 Ⓢ 🅰
🏊 🕎 🅲 All major cards

🏨 **WESLEY**
$$
22 HENNESSEY RD.
TEL 2866-6688
FAX 2866-6633
The Wesley stands on the very busy night-and-day Hennessy Road in the heart of Wan Chai District. This is a popular choice for budget tourists with smallish rooms but reasonable rates. Try asking for an upgrade when you make your reservation.

(i) 251 🛗 Ⓢ 🅰 🅲 All major cards

🏨 **CHARTERHOUSE**
$
209–219 WAN CHAI RD.
TEL 2833-5566
FAX 2833-5888
This attractive boutique hotel, midway between the main shopping and entertainment districts of Causeway Bay and Wan Chai, offers six suites, a restaurant, and two bars. Soft colors and dark timber furniture give the rooms a warm, cozy feel. Avoid the Nightingale if you don't like karaoke.

(i) 277 **P** 🛗 Ⓢ 🅰
🕎 🅲 All major cards

🏨 **WHARNEY**
$
57–73 LOCKHART RD.
TEL 2861-1000
FAX 2865-6023
If you want to be among the thick of things in the neon nightlife of Lockhart Road, you can't get much closer. Prices are reasonable, but rooms are small and somewhat shabby.

(i) 361 **P** 🛗 Ⓢ 🅰
🕎 🅲 All major cards

🍴 **KAETSU**
$$$$$
GRAND HYATT
1 HARBOR RD.
TEL 2588-1234 EXT. 7088

Hong Kong's most upscale Japanese dining venue. Tables are arranged in private booths around a central sushi bar. The sushi, along with scallop sashimi, is the best you'll find anywhere. Ingredients are specially flown in from Japan and the menu changes with the seasons. The Kaetsu's set course of nine dishes is a good bet. There is a comprehensive sake menu, offering warm or cold varieties.

🍴 90 **P** Ⓢ 🅰 🅲 All major cards

🍴 **AMERICAN PEKING**
$$$
20 LOCKHART RD.
TEL 2527-1000
A local institution since 1948, serving Peking cuisine in a bright and boisterous setting on two floors. Beggar's chicken is an old favorite, but has to be ordered a day in advance. It consists of chicken stuffed with vegetables, shredded mushrooms, and a little pork, marinated for two hours then wrapped in lotus leaves and baked. For dessert, try the soufflé balls and red bean stuffing.

🍴 140 Ⓢ 🅰 🅲 All major cards

🍴 **HK LAO SHANG HAI**
$$$
CENTURY HONG KONG
238 JAFFE RD.
TEL 2827-9339
The entrance to this large Shanghainese establishment is guarded by large clay pots in which Chinese rice wine is maturing. Several vintage varieties feature on the wine list. Try the drunken Shanghai crab marinated in Chinese wine, spiced duck, or lightly stir-fried freshwater shrimps.

🍴 160 Ⓢ 🅰 🅲 All major cards

🍴 **LIU YUAN**
$$$
303 HENNESSY RD.
TEL 2510-0483

The appeal of Liu Yuan's Shanghainese dishes regularly attracts visitors from Shanghai. Crispy eel is a favorite, along with shredded dried bean curd with ham and chicken sauce. The sesame dessert dumplings are extremely popular.

🍴 90 Ⓢ 🅰 🅲 All major cards

🍴 **EIGHTEEN BROOK**
$$
CONVENTION PLAZA,
8TH FLOOR
1 HARBOR RD.
TEL 2827-8802
Cantonese style cuisine but with a slightly spicy and nouveau twist is served in a modern, elegant setting in a glass-and-concrete tower block. Specialties include sauteed shrimp with spices mixed with bamboo shoots, radish, celery, and chilis.

🍴 90 Ⓢ 🅰 🅲 All major cards

🍴 **VICEROY**
$$
SUN HUNG KAI CENTER,
2ND FLOOR
30 HARBOR RD.
TEL 2827-7777
A rich mix of south and Southeast Asian dishes, ranging from India to Indonesia. The emphasis is on spice, but the tandoori specialties are tasty without being explosively hot. Indian vegetarian dishes are plentiful. In the evenings, a nightclub atmosphere prevails, with music and dancing, and there's an outdoor terrace for cooler, dry weather.

🍴 90 Ⓢ 🅰 🅲 All major cards

🍴 **STEAM AND STEW INN**
$
21-23 TAI WONG ST. EAST,
WAN CHAI
TEL 0852 2529-3913
The air heavy with steamy aromas and the boiled infusion of Cantonese herbs

and spices, the emphasis here is not so much on elegance as on authentic, healthy dinner preparations. Highly popular. MSG-free dining. Prix fixe meals. No wine. English menu.

🛏 100 🗋 MC, V

CAUSEWAY BAY

🏨 EXCELSIOR
$$$
281 GLOUCESTER RD.
TEL 2894-8888
FAX 2895-6459
The Excelsior overlooks Victoria Harbor but fronts an extremely busy six-lane highway. The best views of the harbor are from the 21 spacious suites on the top floor. The rear entrance leads straight into the heart of Causeway Bay's shop-till-you-drop scene. Excelsior's Talk of the Town grill bar is a popular nightspot with wide views of the night skyline, live entertainment, and dancing. Its basement sports bar is popular for its big screen showing of major world sporting events.

ℹ️ 887 🅿 🛗 🚭 🚫
📺 🗋 All major cards

🏨 PARK LANE
$$$
310 GLOUCESTER RD.
TEL 2293-8888
FAX 2576-7853
The Park Lane borders Causeway Bay shopping center, overlooking the harbor and one of the area's few oases of green, Victoria Park. Rooms are spacious compared to many other hotels in the area.

ℹ️ 792 🅿 🛗 🚭 🚫
📺 🗋 All major cards

🏨 REGAL HONGKONG
$$$
88 YEE WO ST.
TEL 2890-6633
FAX 2881-0777
The Regal lies in the heart of the Causeway Bay's frenetic shopping, eating, and entertainment scene, close to Victoria

Park and the subway and bus transportation systems. Rooms in this smart hotel have a stylish mixture of European and Asian furnishings.

ℹ️ 425 🅿 🛗 🚭 🚫
🏊 🗋 🗋 All major cards

🏨 ROSEDALE ON THE PARK
$$
8 SHELTER ST.
TEL 2127-8888
FAX 2127-3333
Located close to Causeway Bay's shopping, entertainment, and dining district, the Rosedale offers a peaceful haven from the hustle and bustle of the area. The hotel's 43 suites have kitchenettes and sofa beds, and its restaurant, Sonata Bistro, offers a mix of international and Asian dishes.

ℹ️ 274 🅿 🛗 🚭 🚫
🗋 All major cards

🏨 EMPEROR
$
1A WANG TAK ST.
HAPPY VALLEY
TEL 2893-3693
FAX 2834-6700
A small hotel in the relatively quiet residential Happy Valley District, close to the Happy Valley racetrack and Hong Kong Stadium. Rooms, although not big, are tastefully furnished.

ℹ️ 157 🅿 🛗 🚭 🚫
🗋 All major cards

🍴 W'S ENTRECOTE
$$$$
33 SHARP ST., EAST
TEL 2506-0133
A French steakhouse pure and simple. Charbroiled rib-eye in herb butter sauce is a favorite. The wine is also exclusively French.

🛏 90 🚭 🚫 🗋 All major cards

🍴 COVA
$$$
THE LEE GARDENS
33 HYSAN AVE.
TEL 2907-3399
Dishes from all over the Italian peninsula feature

PRICES

HOTELS
An indication of the cost of a double room without breakfast in U.S. dollars is given by $ signs.
$$$$$ Over $400
$$$$ $300–$400
$$$ $200–$300
$$ $100–$200
$ Under $100

RESTAURANTS
An indication of the cost of a three-course dinner without drinks in U.S. dollars is given by $ signs.
$$$$$ Over $90
$$$$ $60–$90
$$$ $35–$60
$$ $20–$35
$ Under $20

on the menu, such as fresh mozzarella flown in from Italy. Main course specialties include homemade noodles with smoked salmon and caviar, venison with juniper in Barolo wine, and sea bass with olives and tomatoes.

🛏 80 🚭 🚫 🗋 All major cards

🍴 FORUM
$$$
485 LOCKHART RD.
TEL 2891-2516
The large Cantonese menu ranges from simple dishes to the expensively exotic. Aim for the latter.—it's a good place to try those much talked-about dishes such as abalone, shark's fin soup, and bird's-nest soup, all specialties of chief chef Ah Yat.

🛏 80 🚭 🚫 🗋 All major cards

🍴 MYUNG GA
$$$
WORLD TRADE CENTER
280 GLOUCESTER RD.
TEL 2882-5056
Tables have cooking plates to prepare individual hotpots or cook-to-order barbecues, in

Korean style. Many dishes are very spicy, but all use fresh ingredients. Seafood hotpot and a variety of spicy vegetable pancakes are some of the most popular choices in this constantly busy restaurant.
🕃 90 ⬛ 🔄 🅰All major cards

🍴 SNOW GARDEN
$$$
MING AN PLAZA, 2ND FLOOR
8 SUNNING RD.
TEL 2881-6837
A welcome change from Cantonese cuisine can be found at this popular Shanghainese establishment in the form of the curious-sounding drunken pigeon (the bird is soaked in rice wine). Dim sum are served all day.
🕃 110 ⬛ 🔄 🅰All major cards

🍴 BANANA LEAF
440 JAFFE RD.
TEL 2573-8187
$$
Most dishes are eaten off banana leaves in this large, noisy, college canteen-style setting. Malaysian is the food tag, but it's really a spicy mix of Indian, Malay, Thai, and Indonesian. Worth trying are the fried chicken in pandanus leaf, crab curry, and the non-alcoholic exotic fruit drinks.
🕃 140 ⬛ 🔄 🅰All major cards

🍴 DIM SUM
$$
63 SING WOO RD.
HAPPY VALLEY
TEL 2834-8893
A huge dim sum selection, including the noteworthy steamed lobster and shrimp dumplings, brings lines of loyal customers, awaiting the latest dishes. Another specialty, more Sichuan than Cantonese, is pan-fried scallops and prawns with chili sauce and asparagus.
🕃 160 ⬛ 🔄 🅰All major cards

🍴 KUNG TAK LAM
$$
31 YEE WO ST.
TEL 2890-3127
This rare Chinese vegetarian eatery does a great job of imitating meat dishes with its vegetarian Shanghainese deep-fried eel, goose, and chicken. Try the eggplant in Sichuan sauce, Shanghai cold noodles with seven sauces, and, for dessert, rice flour dumplings with black sesame.
🕃 90 ⬛ 🔄 🅰All major cards

🍴 OUTBACK STEAKHOUSE
$$
2/F JP PLAZA
22–36 PATERSON ST.
CAUSEWAY BAY
TEL 2881-8012
This chain faux-Australian restaurant (owned by a U.S. outfit) serves good steak, plus seafood, pasta, and salad to keep the noncarnivores happy. Expect a relaxed atmosphere.
🕃 90 ⬛ 🅰All major cards

HONG KONG ISLAND SOUTH

STANLEY

🍴 LUCY'S
$$
64 MAIN ST.
TEL 2813-9055
This Mediterranean-style café matches the seaside setting. Relaxing wicker chairs set the tone for the lazy Sunday afternoon menu of mozzarella salad, saffron gnocchi and white wine sauce, or leek and gruyère soufflé. Wine is sold by the glass.
🕃 40 ⬛ 🔄 🅰All major cards

REPULSE BAY

SOMETHING SPECIAL

🍴 THE VERANDAH
Overlooking the sea, The Verandah is a delightful

open-air spot to take afternoon tea (3–5:30 p.m.) and is popular for Sunday brunch (11–2:30). A huge buffet ranges from sushi and salmon to eggs Benedict with caviar, roast lamb and beef, and salads. In the evening it becomes a more sophisticated venue for quiet dining, with piano accompaniment.
$$$$
REPULSE BAY
THE ARCADE
109 REPULSE BAY
TEL 2812-2722
🕃 80 ⬛ 🔄 🅰All major cards

🍴 SPICES
$$
THE ARCADE
109 REPULSE BAY
TEL 2812-2711
Typical dishes from India, Singapore, Indonesia, and Korea fill the menu. A big plus is the large garden patio that allows outdoor dining at this pretty bayside location.
🕃 60 ⬛ 🔄 🅰All major cards

KOWLOON

SOMETHING SPECIAL

🏨 THE PENINSULA
The famous Peninsula is a towering tribute to opulence. It still overlooks Victoria Harbor, but owing to development and land reclamation it is no longer directly on the waterfront. The hotel caters to every whim, including a rooftop heliport to bring guests directly from the airport. The large rooms have marble bathrooms, with TVs built into the wall at the end of the bathtub. There are 54 suites, three bar-lounges, and six restaurants, including the renowned Philippe Starck creation, **Felix** (see p. 254), serving Pacific Rim fare, **Gaddi's** (see p.254–55), and **Chesa** (see p. 255). Afternoon tea in the lobby is a must, even if you are not staying at the Peninsula.

HOTELS & RESTAURANTS

$$$$$
SALISBURY RD.
TSIM SHA TSUI
TEL 2920-2888
FAX 2722-4170
📞 300 🅿️ 🔁 🚫 🅢
☎️ 📺 💳 All major cards

🏨 INTERCONTINENTAL 🍴 HONG KONG
$$$$
18 SALISBURY RD.
TSIM SHA TSUI
TEL 2721-1211
FAX 2739-4546
This harborfront Four Seasons hotel offers spacious rooms and lavish suites with marble bathrooms, and some of the best views of the harbor and Hong Kong Island. It has 92 suites, two bars, and six restaurants, including the **Lai Ching Heen** (see p. 255) and **Yu** (see p. 255), serving everything from seafood to charcoal-grilled steaks.
📞 510 🅿️ 🔁 🚫 🅢
☎️ 📺 💳 All major cards

🏨 SHERATON HONG KONG
$$$$
20 NATHAN RD.
TSIM SHA TSUI
TEL 2369-1111
FAX 2739-8707
Right in the heart of Tsim Sha Tsui, surrounded by shopping streets that bustle all day and half the night, this hotel has good-size rooms which are soundproofed to protect guests from the constant noise from Nathan Road below. The Oyster & Wine Bar is popular with Hong Kong's Chinese yuppies.
📞 780 🅿️ 🔁 🚫 🅢
☎️ 📺 💳 All major cards

🏨 KOWLOON SHANGRI-LA
$$$
64 MODY RD.
TSIM SHA TSUI EAST
TEL 2721-2111
FAX 2723-8686
A cozy hotel close to the waterfront, with views across

Victoria Harbor. The rooms are elegant and among the largest you will find in Kowloon. The Margaux, which serves French Mediterranean dishes, is highly regarded.
📞 725 🅿️ 🔁 🚫 🅢
☎️ 📺 💳 All major cards

🏨 LANGHAM HOTEL HK
$$$
8 PEKING RD.
TSIM SHA TSUI
TEL 2375-1133
FAX 2375-6611
The glittering chandeliers, domed ceiling, and marble floors in the lobby are impressive, while the rooms are light and airy. This friendly hotel has three restaurants which serve both Cantonese and American-style cuisine.
📞 487 🅿️ 🔁 🚫 🅢
☎️ 📺 💳 All major cards

🏨 MIRAMAR
$$$
118–130 NATHAN RD.
TSIM SHA TSUI
TEL 2368-1111
FAX 2369-1788
The Miramar is a deluxe hotel offering genuine Oriental hospitality with a dash of glamour and charm, ideally located in the main Tsim Sha Tsui tourist district. It has its own shopping arcade, a bar and five restaurants, three of them Chinese, each serving a distinct regional cuisine.
📞 525 🅿️ 🔁 🚫 🅢
☎️ 📺 💳 All major cards

🏨 NIKKO HONG KONG
$$$
72 MODY RD.
TSIM SHA TSUI EAST
TEL 2739-1111
FAX 2311-3122
The Nikko is a favorite with Japanese visitors, so expect discreet but excellent service. The uncluttered rooms are decorated in soft neutral colors, with full length windows overlooking the harbor. With comprehensive business facilities, three bars, and four restaurants, it is within

walking distance of the main Tsim Sha Tsui shopping district.
📞 461 🅿️ 🔁 🚫 🅢
☎️ 📺 💳 All major cards

🏨 PRUDENTIAL HOTEL
$$$
222 NATHAN ROAD
TSIM SHA TSUI
TEL 852 2736-0922
FAX 852 2405-0922
A quiet haven amid the busy streets of Tsim Shat Sui, the Prudential's muted, sophisticated decor and rooftop pool help promote relaxation. While all of the hotel's rooms are sleek and stylish, certain suites on higher floors feature floor-to-ceiling windows that provide wonderful views of the area. The hotel is conveniently situated above a 6-story shopping complex and provides direct access to the MTR.
📞 431 🔁 🚫 🅢 ☎️ 📺
💳 All major cards

🏨 ROYAL GARDEN
$$$
69 MODY RD.
TSIM SHA TSUI EAST
TEL 2721-5215
FAX 2369-9976
The Royal Garden provides a refuge from Tsim Sha Tsui's frenetic pace, close to most Kowloon-side attractions. Rooms tend to be a little garish and overfurnished for their small size. It has 45 suites, four bars, and five restaurants, both Western and Cantonese.
📞 422 🅿️ 🔁 🚫 🅢
☎️ 📺 💳 All major cards

🏨 EMPIRE KOWLOON
$$
62 KIMBERLY RD.
TSIM SHA TSUI
TEL 2685-3000
FAX 2685-3685
Ten-foot-high ceilings give the otherwise standard rooms in this hotel an airy feel. Close to shopping, dining, museums, and other attractions, the Empire has 23 suites, two bars, and two restaurants

---

KEY 🏨 Hotel 🍴 Restaurant 📞 No. of bedrooms 🔧 No. of seats 🅿️ Parking 🕐 Closed 🔁 Elevator

featuring Japanese and international cuisine.

① 315 **P** 🔁 🚫 💠
📞 💟 💳 All major cards

🏨 GRAND STANFORD 🍴 INTER-CONTINENTAL $$
70 MODY RD.
TSIM SHA TSUI EAST
TEL 2721-5161
FAX 2732-2233
The Grand Standford lies on the Victoria Harbor waterfront and there are great views to the Hong Kong Island skyline from most of the rooms and from the 18th-floor swimming pool. The **Belvedere** restaurant (see p. 255) specializes in French regional cooking.

① 579 **P** 🔁 🚫 💠
📞 💟 💳 All major cards

🏨 HARBOR PLAZA HONG KONG $$
20 TAK FUNG ST.
HUNG HOM
TEL 2621-3188
FAX 2621-3311
The Harbor Plaza is on the Hung Hom waterfront, only five minutes from the main Tsim Sha Tsui tourist area and connecting transportation. It has 101 roomy serviced suites with kitchens and maid service for longer stays. The Pit Stop restaurant and bar serves up hearty U.S. dishes and live music in the evenings.

① 417 **P** 🔁 🚫 💠
📞 💟 💳 All major cards

🏨 HOLIDAY INN GOLDEN MILE $$
50 NATHAN RD.
TSIM SHA TSUI
TEL 2369-3111
FAX 2369-8016
A standard Holiday Inn tower in downtown Kowloon with its own shopping arcade, five restaurants, and lounges. Light timber furnishings, neutral color schemes and floor-to-ceiling windows give a spacious feel to the moderately sized rooms. The Café

Vienna's constantly changing buffet attracts Chinese lunchtime crowds and evening shoppers.

① 600 **P** 🔁 🚫 💠
📞 💟 💳 All major cards

🏨 HYATT REGENCY 🍴 $$
67 NATHAN RD.
TSIM SHA TSUI
TEL 2311-1234
FAX 2739-8701
Much attention has been paid to *feng shui* in the redesign of this hotel, particularly in the positioning of furniture in the rooms. It offers a range of dining choices in its four restaurants, including **Hugo's** (see p. 255), and two bars.

① 723 **P** 🔁 🚫 💠
💳 All major cards

🏨 KIMBERLEY $$
28 KIMBERLEY RD.
TSIM SHA TSUI
TEL 2723-3888
FAX 2723-1318
The deluxe rooms and suites are large and comfortable but standard rooms tend to be small. The Hanamizuki Japanese restaurant is a popular venue.

① 546 **P** 🔁 🚫 💠
💟 💳 All major cards

🏨 KOWLOON $$
19–21 NATHAN RD.
TSIM SHA TSUI
TEL 2929-2888
FAX 2739-9811
This cost-conscious Peninsula Group hotel offers excellent bargains for stays of seven days or longer. The rooms are a bit small but well appointed. Guests can charge services received at the nearby upscale Peninsula directly to their Kowloon hotel bill.

① 736 **P** 🔁 🚫 💠
💳 All major cards

🏨 MAJESTIC $$
348 NATHAN RD.
YAU MA TEI

TEL 2781-1333
FAX 2781-1773
The Majestic offers quality accommodations and dining. This pleasantly appointed hotel is run by a friendly and helpful staff in the bustling Yau Ma Tei District.

① 387 **P** 🔁 🚫 💠
💳 All major cards

🏨 MARCO POLO GATEWAY $$
HARBOR CITY, CANTON RD.
TSIM SHA TSUI
TEL 2113-0888
FAX 2113-0022
One of three adjacent Marco Polo properties in the Harbor City complex, the Gateway offers a combination of efficiency and comfort. Rooms are tastefully decorated in subdued tones and are a decent size. The Parisian Brasseries is the pick of its three restaurants.

① 440 **P** 🔁 🚫 💠
💳 All major cards

🏨 MARCO POLO HONG KONG $$
HARBOR CITY, CANTON RD.
TSIM SHA TSUI
TEL 2113-0088
FAX 2113-0011
The pick of the three Marco Polos, the Hong Kong has a higher standard of style and comfort and bigger rooms than its sister hostelries. This one has 44 suites, and a tempting range of cuisines in its six restaurants, from Chinese Chiu Chow to American.

① 665 **P** 🔁 🚫 💠
📞 💟 💳 All major cards

🏨 MARCO POLO PRINCE $$
HARBOR CITY, CANTON RD.
TSIM SHA TSUI
TEL 2113-1888
FAX 2113-0066
Superbly located in one of Hong Kong's largest shopping and commercial complexes in downtown Tsim Sha Tsui,

this hotel is ideal for both business and leisure travelers. Room rates, decor, and service compare well with its neighbor, the Marco Polo Gateway. It has more than 50 suites, a lounge-bar, and two restaurants, including The Spice Market, which specializes in Southeast Asian dishes.

ⓘ 396 🅿 ⬍ Ⓢ Ⓢ
⬥ All major cards

🏨 NEW WORLD RENAISSANCE
$$
22 SALISBURY RD.
TSIM SHA TSUI
TEL 2369-4111
FAX 2369-9387
The New World is in a perfect position on the Tsim Sha Tsui harborfront. Rooms are tastefully decorated and spacious, with floor-to-ceiling windows. The Panorama Restaurant has great nighttime views across to Hong Kong Island's brightly illuminated skyscraper architecture.

ⓘ 525 🅿 ⬍ Ⓢ Ⓢ
⬛ 🏮 ⬥ All major cards

🏨 REGAL KOWLOON
🍴 $$
71 MODY RD.
TSIM SHA TSUI EAST
TEL 2722-1818
FAX 2369-6950
The Regal Kowloon offers elegance and comfort, with 34 suites, two bar-lounges, and four restaurants. It has a small art gallery on the first floor and a playroom for the kids. The exclusive **Mamman** wine bar and restaurant (see p. 255) serves traditional French cuisine.

ⓘ 593 🅿 ⬍ Ⓢ Ⓢ
🏮 ⬥ All major cards

🏨 EATON
$
380 NATHAN RD.
KOWLOON
TEL 2782-1818
FAX 2782-5563
This modern, well-appointed hotel lies in downtown Kowloon, in the heart of the Nathan Road Golden Mile shopping mecca. Ask for a corner deluxe room with large windows and terrific views of Kowloon Park..

ⓘ 468, 🅿 , ⬍ Ⓢ Ⓢ
⬛ 🏮 ⬥ All major cards

🏨 PARK
$
61–65 CHATHAM RD. SOUTH
TSIM SHA TSUI
TEL 2366-1371
FAX 2739-7259
A well-appointed and comfortable, if uninspiring, hotel, offering minimal luxuries and facilities, but close to museums, shopping, and other tourist attractions. There are 29 suites, two bar-lounges, and three restaurants.

ⓘ 1,026 🅿 ⬍ Ⓢ Ⓢ
⬥ All major cards

🍴 FELIX
$$$$$
THE PENINSULA
SALISBURY RD.
TSIM SHA TSUI
TEL 2315-3188
The renowned Felix is well known for its dramatic views across Hong Kong from the 28th floor. But perhaps more dramatic is its East–West fusion cuisine—big-eye tuna with pineapple mixed with spices, chargrilled cod in sake sauce, and roasted duck with Shanghai rice.

🪑 76 🅿 🕐 Closed L Ⓢ
Ⓢ ⬥ All major cards

🍴 GADDI'S
$$$$$
THE PENINSULA
SALISBURY RD.
TSIM SHA TSUI
TEL 2315-3171
One of Hong Kong's most exclusive and elegant French restaurants, visited mostly by the rich and famous. It boasts its own entrance, separate from the exclusivity of the Peninsula. Try the Atlantic sea bass in Chateau Chalon sauce, roast Scottish lamb, or warm lobster salad. The wine list, predominantly but not exclusively French, equals the quality of the cuisine.

🪑 80 🅿 Ⓢ Ⓢ ⬥ All major cards

🍴 YU
$$$$$
INTERCONTINENTAL HONG KONG
18 SALISBURY RD.
TSIM SHA TSUI
TEL 2721-1211
Probably the best, if also the most expensive, place to eat seafood in Hong Kong. Several fishing vessels are permanently assigned to supply seafood from the South China Sea. Yu's kitchen will cook to the customer's instructions, or the knowledgeable waiters can advise and recommend. The cuisine is European with Asian touches, such as lobster in black bean sauce. Another treat is oysters glazed with champagne. Window tables give panoramic views of Hong Kong Harbor.

🪑 90 Ⓢ Ⓢ ⬥ All major cards

PRICES

HOTELS
An indication of the cost of a double room without breakfast in U.S. dollars is given by $ signs.

$$$$$	Over $400
$$$$	$300–$400
$$$	$200–$300
$$	$100–$200
$	Under $100

RESTAURANTS
An indication of the cost of a three-course dinner without drinks in U.S. dollars is given by $ signs.

$$$$$	Over $90
$$$$	$60–$90
$$$	$35–$60
$$	$20–$35
$	Under $20

Ⓨ BELVEDERE
$$$$
GRAND STANFORD
HARBOR VIEW
70 MODY RD.
TSIM SHA TSUI
TEL 2731-2880
A romantic ambience and
discreetly attentive staff,
coupled with the high-quality
French provincial cuisine and
wines, make this a perfect
venue for a celebratory
dinner. Stir-fried duck's liver,
snails in garlic, and spit-
roasted lamb are country-
style staples.
🛏 50 🅿 🔲 🔲 🔲 All
major cards

Ⓨ CHESA
$$$$
THE PENINSULA, 1ST FLOOR
SALISBURY RD.
TSIM SHA TSUI
TEL 2315-3169
Well worth exploring for its
excellent representation of
Switzerland's Italian, German,
and French influences. Try
Zurich-style roesti with snails
and herbs, mountain-cured
ham and beef, veal sausage,
and the gruyère-and-
Emmentaal cheese fondue.
🛏 80 🔲 🔲 🔲 All major
cards

Ⓨ FOOK LAM MOON
$$$$
53-59 KIMBERLEY ROAD
TSIM SHA TSUI
TEL 852 2-366-0286
A venerable Hong Kong
institute specializing in exotic
Cantonese dishes. The menu
tends to be rather expensive,
but for delicacies such as
shark's fin and double boiled
bird's nest, both locals and a
high-profile clientele swear
that Fook Lam Moon is the
only place to go.
🔲 All major cards

Ⓨ HUGO'S
$$$$
HYATT REGENCY
67 NATHAN RD.
TSIM SHA TSUI
TEL 2311-1234

Enjoy the splendor of an
English castle hall in Chinese
Hong Kong, with stag heads
and suits of armor lining the
walls and metal portcullises
separating tables. Troubadours
meander around the place
strumming and gently singing.
The food is Continental, with
some English flavor. Dover
sole and roast beef
complement the setting.
🛏 90 🔲 🔲 🔲 All major
cards

Ⓨ HOI KING HEEN
$$$
70 MODY RD.
TSIM SHA TSUI
TEL 2731-2883
Excellent Cantonese cuisine
with some unusual vegetarian
dishes, such as braised black
moss with mushrooms and
bamboo. The killed-to-order
steamed garoupa fish is a
delightful delicacy, as are the
poached prawns mixed with
Chinese herbs. An interesting
collection of wines from
countries such as Austria,
Germany, and Switzerland.
🛏 110 🔲 🔲 🔲 All
major cards

Ⓨ YAN TOH HEEN
$$$
INTERCONTINENTAL
HONG KONG
18 SALISBURY RD.
TSIM SHA TSUI
TEL 2721-1211 EXT. 2243
Fascinating and sometimes
unusual Cantonese dishes can
be found in this classy harborside restaurant, such as stewed
frog with eggplant and bean
paste. More conventional
dishes include barbecued
suckling pig.
🛏 90 🔲 🔲 🔲 All major
cards

Ⓨ SAKURADA
$$$
ROYAL PLAZA
193 PRINCE EDWARD RD.
KOWLOON
TEL 2622-6164
Sakurada lies a few miles up
Nathan Road from the harbor

and onto Prince Edward
Road, but is worth the effort
for the Japanese food and
the peaceful and elegant
setting of red and black
colors and Japanese
woodwork. Sakurada's chefs
use traditional methods and
ingredients. Look for crab egg
salad, tuna and wasabi, and
teppanyaki Matsuzaka beef.
🛏 80 🔲 🔲 🔲 All major
cards

Ⓨ SPRING DEER
42 MODY RD.
TSIM SHA TSUI
TEL 2366-4012
$$$
Peking duck is a must at this
highly regarded Pekingese
restaurant, the hot and sour
soup is very rich and tasty, and
the stewed ham with Tientsin
cabbage is classic. The menu
offers small, medium, and
large portions of most dishes,
but only the biggest appetites
should tackle the large sizes.
🛏 110 🔲 🔲 🔲 All
major cards

Ⓨ TAI PAN GRILL
$$$
MARCO POLO HONG KONG,
6TH FLOOR
3 CANTON RD.
TSIM SHA TSUI
TEL 2113-0088
An elegant evening venue
with piano accompaniment.
Some window tables give
views of Hong Kong Island.
The menu is mostly European:
goose liver pâté, grills, steak
Diane, and excellent cheeses.
More bustling at lunchtime,
when an extensive buffet
is served.
🛏 80 🔲 🔲 🔲 All major
cards

Ⓨ WU KONG
$$$
27 NATHAN RD.
TSIM SHA TSUI
TEL 2366-7244
Popular basement
Shanghainese restaurant with
friendly, attentive staff. Sautéed
fresh shrimps and steamed

HOTELS & RESTAURANTS

pork dumplings are two old established favorites, as is the pigeon in wine.

🪑 120 ◻ ◻ ◻ All major cards

🏨 **GOLD COAST**
$$
1 CASTLE PEAK RD.
TEL 2452-8888
FAX 2440-7368
A beach resort hotel in the far western reaches of the Kowloon peninsula, the Gold Coast offers leisure facilities set in palm-tree-covered gardens, and there's a marina and private beach. Spacious rooms come with sea views and private balconies. Good entertainment, dining, and a shopping mall are designed to keep guests on site. Reasonable road and train connections to Tsim Sha Tsui.

🛏 450 🅿 ◻ ◻ ◻
◻ ◻ All major cards

🏨 **REGAL AIRPORT**
$$
9 CHEONG TAT RD.
CHEK LAP KOK
LANTAU
TEL 2286-8888
FAX 2286-8686
One of the largest airport hotels in the world, the Regal is a superbly equipped resort property at Hong Kong International Airport. Landscaped, fully sound-proofed, and with a covered sky bridge to the terminal, it offers 26 suites, two bar-lounges and six restaurants serving Beijing, Shanghai, Sichuan, Japanese, Western, and many other specialties.

🛏 1,103 🅿 ◻ ◻ ◻
◻ ◻ ◻ All major cards

🏨 **ROYAL PARK**
$$
8 PAK HOK TING ST.
SHA TIN
TEL 2601-2111
FAX 2601-3666
Renowned for its attentive

service, and for its business and recreational facilities, the Royal Park is located on the Kowloon–Canton Railway line with easy access to downtown and the Chinese border. Rooms are large, light, and airy, and its Sakurada Japanese restaurant is popular with businesspeople.

🛏 448 🅿 ◻ ◻ ◻
◻ ◻ All major cards

🏨 **PANDA**
3 TSUEN WAH ST.
TSUEN WAN
TEL 2409-1111
FAX 2409-1818
$
This monolith of a building is set off by a curious piece of modern art illuminated at night all down one side of its 30 stories. Its out-of-the-way location means you can get good deals on rooms rates. The restaurant serves Cantonese and Italian cuisine, and the delicatessen produces a big range of pastries and chocolate.

🛏 1,026 🅿 ◻ ◻ ◻
◻ ◻ All major cards

🏨 **REGAL RIVERSIDE**
$
34–36 TAI CHUNG KIU RD.
SHA TIN
TEL 2649-7878
FAX 2637-4748
One of the few Hong Kong hotels set amid the greenery of a semirural environment, the Regal Riverside lies close to the Kowloon–Canton Railway line for easy access to downtown and the border with mainland China.

🛏 830 🅿 ◻ ◻ ◻
◻ ◻ All major cards

LAMMA ISLAND

🍽 **SAMPAN SEAFOOD RESTAURANT**
$$
16 MAIN STREET
YUNG SHUE WAN

TEL 0852 2982-2388
A trip to Lamma Island should really include a sampling of seafood to accompany the splendid views. Go no farther than this restaurant in Yung Shue Wan's main street for Cantonese maritime fare and excellent vistas out to sea. Dim sum in mornings. English menu.

🪑 200 ◻ All major cards

LANTAU ISLAND

🏨 **HONG KONG DISNEYLAND HOTEL**
$$$
TEL 852 1-830-830
FAX 852 3510-6333
With typical Disney Flair, the Disneyland Hotel presents a sumptuous Victorian fantasy with modern-day luxuries throughout. Rooms feature high-speed internet and flat-screen TVs, while a Victorian spa, and afternoon tea help maintain an old-world sense of charm. The Disneyland features six restaurants and provides transportation to the theme park.

🛏 400 🅿 ◻ ◻ ◻ ◻
◻ ◻ All major cards

🏨 **DISNEY'S HOLLYWOOD HOTEL**
$$
TEL 852 1-830-830
FAX 852 3510-5333
The Hollywood Hotel is a good option for those wishing to extend their Disney experience beyond the standard theme-park visit. With its bright blue exterior and colorful, lively decor, the hotel is Disney's exuberant take on 1930s Hollywood glamour. Five restaurants are located within the hotel and transportation to Disneyland is provided.

🛏 600 🅿 ◻ ◻ ◻ ◻
◻ ◻ All major cards

EXCURSIONS

MACAU

🏨 MANDARIN ORIENTAL
🍴 $$$$
956–1110 AVENIDA DA
AMIZADE
TEL 853/567-888
FAX 853/594-589
Portuguese architectural and
design influences can be seen
throughout the hotel. Rooms
make good use of Portuguese
fabrics and teak furnishings.
There are 28 suites, and eight
restaurants (see **Dynasty,**
opposite), and cafés, notably
Café Girassol, serving
Macanese cuisine. Close to
the waterfront, within walking
distance of the ferry terminal
from Hong Kong and the
main shopping district.
🛈 435 🅿 🔁 🚭 🅐
🏊 🎽 🅐 All major cards

SOMETHING SPECIAL

🏨 POUSADA DE
SAO TIAGO
A converted fortress built by
the Portuguese in the 17th
century to defend their colonial
possession, this charmingly
romantic hotel drips with
history. The old fortress's chapel
has been preserved within the
complex, and renovated hand-
hewn sandstones form much of
the conversion. Guests enter via
a cobblestone passage through
the old fortress battlements.
Rooms, swimming pool, and
dining terrace look out over the
sea and the entrance to the
harbor. There are two restaurants.
$$$
AVENIDA DA REPUBLICA
FORTALEZA DE SAO TIAGO
DA BARRA
TEL 853/378-111
FAX 853/552-170
🛈 23 🅿 🔁 🚭 🅐 🏊
🅐 All major cards

🏨 HYATT REGENCY
$$
2 ESTRADA ALMIRANTE
MARQUES ESPARTEIRO
TAIPA ISLAND
TEL 853/831-234
FAX: 853/830-195
Rooms are bright and
spacious at this hotel, located
on the island of Taipa, and
connected to maintown
Macau via a long bridge. The
property is set on acres of
lush greenery.
🛈 326 🅿 🔁 🚭 🅐
🏊 🎽 🅐 All major cards

🏨 LISBOA
$$
2–4 AVENIDA DE LISBOS
TEL 853/577-666 OR 853/377-666
FAX 853/567-193
The Lisboa is a landmark
cylindrical building which also
houses Macau's most famous
casino. Most of the rooms
have great views of the South
China Sea and surrounding
townscape. There's a large
range of facilities, including a
nightclub, 13 restaurants, and
a shopping arcade.
🛈 1,017 🅿 🔁 🚭 🅐
🏊 🎽 🅐 All major cards

🏨 SINTRA
$$
AVENIDA D. JOAO IV MACAU
TEL 853/710-111
FAX 853/510-527
Conveniently located in the
heart of Macau overlooking
Praia Grande Bay, the Sintra
has comfortable, albeit small,
rooms. The Sintra restaurant
is a 24-hour steakhouse. The
menu also has Macanese and
Portuguese dishes.
🛈 220 🅿 🔁 🚭 🅐
🅐 All major cards

🍴 TUNG YEE HEEN
$$$$
MANDARIN ORIENTAL
956 AVENIDA DA AMIZADE
TEL 853/567-888
Unusual flavors and an
experimental Cantonese style
contrast with the bustling,
sometimes smoky atmosphere
associated more with a street

market café than an upscale
hotel restaurant. But the
kitchen's efforts prevail: sour
Macau shrimp paste blended
with shellfish dishes, pigeon in
tofu sauce, yellow beans, and
ginger topping over steamed
seafood. A large selection of
exotic Chinese teas.
🍴 160 🅿 🚭 🅐 All
major cards

🍴 A LORCHA
$$$
289A RUA DO ALMIRANTE
SERGIO
INNER HARBOR
TEL 853/313-195
Owner Adriano Neves
catches his own fish, thus
ensuring freshness. But equally
good in this long-time popular
Portuguese restaurant are the
feijoada (pork and bean stew)
and *arroz de marisco* (stuffed
squid). Try the chocolate
mousse in Portuguese
brandy to finish.
🍴 70 🕐 Closed Tues. 🚭
🅐 🅐 All major cards

🍴 CLUBE MILITAR DE
MACAU
$$$
795 AVENIDA DA PRAIA
GRANDE
TEL 853/714-000
A delightful and airy dining
room in a renovated 19th-
century colonial building that
used to be the Portuguese
military club. It's still a private
members' club, but the restaurant is public. The menu is
Portuguese, although some
Macanese dishes creep in.
Look for *bacalhau a bras,* cod
cooked with julienne potatoes
and onions. Clube Militar has
one of Macau's best Portuguese wine lists, and serves
wonderfully rich, thick coffee.
🍴 70 🚭 🅐 🅐 All major
cards

🍴 LITORAL
$$$
261A RUA DO ALMIRANTE
SERGIO
INNER HARBOR
TEL 853/967-878

Sophisticated Macanese cuisine—a blend of cuisine evolved over the past 400 years from Portugal's colonial empire—is served in a fanciful setting that is much liked and visited by the well-heeled fashion setters of both Macau and Hong Kong. They come not only to be seen, but also to eat crab curry with quail eggs, chili-spiced *diablo* stews, and *tacho* beef stews.

🍴76 🅿 Ⓢ Ⓢ Ⓢ All major cards

🍴 SAI NAM
$$$
39 RUA DA FELICIDADE
TEL 853/574-072
Aficionados of shark's fin soup gladly travel here from Hong Kong, where it's much more expensive. Other Cantonese favorites in this restaurant, which still bears the hallmarks of its 1960s-era foundation, are fried chicken, steamed fish, and an unusual fried rice with pungent lotus leaves. Sai Nam also panders to Macau's taste for star-fruit juice.

🍴120 Ⓢ Ⓢ Ⓢ All major cards

SOMETHING SPECIAL

🍴 FERNANDO'S

A visit to Macau is not complete without a meal in the legendary Fernando's. Hong Kong's cognoscenti come here on weekends to eat, drink, and laze in the fresh air—not easy in Hong Kong. The Portuguese food is not the best in Macau, but it doesn't stop people lining up for garden tables to dine on the clams, sardines, roast chicken, and shrimp.

$$
9 HAN SA BEACH
COLOANE ISLAND
TEL 853/882-264
🍴50 Ⓢ Ⓢ Ⓢ No credit cards - check

🍴 POUSADA DE COLOANE
$$
PRAIA DE CHEOC VAN
COLOANE ISLAND
TEL 853/882-143
The Portuguese–Macanese food may not be the best in Macau, but people flock here to sip Portuguese wine and watch night fall across the South China Sea. The restaurant is part of a small hotel built into the cliffs above a beach well away from the hustle and bustle of Hong Kong. The Sunday buffet lunch is excellent value.

🍴80 🅿 Ⓢ Ⓢ Ⓢ All major cards

🍴 BOLO DE ARROZ
$
11 TRAVESSA DE SAO DOMINGOS
TEL 853/339-089
A Portuguese village coffee shop on the South China Sea. Homemade pastries are accompanied by rich espresso in simple, gossipy surroundings, where some people linger over lunch and others pop in for five minutes for a counter coffee and a cigarette.

🍴30 Ⓢ Ⓢ Ⓢ No credit cards - check

🍴 RIQUEXO
$
69 AVENIDA SIDONIO PAIS
TEL 853/565-655
Macau's dwindling population of Macanese gather at the sign of the rickshaw (*riquexo*) to swap and share their culinary heritage. Simple but flavorful Macanese household dishes, prepared by aging housewives, are served in this simple, cozy café over a supermarket that stocks a big selection of Portuguese wines and ports.

🍴40 Ⓢ Ⓢ Ⓢ All major cards

GUANGZHOU

🏨 MARRIOTT CHINA
$$$
LIU HUA LU
TEL 86-20-8666-6888
FAX 86-20-8667-7288
This upscale complex includes a hotel tower, an office tower, two serviced apartments blocks, and a shopping arcade. The rooms are well appointed and the lobby is grand. There are 168 luxury suites and four restaurants, including a Hard Rock Café.

ⓘ885 🅿 Ⓢ Ⓢ Ⓢ Ⓢ 🞤 All major cards

🏨 FURAMA
$$
316 CHANGDI LU
TEL 86-20-8186-3288
FAX 86-20-8186-3388
Facing the picturesque Pearl River in Guangzhou's hectic commercial and shopping area, the Furama has comfortable rooms, a popular, noisy disco, and three restaurants that serve both Chinese and international dishes.

ⓘ360 🅿 Ⓢ Ⓢ Ⓢ Ⓢ 🞤 All major cards

🏨 GARDEN
$$
368 HUANSHI DONG LU
TEL 86-20-8333-8989
FAX 86-20-8332-5334
Guests are greeted by spouting fountains at the main entrance to this huge, modern, and sometimes over-the-top hotel. The large gilded mural in the lobby is an attraction in itself. There are eight restaurants, ranging from the European cuisine of the Connoisseur to the Cantonese Peach Blossom, as well as several bars and a nightclub. Centrally located in the commercial and financial hub of Guangzhou, and close to the Trade Fair Center, airport, and rail and ferry terminals.

ⓘ1,003 🅿 Ⓢ Ⓢ Ⓢ Ⓢ 🞤 All major cards

SHOPPING IN HONG KONG

As a duty-free port, Hong Kong is a shoppers' paradise, although not quite as cheap as popular myth suggests. You can buy anything from clothes made to measure in 24 hours to a Ming dynasty vase. Government efforts have been made to stamp out counterfeiting, but Hong Kong is still inundated with low-price, copycat goods, usually made in southern China and bearing the expensive brand names and labels of Japanese and Western producers. The street markets are often the source of counterfeit designer-label clothes, watches, CDs, and some electronic equipment.

Guaranteed genuine goods are sold at shops where you see a red junk sign supported by the Hong Kong Tourism Board (HKTB).

If you are looking for genuine Chinese antiques, you can usually find what you want, at a price, in the Hollywood Road district of Hong Kong Island.

Elsewhere, good bargains in jade, gold, pearls, and silk are possible because of Hong Kong's free port status and the large number of retailers. Check several shops before making a final selection.

There are plenty of lively street markets and discount stores where you can pick up cheap clothing, bags, shoes, souvenirs, and knick-knacks.

There are two cut-price sales periods each year—July to September and December to February.

Local clothes and jewelry designers and contractors producing for big-name international clothes brands sometimes have sales of excess production or slightly flawed goods at their factories, with prices much lower than in the stores. Tourist offices issue pamphlets giving details of these factory outlets. In Central, the Pedder Building on Pedder Street offers European fashion bargains.

Bargaining

Goods in department stores and some other retailers have price tags and are fixed, but at markets, electronic outlets, and some smaller stores bargaining is expected. When buying electronics, always visit a few stores to price goods.

Opening times

Most shops are open seven days, only closed during a few days at Chinese New Year (see p. 47). Big stores open from 10 a.m. until 8 or 9 p.m. Smaller shops, especially in Kowloon, Wan Chai, and Causeway Bay stay open as late as 11 p.m.

ANTIQUES & ARTIFACTS

A large selection of Chinese and other Asian antiques and artifacts is available in Hong Kong. The biggest concentration of specialist shops is found on and around Hollywood Road, in Central on Hong Kong Island. In addition to rare porcelain, jade, and furnishings, there is a wealth of inexpensive but evocative curios from China, such as opium pipes and old photographs. The Hollywood Road district also has art from Myanmar (Burma), Thailand, Indonesia, and India.

Mainland China-owned department stores such as the Chinese Arts and Crafts stores stock Chinese antiques and art as well as jade, porcelain, and silk.

Chinese and other East Asian antiques are sold by auction in Hong Kong from time to time. Christie's holds auctions from April to May and October to November. The focus is on Chinese art and jewelry, particularly jade.

Cat Street Galleries

38 Luk Ku Rd., Sheung Wan, Hong Kong Island, tel 2543-1609, open 10 a.m.–7 p.m. Five floors of retail outlets selling Chinese and other Asian antiques, artifacts, and handicrafts. A convenient one-stop-shop.

AUCTION HOUSES

Christie's

Alexandra House, 16–20 Chater Rd., Central, Hong Kong Island, tel 2521-5396, fax 2845-2646

Sotheby's

Standard Chartered Bank Building, 5th floor, 4–4A Des Voeux Rd., Central, Hong Kong Island, tel 2524-8121, fax 2810-6238

ARCADES & MALLS

Shopping malls offer a convenient way to shop in Hong Kong. Most malls have an excellent range of department stores, boutiques, and camera, jewelry, and electronic goods outlets. Prices are fixed and displayed on the goods, so there is no bargaining here.

Shopping malls also have a good selection of restaurants and food halls where you can relax and replenish your energy levels, and most have multiple-screen cinema centers attached.

HONG KONG

Cityplaza

18 Tai Koo Shing Rd., Quarry Bay, tel 2568-8665, open 10 a.m.–9 p.m.

One of Hong Kong's largest shopping centers, with department stores and retail outlets selling clothes, accessories, jewelry, watches, electronic goods, and cameras. There are also plenty of restaurants as well as a movie theater complex.

Pacific Place

88 Queensway, Admiralty, tel 2844-8988, open 10 a.m.–9 p.m. Hong Kong's premier shopping center. This vast mall was one of the first of its kind in Asia and a benchmark for retail complexes throughout the region. There are floors of boutiques, specialist electronics shops, cafés, bars, and a movie complex.

The Peak Galleria
118 Peak Rd., The Peak, tel 2849-4113, open 10 a.m.–11 p.m.
Spectacular setting for clothes shops, souvenir outlets, restaurants (some with a view over Hong Kong Harbor), and a huge Park 'n' Shop supermarket. Be prepared to pay generously for your purchases—the prices here can be as lofty as the view.

KOWLOON
Festival Walk
80 Tat Chee Ave., Kowloon Tong, tel 2844-2200, open 10 a.m.–9 p.m.
One of Hong Kong's newer megamalls, with 200 shops, boutiques, department stores, restaurants, and a massive food court. The complex also has an 11-screen movie complex.

Harbor City
Ocean Terminal, 3 Canton Rd., Tsim Sha Tsui, tel 2118-8668, open 10 a.m.–8 p.m.
A huge shopping mall with outlets selling upscale fashion, formal wear, bespoke tailoring, electronics, shoes, and artifacts.

Kowloon City Plaza
128 Carpenter Rd., Kowloon City, tel 2383-3608, open 10 a.m.–9 p.m.
More down-market than some of the other malls, but stocked with casual clothes, electronic equipment, cameras, bags, and shoes, with the advantage of unglitzy prices.

ARTS & CRAFTS

Hong Kong has a fine selection of traditional crafts, not least porcelain from China, carpets and rugs from Turkey and Iran, silk garments from China and Thailand, Indonesian batik, and teak furniture from Myanmar. Chinese calligraphists work in several of the open-air markets.

Calligraphy
Some of the best craftsmen work at bustling Stanley Market on Hong Kong Island South. Popular items to purchase as

souvenirs include book-size name cards drawn to order in Chinese characters.

Carpets
There are numerous carpet shops along Wyndham Street and Hollywood Road in Central, Hong Kong Island.

Rattan and rosewood furniture
Sold in many shops along Queen's Road East, Wan Chai.

Silk
On sale in Chinese Arts and Crafts stores, Western Market, and Stanley Market on Hong Kong Island.

BOOKS & PRINTS

HONG KONG
Bookazine
Basement, Canton House, 54–56 Queen's Rd., Central, tel 2521-1649, open 10 a.m.–7 p.m.

Page One Bookshop
9/F, Times Sq., 1 Matheson St., Causeway Bay, tel 2506-0383, open 10:50 a.m.–10 p.m. (10:50 p.m. Sat. and Sun.)

KOWLOON
Page One Bookshop
Shop 3002, Level 3, Harbor City, Tsim Sha Tsui, Kowloon, tel 2778-2808, open 10:30 a.m.–10 p.m.

CAMERAS

Hong Kong is a genuine bargain basement for all makes and types of cameras—from compacts and 35mm single lens reflex to digital and video cameras—so it is worth waiting until you arrive to purchase a new camera to record your visit.
On Hong Kong Island, check the shops on Stanley Street, Central, and in Causeway Bay. On the other side of the harbor, visit Nathan Road in Tsim Sha Tsui and Sai Yeung Choi Street in Mong Kok. Make sure your purchase includes full international warranty documentation and guide booklet.

CLOTHING & ACCESSORIES

Tailoring has always been one of Hong Kong's trademarks. Suits, evening gowns, shirts, and hats are made to measure by small-shop tailors, and your favorite designs can be copied.
Some of the major hotels have tailor services within their own shopping arcades. Other notable locations, especially for the Indian tailoring community, are in Tsim Sha Tsui. Suits can often be prepared in 24 hours, but make sure you have more than one fitting after the initial measuring.
Shoes and other leather goods are also made to measure.
In addition to all the international Western designer brands on sale in the major stores and upscale boutiques in Causeway Bay, Hong Kong has spawned a number of its own fashion designers—notably Vivienne Tam, William Tang, Walter Ma, and Barney Cheng.

Allan Tom & Co.
Shop 1109B, 1st floor, Peninsular Center, 67 Mody Rd., Tsim Sha Tsui East, Kowloon, tel 2366-6690

Island Beverley
Island Center, 26th floor, 1 Great George St., Causeway Bay, tel 2890-6823.
Young fashion.

Marks & Spencer
Ocean Center, 5 Canton Rd., Tsim Sha Tsui, tel 2929-3346, open 10 a.m.–8:30 p.m.
M&S's own-brand clothes and accessories.

Princeton Custom Tailors
71 Peking Rd., Tsim Sha Tsui (opposite Hyatt Hotel), tel 2721-0082

Shanghai Tang
Ground Floor, Pedder Building, 12 Pedder St., Central, tel 2525-7333, open 10 a.m.–8 p.m. (11 a.m.–7 p.m. Sat. and Sun.)

Fashionable clothes Hong Kong-style.

DEPARTMENT STORES

Lane Crawford
Podium 3, ifc, Central,
tel 2118-3388, open 10 a.m.–9 p.m.
and
Times Sq., 1 Matheson St.,
Causeway Bay, tel 2118-3638,
open 10 a.m.–9 p.m.
Good source of high fashion,
featuring labels from the major
international and local designers,
as well as a good selection of
jewelry and perfumes.

Sogo
555 Hennessy Rd., Causeway
Bay, tel 2833-8338, open
10 a.m.–10 p.m.
Huge Japanese department store
selling clothes, electronic goods,
and Japanese food.

FOOD & DRINK

Oliver's Delicatessen
Prince's Building, 2nd floor,
10 Chater Rd., Central, Hong
Kong Island, tel 2869-5119,
open 8:30 a.m.–8 p.m.
Probably the biggest selection of
Scotch malt whisky in east Asia,
including many single malts.
A fine range of wines is also
available here.

Seibu
Pacific Place, 88 Queensway,
Hong Kong Island, tel 2971-3888,
open 10:30 a.m.–8 p.m.
The basement of this Japanese
department store has a colorful
range of Japanese and Chinese
delicacies and dried foods, as
well as Japanese sake and
Chinese rice wine.

GIFTS

JEWELRY & GEMS
Jade holds a special fascination
for the Chinese—they believe it
has spiritual properties—so it is
on sale in many forms. Colors
range from white and dark
orange to numerous shades of

the familiar jade green.
   The quality of jade is judged
by its translucence and color
consistency. A receipt detailing
the stone's type and origin
should accompany the more
expensive pieces.
   The best selection of jade
is found at the Jade Market in
Kowloon. (see Markets). Take the
subway (MTR) to Yau Ma Tei and
follow exit C.
   Gold is also highly prized,
as are pearls. There are many
stores that sell them along
Queen's Road Central and
Des Voeux Road on Hong Kong
Island, as well as along Nathan
Road, Tsim Sha Tsui.

DFS Galleria
Sun Plaza, 8 Peking Rd.,
Tsim Sha Tsui, tel 2302-6888,
open 9 a.m.–11 p.m.
Electronics, gems, and watches.

Duty Free Shoppers
Hong Kong International
Airport, tel 2383-1474, open
7 a.m.–11:30 p.m.
Large range of jewelry, perfumes,
wines, spirits, and tobacco.

MARKETS

Hong Kong is renowned for its
street markets, selling all manner
of goods. Bargaining is an
essential part of a market visit,
whether you are buying clothes,
watches, Chinese medicine, or
inexpensive jade trinkets.
   Beware of pickpockets
when shopping in markets, and
be cautious when purchasing
what appears to be an
exceptionally good bargain: The
actual music on your chosen
CD, for example, may turn out
not to have been recorded by
the famous performer pictured
on the cover.

HONG KONG ISLAND
Stanley Market
Market Rd., Stanley,
open 10 a.m.–6 p.m.
Packed with Chinese artwork,
silk, curios, and casual clothes.

Wan Chai Market
Between Johnson St. and

Queen's Rd. East, Wan Chai,
open 7 a.m.–7 p.m.
A "wet" market, primarily selling
fresh food, especially fish, but
there are also clothing stands,
and a number of Chinese
apothecaries.

Western Market
323 Des Voeux Rd., Sheung
Wan, open 10 a.m.–7 p.m.
A paradise for silk seekers in
the setting of an attractive
Edwardian building.

KOWLOON
Bird Market
Yuen Po St., Mong Kok,
open 7 a.m.–8 p.m.
Exotic bird song amid the ornate
cages and bric-a-brac.

Flower Market
Flower Market Rd., Mong Kok,
open 7 a.m.–7 p.m.
Huge variety of cut flowers and
fortune-bringing houseplants
favored by the Chinese. Sweet
scents and exotic blossoms.

Jade Market
Corner of Kansu and Battery
Sts., Yau Ma Tei, next to Tin Hau
temple, open 10 a.m.–3:30 p.m.
A lively market for purveyors of
jade, selling a wide range from
inexpensive trinkets to pieces
costing a small fortune.
Unless you have an extensive
knowledge of jade, it is wise to
settle for a trinket.

Temple Street Night Market
Tsim Sha Tsui, open 3 p.m.–
midnight.
Hong Kong's favorite night
market. Everything under the
moon for sale, including casual
clothes, electronics, watches,
toys, CDs, and bric-a-brac.
There are many Chinese cafés
and restaurants along the street.

ENTERTAINMENT & ACTIVITIES

Hong Kong's seasons are marked with a variety of cultural and sporting events and festivals, both Chinese and Western. There always seems to be some excuse for a big fireworks display to light up the harbor. The city's moviemaking heritage is enjoying a renaissance with the emergence of quality film producers and directors making their mark internationally. The thousand-year-old art of Chinese opera, which portrays Chinese folklore, is still practiced and forms part of the local cultural heritage.

Ticket Agency
URBTIX, tel 2734-9009

BALLET & DANCE

Hong Kong Ballet Company
G/F, 60 Blue Pool Rd., Happy Valley, tel 2573–7398, open 10 a.m.–11 p.m.
Focuses on modern Western performances.

Hong Kong Dance Company
4/F Sheung Wan Municipal Services Bldg., 345 Queen's Rd., Central, tel 3103-1888.
Concentrates on traditional Chinese dance.

CHINESE OPERA

Chinese opera (see p. 42) can last up to three hours, but it's possible to watch for shorter periods to enjoy the mix of extravagant costumes, makeup, singing, and martial arts. The performers' tone and body language help spectators even if the words cannot be understood.

Traveling operatic companies perform on makeshift stages across the territory throughout the year. The Hong Kong Tourism Board, tel 2508-1234, can give details of performances.

Regular performing venues:
City Hall
Edinburgh Pl., Central, tel 2921-2840

Hong Kong Cultural Center
Salisbury Rd., Tsim Sha Tsui, (next to the Star Ferry Pier), tel 2734-2820

Ko Shan Theater
77 Ko Shan Rd., Hung Hom, Kowloon, tel 2740-9222.

CINEMA

Hong Kong is dominated by two big distributor chains. Multiple-screen centers are attached to most shopping centers (see pp. 259–260). The *South China Morning Post* newspaper has daily *What's On* listings.

Golden Harvest Cinemas
The Gateway, 25 Canton Rd., Tsim Sha Tsui, tel 2956-2471, or Ocean, 3 Canton Rd., Tsim Sha Tsui, tel 2956-2003.
Both theaters show mainstream Hollywood as well as locally produced movies.

UA Cinemas
1 Pacific Place, 88 Queensway, tel 2869-0322, or Times Sq., Causeway Bay, tel 2506-2822.
Both multiplex venues showing mainstream Hollywood-dominated, English-language films.

Cine-Art House
G/F Sun Hung Kai Center, Wan Chai, tel 2827-4820.
Off-beat Western and Chinese movies.

ENTERTAINMENT CENTERS

Convention & Exhibition Center
1 Expo Dr., Wan Chai, tel 2582-8888.
A huge complex on the harbor with its distinctive "butterfly" roof. Numerous exhibitions and fairs are held here throughout the year. The center also has seven cafés and restaurants, some, notably the Harbor Lounge, with tables offering dramatic views over the harbor.

The Fringe Club
2 Lower Albert Rd., Central, tel 2521-7251.
Stage plays, comedy, and lunchtime art exhibitions in a slightly avant-garde setting next door to the Foreign Correspondents' Club (see opposite). Good-value lunches and lively early evening bar.

Hong Kong Arts Center
2 Harbor Rd., Wan Chai, tel 2582-0200.
Locally written and produced plays and specialty films.

Hong Kong Cultural Center
Salisbury Rd., Tsim Sha Tsui, tel 2734-2820.
The Hong Kong Philharmonic Orchestra is in residence here between September and July. The Hong Kong Chinese Orchestra—one of the world's largest using traditional Chinese instruments—also performs regularly at the center.

Ocean Park
Aberdeen, Hong Kong Island, tel 2552-0291. Open 10 a.m.–6 p.m. Entrance: HK$185 ($24) per person, children HK$93 ($12). Ocean Park offers a full day of family entertainment, including cable-car rides overlooking Hong Kong Island's spectacular southern coastline, shark aquarium, butterfly house, giant-panda enclosure, and a goldfish pagoda, which is home to 110 species of brilliantly colored fish. There are also daily dolphin, killer whale, and sea lion shows.

Yuen Long Theater
9 Yuen Long Tai Yuk Rd., New Territories, tel 2477-5324.
An arts venue outside the main conurbations, which concentrates on Chinese opera, music, and dance.

NIGHTLIFE

CENTRAL
Foreign Correspondents' Club
2 Lower Albert Rd., North Block, Central, Hong Kong

Island, tel 2521-1511.
Lively and clubby hang-out of journalists in a converted ice factory. The huge circular bar is the focal point. Western and Chinese food. Live jazz Thursdays, Fridays, and Saturdays. Temporary membership can be obtained for a modest price.

LAN KWAI FONG
Hong Kong's newest night-scene venue—a concentration of late-night bars, nightclubs, and restaurants on the narrow, steep streets clustered around D'Aguilar Street, Central (close to the Fringe and Foreign Correspondents' Club).

Club 97
24–26 Lan Kwai Fong,
Ground floor, tel 2810-9333.
A nightclub institution in Hong Kong. DJs play funk, soul, jazz. Open to the early hours.

SOHO
Similar to Lan Kwai Fong.
This area, in the shadow of the Central-to-Mid-Levels Escalator around Staunton, Elgin, and Shelley Streets, is full of bars and restaurants.

WAN CHAI
Made internationally famous by the book and movie *The World of Suzy Wong*, and a haunt of visiting shore-leave sailors for most of the 20th century. Today's neon-lit pubs, discos, and hostess bars, some offering floor shows with scantily clad girls, occupy several small streets around the junction of Lockhart and Luard Roads. More salubrious bars include:

Delaney's
1 Capital Pl., 2nd fl., 18 Luard Rd., tel 2804-2880. Irish theme pub with live Irish music and Guinness.

Devil's Advocate
48 Lockhart Rd., tel 2865-7271.
A British-style pub that sells the locally brewed Dragon's Back ale and serves good food, notably steaks. Happy Hour lasts from noon until 9:30 p.m.

Dusk Till Dawn
76 Jaffe Rd., Wan Chai,
tel 2528-4689.
A smart, well-managed late-night bar that attracts a broad mix of people.

JJs
M/F, Grand Hyatt, 1 Harbour Rd., tel 2588-1234.
One of Hong Kong's most popular nightclubs. It's a cavernous place populated by the young and wealthy, and is as elegant as the hotel it's located in.

HARBOR CRUISES

Watertours of Hong Kong Ltd.
Star House, 3 Salisbury Rd., Tsim Sha Tsui, tel 2926-3868, open daily. Offers a variety of tours, including:

Sunset Drinks Cruise
Price per person for 90 minutes, including drinks, HK$290.
Departure points Central, Hong Kong Island (6:15 p.m.) or Tsim Sha Tsui (6:30 p.m.).

Dinner Cruise
The daily tour, including dinner at Lei Yue Mun Seafood Village, lasts three hours. Price per person HK$390 (US$50).

AERIAL RIDES

Helicopters can be rented for tours over Hong Kong and adjoining islands and to fly to Macau (a 30-minute ride).

HeliExpress
Tel 2108-9899

Heliservices Limited
Tel 2802-0200

ACTIVE SPORTS

GOLF
Clearwater Bay Golf & Country Club
Sai Kung, tel 2335-3888.
An 18-hole course. The club accepts reservations from overseas visitors three days in advance, on weekdays only.

The Hong Kong Golf Club
Fanling, tel 2670-1211.
Perhaps the territory's most exclusive golf club. Overseas visitors are permitted to play on weekdays by prior arrangement.

Jockey Club Golf Course
Kau Sai Chau Island, Sai Kung, tel 2791-3380 (9:30 a.m.– 12:30 p.m. only).
This 36-hole course is on an island in a spectacular bay setting a short ferry ride from Sai Kung. The club accepts visitor reservations on weekdays if made seven days in advance.

HIKING
Almost 40 percent of Hong Kong territory is protected in 23 country parks with more flora and fauna than some much larger countries. Hiking trails crisscross most of the parks. On Hong Kong Island South, a 30-mile (50 km) hiking trail snakes over several peaks and through lush subtropical valley flora. A good starting point is Victoria Peak.
  A general guide, *Exploring Hong Kong's Countryside,* is sold by tourist offices, or contact the Country Parks Management Office, 303 Cheung Sha Wan Rd., Kowloon, tel 2708-8885.
  To take a guided walk contact the Education Unit, Country Park Ranger Services Division, tel 2428-7137.

SWIMMING
Hong Kong has numerous public swimming pools. All are closed between November and March.

Victoria Park Swimming Pool
Victoria Park, Hing Fat St., Causeway Bay, tel 2570-8347, open daily 6:30 a.m.–10 p.m., closed noon–1 p.m. and 5–6 p.m. One Olympic-size pool as well as several smaller and shallower ones.

Kowloon Park Swimming Pool
Kowloon Park, 22 Austin Rd., Tsim Sha Tsui, tel 2724-3577, open daily 6:30 a.m.–10 p.m.,

closed noon–1 p.m. and 5–6 p.m. Indoor Olympic-size pool and several interconnected pools set in gardens.

TAI CHI
Garden Plaza, Hong Kong Park, Admiralty, Hong Kong Island. Open Tuesdays, Fridays, and Sundays, 8:15 a.m.–9:15 a.m. Tel 2508-1234 for free lessons.

TENNIS
Victoria Park, Causeway Bay, Hong Kong Island, tel 2570-6186, open 6 a.m.–11 p.m., closed noon–1 p.m. and 5–6 p.m. Five public courts which get crowded on weekends, so reserve in advance in person. You will need your passport.

WATER SKIING & SAILING
Despite being perceived as a big, crowded city, the territory of Hong Kong has almost 40 beaches. Equipment can be rented from beachside stores. Some beaches are subject to seasonal conditions such as a heavy swell caused by storms elsewhere. Tel 1823 for details of the best equipped and safest beaches during your visit.

WINDSURFING
Cheung Chau Windsurfing Center
Cheung Chau Island, tel 2981-2772.
The sport has become popular in Hong Kong since Lee Lai Shan won an Olympic gold medal—a first for Hong Kong—in Atlanta in 1996. She trained at the Cheung Chau beach.

SPECTATOR SPORTS

DRAGON BOAT RACING
This exciting sporting event is special to Hong Kong. The main races are held in June when more than one hundred boat teams participate at numerous locations around Hong Kong's sheltered coastline.

The 50-foot-long narrow wooden boats have bows shaped like dragons heads. The Tuen Ng Dragon Boat Festival celebrates

Qu Yuan, a Chinese hero who died 2,300 years ago.

Training and racing can be seen at Aberdeen and Stanley on Hong Kong Island; at Sai Kung, Sha Tin, Tai Po, and Tuen Mun on the Kowloon side; and around the islands of Lantau and Cheung Chau.

Some tour companies organize spectator boats to follow the races: Gray Line Tours, tel 2368-7111 and Panda Travel, tel 2724-4440, or contact tourist offices for dates and times, tel 2508-1234.

GOLF
The Hong Kong Open, which takes place in November and December, is a major international sports event. It is held across several of the territory's best courses and has featured such prominent players as Tiger Woods. Contact tourist offices for competition schedules, tel 2508-1234.

HORSE RACING
Hong Kong's biggest spectator sport is horse racing, which was introduced by the British in the mid-19th century. Between mid-September and mid-June, tens of thousands of people flock to the two race courses, at Happy Valley and at Sha Tin, every Wednesday evening and Saturday afternoon. Race meetings usually last several hours and cause considerable traffic disruption in the vicinity of the courses. Hundreds of thousands more listen on radios or watch TV to follow the races on which tens of millions of Hong Kong dollars are wagered.

The two biggest events of the local racing calendar are the Queen Elizabeth II Cup, in April, in which horses and jockeys from around the world partici-pate, and the Hong Kong Inter-national Races in December— the final leg of the Emirates World Racing Championship.

The Hong Kong Tourism Board organizes tours to the races. The price per person of HK$490 (US$63) includes hotel

pick-up by air-conditioned bus, guided tour, buffet meal, drinks, admission badge, and race card. Tel 2508-1234 to reserve.

Happy Valley Racecourse
1 Sports Rd., Happy Valley, tel 2966-8345 for admission badge prices. Races start at 7 p.m. on Wednesdays. To get there, take the Happy Valley tram, bus 1M from Admiralty, or taxi.
The Hong Kong Racing Museum is located here. Closed Mondays.

Sha Tin Race Course
Penfold Park, Sha Tin, New Territories, tel 2966-8345 for admission badge prices. Races start at 2:30 p.m. Saturdays (sometimes Sun.). To get there, take bus 891 from Tsim Sha Tsui Star Ferry Pier, or the KCR East Racecourse station (open only during racing days).

RUGBY & SOCCER
Hong Kong Stadium, 55 Eastern Hospital Rd., Hong Kong Island, tel 2895-7895.
The World Sevens Series rugby competition is held in the 40,000-seat stadium every spring, as well as smaller events at other times. The stadium is also the venue for soccer and cricket tournaments.

INDEX

Bold page numbers
indicate illustrations

ILLUSTRATIONS CREDITS

Abbreviations for terms appearing below: (t) top; (b) bottom; (l) left; (r) right; (c) center.

Cover: (l) ImageState. (c) Trip Photo Library. (r) Pictor International, London.

1, Robert Harding Picture Library (RHPL). 2/3, Bob Krist/Corbis. 4, Catherine Karnow. 9, Powerstock/ Zefa. 11, RHPL. 12/13, Nigel Hicks/AA Photo Library. 14, Philip Harle. 15, Nigel Hicks. 16/17, Gareth Jones/Getty Images. 18, Justin Guariglia/National Geographic. 19, Nigel Hicks. 20/21, Catherine Karnow. 22/23, Travel Ink/Robin Adshead. 24, Nigel Hicks. 25, Impact Photos. 27, Hulton Archive. 29, Hulton Archive. 30/31, Roy Miles Fine Paintings/Bridgeman Art Library, London. 32, Royal Geographical Society Picture Library. 33, Hulton Archive. 35, Jodi Cobb/National Geographic Society. 36/37, Associated Press. 39, Nigel Hicks. 40/41, RHPL. 43, RHPL. 44/45, RHPL. 46/47, Jodi Cobb/National Geographic Society. 49, Panos Pictures. 50/51, Travel Ink/Derek Allan. 52, Nigel Hicks/AA Photo Library. 53, RHPL. 54(t), Nigel Hicks/AA Photo Library. 54(b) Bruce Coleman Collection. 55, Philip Harle. 56, Nigel Hicks/AA Photo Library. 57, Catherine Karnow. 58, Nigel Hicks/AA Photo Library. 59, Nigel Hicks. 60, Nigel Hicks/AA Photo Library. 62, Nigel Hicks. 64, Nigel Hicks/AA Photo Library. 65, Nigel Hicks. 66, Nigel Hicks/AA Photo Library. 67(t), Nigel Hicks/AA Photo Library. 67(b), RHPL. 68/69, Stefan Irvine/OnAsia. 70, Hutchison Picture Library. 71, Panos Pictures. 72, Nigel Hicks/ AA Photo Library. 73, RHPL. 74, Nigel Hicks/AA Photo Library. 75, Panos Pictures. 76, Nigel Hicks. 77, Nigel Hicks/AA Photo Library. 79, Nigel Hicks/AA Photo Library. 80, Nigel Hicks. 81(t), Nigel Hicks/AA Photo Library. 81(b), Sally & Richard Greenhill. 82, Travel Ink/Derek Allan. 83, Rex Butcher/Stone. 85(t), Nigel Hicks. 85(b), Nigel Hicks/AA Photo Library. 86/87, Nigel Hicks/AA Photo Library. 88, Art Directors and TRIP Photo Library. 89, Terry Duckham/Asiapix. 90/91, Travel Ink/Derek Allan. 91(bl), Art Directors and TRIP Photo Library. 91(br), Hutchison Picture Library. 92/93, Travel Ink/Derek Allan. 93, Nigel Hicks/AA Photo Library. 94, Hutchison Picture Library. 95, Nigel Hicks/AA Photo Library. 96, Nigel Hicks/AA Photo Library. 97, Hong Kong Academy for Performing Arts. 98, Hutchison Picture Library. 99, Catherine Karnow. 101, Terry Duckham/ Asiapix. 102, Art Directors and TRIP Photo Library. 103, Hutchison Picture Library. 104/105, Catherine Karnow. 105, Catherine Karnow. 106, Catherine Karnow. 107, Hong Kong Tourism Board. 108, Hutchison Picture Library. 109, Catherine Karnow. 110, Nigel Hicks. 111(t), Nigel Hicks/AA Photo Library. 111(b), Art Directors and TRIP Photo Library. 112, Travel Ink/Derek Allan. 113, Hutchison Picture Library. 114, Hutchison Picture Library. 115, Sally & Richard Greenhill. 116, Hutchison Picture Library. 117, Travel Ink/Derek Allan. 118, Nigel Hicks/AA Photo Library. 120, Catherine Karnow. 121, Art Directors and TRIP Photo Library. 122, Art Directors and TRIP Photo Library. 123, Nigel Hicks. 124, Nigel Hicks/AA Photo Library. 126, RHPL. 127, Nigel Hicks/AA Photo Library. 128/129, Nigel Hicks/ AA Photo Library. 130, Nigel Hicks/ AA Photo Library. 131, Nigel Hicks/ AA Photo Library. 132, Hong Kong Museum of History. 133, Hong Kong Museum of History. 134, Nigel Hicks/AA Photo Library. 135, Hong Kong Tourism Board. 136/137, Jake Wyman/Getty Images. 137(b), RHPL. 138, Nigel Hicks. 139, Nigel Hicks. 140/141, Michael Yamashita/National Geographic Society. 142/143, Travel Ink/Mark Reeve. 143(r), Nigel Hicks. 144(l), Panos Pictures. 144/145, Randall van der Woning. 146, Ronald Grant Archive. 147(t), David Appleby/Buena Vista/Everett Collection. 147(b), RHPL. 148/149, Randall van der Woning. 150, Randall van der Woning. 152, Travel Ink/Derek Allan. 153, RHPL, 156, Nigel Hicks. 157, Hutchison Picture Library. 158, Nigel Hicks. 159, Impact Photos. 160, Nigel Hicks. 161, RHPL. 162, RHPL. 163, Nigel Hicks. 164, Nigel Hicks.

165(t), Hong Kong Tourism Board. 165(b) Impact Photos. 166/167. Nigel Hicks. 167(r), NHPA/J Blossom. 168, Nigel Hicks. 169, Nigel Hicks. 170, Nigel Hicks. 172, RHPL. 173, Nigel Hicks. 174/175 Harry How/Getty Images. 176/177, Nigel Hicks/AA Photo Library. 177(r), Impact Photos. 178(l), China Photo Library. 178/179, James Davis Travel Photo Library. 180, The Charles Walker Collection. 181, The Charles Walker Collection. 182, Panos Pictures. 183, Nigel Hicks. 184(l), Nigel Hicks. 184/185, Nigel Hicks/AA Photo Library. 186, RHPL. 188(l), Nigel Hicks. 188/189, China Photo Library. 190, Travel Ink/Derek Allan. 191, Michael S. Yamashita/CORBIS. 192/193, Travel Ink/Derek Allan. 194, Hong Kong Tourism Board. 195(tr), Travel Ink/Derek Allan. 195(br), RHPL. 196, Hong Kong Tourism Board. 197, Nigel Hicks. 198, Impact Photos. 199, China Photo Library. 200, Hong Kong Tourism Board. 201, RHPL. 202, Catherine Karnow. 203, Nigel Hicks. 204/205, Nigel Hicks. 205(r), Nigel Hicks/AA Photo Library, 206/207, marinethemes.com/Ken Hoppen. 207(b), Macduff Everton/CORBIS. 208, Hutchison Picture Library. 209, Paul Springett/Alamy. 210, Art Directors and TRIP Photo Library. 211, Hong Kong Disneyland/Handout/ Reuters/Corbis. 212, Travel Ink/Derek Allan. 215, Nigel Hicks. 216, Julien Nieman/Getty Images. 217, Impact Photos. 218/219, Peter Adams/Ace Photo Agency. 220/221, Impact Photos. 222, Stefan Irvine/OnAsia. 223, Impact Photos. 226, Nigel Hicks. 227, Impact Photos. 229, Michael S. Yamashita/Corbis. 230, Nigel Hicks. 231, Bohemian Nomad Picturemakers/CORBIS. 232, Impact Photos. 233, Carl & Ann Purcell/CORBIS. 234, Nigel Hicks. 235, Nigel Hicks/AA Photo Library

The world's largest nonprofit scientific and educational organization, the National Geographic Society was founded in 1888 "for the increase and diffusion of geographic knowledge." Since then it has supported scientific exploration and spread information to its more than nine million members worldwide.

The National Geographic Society educates and inspires millions every day through magazines, books, television programs, videos, maps and atlases, research grants, the National Geography Bee, teacher workshops, and innovative classroom materials.

The Society is supported through membership dues, charitable gifts, and income from the sale of its educational products. Members receive NATIONAL GEOGRAPHIC magazine—the Society's official journal—discounts on Society products, and other benefits.

For more information about the National Geographic Society, its educational programs, publications, or how to support its work, call 1-800-NGS-LINE (647-5463), or write to: National Geographic Society, 1145 17th Street, N.W., Washington, D.C. 20036 U.S.A.

Printed in Spain.

Published by the National Geographic Society

John M. Fahey, Jr., *President and Chief Executive Officer*

Gilbert M. Grosvenor, *Chairman of the Board*

Nina D. Hoffman, *Executive Vice President, President, Books and School Publishing*

Kevin Mulroy, *Vice President and Editor-in-Chief*

Marianne Koszorus, *Design Director*

Kristin Hanneman, *Illustrations Director*

Elizabeth L. Newhouse, *Director of Travel Publishing*

Barbara A. Noe, *Senior Editor and Project Manager*

Cinda Rose, *Art Director*

Carl Mehler, *Director of Maps*

Nicholas P. Rosenbach, *Map Coordinator*

Gary Colbert, *Production Director*

Richard S. Wain, *Production Project Manager*

Rebecca Hinds, *Managing Editor*

Lise Sajewski, *Editorial Consultant*

Allan Fallow, Jane Sunderland, *Contributors*

Jennifer Davis, Steven D. Gardner, Rebecca Gross, Caroline Hickey, Judy Klein, Carol Stroud, Teresa Neva Tate, Ruth Thompson, Mapping Specialists, *Contributors to 2006 edition*

First edition: Edited and designed by AA Publishing (a trading name of Automobile Association Developments Limited, whose registered office is Norfolk House, Priestley Road, Basingstoke, Hampshire, England RG24 9NY. Registered number: 1878835).

Virginia Langer *Project Manager*

David Austin, *Senior Art Editor*

Jenni Davis, *Editor*

Bob Johnson, *Designer*

Keith Brook, *Senior Cartographic Editor*

Cartography by AA Cartographic Production

Richard Firth, *Production Director*

Steve Gilchrist, *Prepress Production Controller*

Liz Allen, *Picture Research Manager*

Picture Research by Zooid Pictures Ltd.

Area and drive maps drawn by Chris Orr Associates, Southampton, England

Cutaway illustrations drawn by Maltings Partnership, Derby, England (pp. 63, 150–151, & 168–169)

Second Edition 2006

ISBN: 0-7922-5369-8

The Library of Congress catalogued the first edition as follows:

ISSN 1538-5493

Printed and bound by Cayfosa Quebecor, Barcelona, Spain. Color separations by Leo Reprographic Ltd., Hong Kong. Cover separations by L.C. Repro, Aldermaston, U.K.

Visit the society's Web site at http://www.nationalgeographic.com

The information in this book has been carefully checked and to the best of our knowledge is accurate. However, details are subject to change, and the National Geographic Society cannot be responsible for such changes, or for errors or omissions. Assessments of sites, hotels, and restaurants are based on the author's subjective opinions, which do not necessarily reflect the publisher's opinion. The publisher cannot be responsible for any consequences arising from the use of this book.

NATIONAL GEOGRAPHIC
TRAVELER

A Century of Travel Expertise in Every Guide

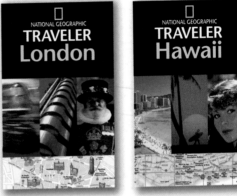